THE ARABIC PARTS IN ASTROLOGY

THE ARABIC PARTS IN ASTROLOGY
THE LOST KEY TO PREDICTION

ROBERT ZOLLER

INNER TRADITIONS INTERNATIONAL
Rochester, Vermont

Inner Traditions International
One Park Street
Rochester, Vermont 05767
www.InnerTraditions.com

LIBRARY OF CONGRESS CATALOGING-IN-PUBLICATION DATA

Zoller, Robert, 1947.
    Arabic parts in astrology : lost key to prediction / by Robert E. Zoller.
        p.   cm.
    Rev. ed. of: The lost key to prediction / Robert Zoller. c1980.
    Bibliography: p.
    Includes index.
    ISBN 978-0-89281-250-9
    1. Astrology. 2. Astrology, Arabic—Miscellanea. I. Zoller, Robert, 1947 Lost key
to prediction. II. Title.
    BF1711.Z65   1989
    135.5—dc19   88-1832
                                                                      CIP

Printed and bound in the United States

12

Dedicated to Saraswati-Minerva.

CONTENTS

ACKNOWLEDGMENTS

Without the constant support, reassurance, and complete faith of my wife, Michelle, this book would not have been written. From the conception to the completion Michelle was always ready as a patient listener, with helpful suggestions and a keen eye for inconsistencies.

Recognition is also due to Mary Valerie Kempinski whose patience, industry, and reliability are extraordinary. Mary typed the greater part of the manuscript and her help is deeply appreciated.

PREFACE

This work sets forth for the intermediate student of astrology the ancient doctrine of Arabic parts. It is assumed that the reader is familiar with the essentials of chart erection and at least the elements of horoscope interpretation relating to the natal chart. He or she would be aware of the fundamental similarity of horary, electional, and natal figures and that the revolutions (solar, lunar, and planetary) of nativities are analogous to the revolutions of the world: that is, the ingresses of the sun into the cardinal signs at the beginning of each of the four seasons and the "returns" of the moon and the sun and of the planets to some point previously held. Finally, though a precise understanding is not required, the reader should be aware that for purposes included in mundane astrology, the conjunctions of the major planets and the eclipses of the luminaries are frequently employed. Thus armed, the reader will find nothing in this book to be outlandishly alien and may speed along quickly from the theoretical considerations to the practical applications of the doctrine of the parts.

INTRODUCTION

2 / THE ARABIC PARTS IN ASTROLOGY

At times astrology seems to me very much like the study of grammar. The vast terminology, the formidable array of planets, aspects, houses, luminaries, decans, dignities, and debilities—all this conjures up memories of school days spent wrestling with parts of speech, syntax, and sentence construction. The analogy is apt, for astrology itself is a language: the language of Nature. Where in grammatical study we have sentence fragments, in astrology we have the void of course moon. What dangling participles are to the grammarian, feral planets are to the astrologer. And just as the student of grammar proceeds from simple to compound and complex sentences, so must the astrologer pass from the elementary concepts to the more advanced and subtle doctrines of his art.

Among the most useful—and lesser-known—of these is the ancient doctrine of the Arabic parts (or "lots," as they are sometimes misleadingly called). These are arithmetically derived points on the ecliptic which represent the synthesis of two or more causal factors acting in the irrational sphere, called by Plato "the circle of the Other." The use of the parts gives the astrologer a profound insight into the "inner" workings of a figure—whether natal, mundane, horary, or electional—as opposed to the "outer" aspect indicated by the arrangement and determination of the planets, stars, signs, and houses. Ninety-seven parts were commonly used, although medieval Arabian and Persian astrologers devised and used many more. This book presents the basic ninety-seven parts as well as seventy-three additional parts from various medieval sources. The parts given deal with all areas of life—from war (part of the military), commodities speculation (part of barley, part of cucumbers), and profession (part of those who are suddenly elevated), to marriage and partnerships (part of craftiness of men toward women).

Despite the practical benefits of the doctrine, it has been all but lost to Western astrological practice since the seventeenth century. The aim of this book is to retrieve this valuable key to prediction and restore it to use by explaining its theoretical foundations and providing a clear and simple guide to its practical application.

In Chapter 1, I offer a brief history of the parts and explain how they were lost with the decline of traditional astrological practice in the West, owing to ignorance of the metaphysical foundations of the art and a misunderstanding of the essentially divine nature of Man.

An astrologer should be no more ignorant of the nature and origin of his art than a grammarian of the ABC's. Thus Chapter 2 is devoted to a discussion of the metaphysical basis of astrology, for an understanding of it is indispensable to the proper use of the parts. I shall show that, contrary to popular misconception, the basis of astrology is not the physical movements of the planets, not some kind of "radiation" from the stars, but is in fact the esoteric nature of *number*. When we astrologers deal with circles such as the ecliptic or right circle, we deal with numbers. When we watch the transits of Jupiter or Mars, it is not the physical hunk of rock in space which accounts for the predictions that are our stock in trade, but something subtle, numerical in essence.

In the metaphysical discussion, we shall consider not only the nature of number, but also its sphere of activity, which is Man, or Mind. We shall see what the great magi of the Renaissance had to say on the nature of Man and, in order to understand the Hermetic doctrine of "As above, so below," shall uncover the common source of the Cosmos, both Macrocosm and Microcosm. Finally, Chapter 2 provides the point of view from which astrology, alchemy, magic, and the liberal arts are all seen to be specialized applications of One Wisdom.

No effort will be made to prove the metaphysical principles set forth, however; my aim is rather to pass on the tradition to those who already have some experience in astrology and an interest in the deeper aspects of it. Such lengthy proofs would be out of place in a work that is intended to facilitate the practical application of the doctrine of the parts.

The exposition of the doctrine itself, in Part II, is constructed around my translation of a section from *Liber astronomiae,* an important thirteenth-century Latin text written by Guido Bonatti. Though Bonatti's work was certainly influenced by the somewhat limited view of his time, his vision and his understanding of the necessary metaphysics are superior to what commonly passes for astrology and mysticism today. Furthermore, the *Liber astronomiae* gives us a complete and accurate picture of astrological practice in the

Middle Ages during the time immediately following its reintroduction into Europe by the Arabs. Bonatti conveys purely to us the traditions of the art as it was practiced for centuries before his time. Thanks to the wide popularity of the work, it did not perish in the intervening centuries, and thus we are able to judge for ourselves the merits of modern astrological innovations compared with the traditional procedures based upon the ancient teachings.

Finally, Part III consists of numerous detailed examples which clearly demonstrate the proper use of the parts. These examples are offered to the reader both as illustrations of possible applications and for future reference or review of the use of the different parts.

I hope that this book will give the reader a working knowledge of a highly useful doctrine that is virtually ignored in this day of "pop" astrology. If, beyond that, he or she is moved to probe more deeply into the laws underlying the art of astrology and so come face to face with the forces that direct the seemingly confused course of human affairs, so much the better. Most desired of all would be that, having been enticed by the allurement of Knowledge, the reader might seek even further and draw closer to the Source of all.

PART I

BACKGROUND

1

HOW THE PARTS
WERE LOST

ORIGIN OF THE PARTS

The doctrine of the so-called Arabic parts is of considerable antiquity. The oldest surviving record of them is found in the famous second-century text *Tetrabiblos* by the Greek astronomer Claudius Ptolemy, who refers there to the part of fortune as one of the five hylegeical places.* The Roman writer Julius Firmicus Maternus, writing in the fourth century, mentions both the part of fortune and its complement, the part of the Sun (which he calls the part of the daemon). The eighth-century Egyptian-Jewish astrologer Masha'allah also discusses the part of fortune, in his book on nativities, which survives in Latin translation.

But the use of the parts surely goes back further than Ptolemy's time. A recorder of astrological method rather than an innovator, Ptolemy repeatedly acknowledged that he drew from Egyptian and Chaldean sources. In the ninth century, the learned Arabic astronomer Albumassar wrote that the Egyptians and Babylonians commonly used ninety-seven parts "as may be seen in their books."[1] Although the books he mentions have not survived, it seems evident that a living

---

*An earlier work, by the poet Marcus Manilius (fl. first century), mentions twelve "lots" which appear on superficial glance to be parts, but in fact they are not, although they begin from the part of fortune and are of essentially the same nature as the parts. See Appendix A for a commentary on the lots of Manilius. A similar system presented by Firmicus is discussed in Appendix B.

astrological tradition, including the doctrine of the parts, existed from some time before Ptolemy's day and extended down as far as Albumassar's.

The exact origin of the parts—whether Babylonian/Egyptian, Hermetic, Magian, or Indian—is uncertain. Yet all these traditions emphasized the esoteric nature of number, which is the fundamental principle at work in the doctrine of the parts. The doctrine could therefore have easily come from any of these schools. In any case, we may assume that Ptolemy, Manilius, and Firmicus drew their information from such ancient sources.

ARABIC ASTROLOGY

The Arabs, overrunning the decaying Byzantine Empire and Persia in the second half of the seventh century, became the inheritors of classical antiquity. Under the Abbasid caliphs of the eighth century, schools of astrology were established in Baghdad. Patrons of culture and education, the Abbasids fostered a climate that was far more favorable to the transmission of esoteric learning than could be found in barbarian Europe, and the ancient philosophic schools continued in the Arab world and Persia long after they had closed in Greece and Europe.

The Arabs, moreover, formed a link between Spain and India. The resulting exchange of philosophic and scientific learning greatly affected the astrological art, which was seen as the practical union of metaphysics and astronomy. It was during the eighth century, for example, that the *siddhantas,* Hindu treatises on astronomy and trigonometry, were translated from Sanskrit into Arabic by the astrologers of the caliph al-Mansur. Traditional astrology as it now stands is largely a product of this period.

The Arabs perpetuated the syncretizing activity in the field of religion and philosophy begun by Alexander, continued through the establishment of the Hellenistic world, and maintained by the Byzantines. Arab astrology therefore drew upon Magian, Hermetic, Vedantic, Gnostic, Chaldean, Egyptian, Neoplatonic, and Aristotelian sources, all of which flourished in the Arab world up to about the eleventh century.

Of all the renowned Arabic astrologers, Albumassar (fl. ninth century) achieved a degree of recognition unmatched before or after his day. His works provided at least as much impetus to the astrological tradition as did those of Ptolemy. Albumassar was a student of the great sage al-Kindi, to whom are attributed about 200 works on subjects ranging from astrology, magic, philosophy, and metaphysics to optics,

mathematics, and meteorology. Al-Kindi also translated the works of
Aristotle into Arabic. The influence of al-Kindi on Albumassar was
enormous. Close reading and comparison of the works of the two men
show that the student incorporated much of the teacher's work into his
own (sometimes without acknowledging his source).

Albumassar or one of his pupils was the author of several works on
astrology. One of them, *De magnis conjunctionibus* (On the Great
Conjunctions), contains the earliest description of the use of the ninety-
five parts other than the part of fortune and the part of the sun. These
parts are easily discovered by finding the ecliptical distances between
various significators and/or other parts and projecting these distances
from a house cusp such as the ascendant. Since the parts were so easy to
discover, the Arab astrologers apparently became too reliant upon
them, and their number proliferated. In time they had grown so
excessive that al-Biruni (973-1048) complained in his *Elements of
Astrology* that "the number of these lots multiplies daily."[2]

Al-Biruni's *Elements* is especially interesting in that it shows a
strongly esoteric mathematical and geometric influence based on
Pythagorean philosophy. The work is essentially a recording of
methodology practiced in the tenth and eleventh centuries in India,
Persia, and the Middle East, and it clearly indicates the presence of
several schools of astrology in those areas. Al-Biruni, himself a Persian
Muslim probably of Zoroastrian (or Magian) descent, had traveled to
India and observed the procedures used by astrologers there. In his book
he frequently compares the practices of the Hindus, Magians, and Arabs
but shows no preference for or understanding of the parts. (What parts
he does list which are not mentioned by Bonatti in *Liber astronomiae*
are given in Appendix E of this book.)

THE SPREAD OF ASTROLOGY TO EUROPE

The doctrine of the parts passed into Europe in the twelfth
century, along with other astrological material, as part of the great
effort of European scholars to translate Arabic treatises into Latin. The
writings of Albumassar and others were eagerly pursued by these
scholars, who were just emerging from the Dark Ages following the fall
of Roman civilization and were beginning to rediscover lost scientific
and philosophic knowledge.

This wave of translations was followed in the thirteenth century by
a period of assimilation and digestion of the new learning. It was then
that European astrologers such as Guido Bonatti began to synthesize
what had been learned and to disseminate and popularize the new art.

Bonatti, who has been called the most influential astrologer of the thirteenth century,[3] was a native of Forlí in what is now northern Italy. He was employed both by Frederick II Hohenstaufen, the Holy Roman Emperor, and by Count Guido Montefeltro. Bonatti's *Liber astronomiae*, written sometime after 1277, was the most important astrological work produced in Latin at that time. It enjoyed a very wide manuscript and, later, printing tradition and was referred to constantly by astrological writers up to the seventeenth century. Among those who paid special attention to Bonatti's book were the Englishman John Dee (1527-1608) and the German Johann Schöner (1477-1547).

Bonatti included a section on the parts in his *Liber astronomiae;* it formed the latter part of his treatment of revolutions of the world (annual ingresses of the sun into the cardinal signs). Largely as a result of this section of the book, knowledge of the parts as an ancillary method of prediction and horoscope delineation spread.*

Unfortunately, the parts were never used as extensively in Europe as they had been in the Arab world. To see why this was so, we now turn to an examination of developments in the Renaissance.

THE DECLINE OF WESTERN ASTROLOGY

With the rise of the Humanist tradition in the Renaissance, astrology came under increasing attack as violating the Christian doctrine of free will and as being founded upon arbitrary or scientifically unsound assumptions. The vigorous condemnation of Arabic astrology coincided with a serious political threat to Western Europe posed by the invasions of the Turks beginning in the fifteenth century; this ensured the acceptance of the Humanist arguments as part of the anti-Islamic propaganda of the period.

Among those who helped to mount the attack against astrology was the philosopher Pico della Mirandola (1463-1494). At first Mirandola had openly espoused a Hermetico-Cabalistic magic, but he later turned against astrology under the pressure of the Inquisition and the influence of his friend, the religious reformer Savonarola. Mirandola specifically mentions Bonatti in disparaging terms in his *Disputationes adversus astrologiam divinatricem* (Disputations Against Astrological Divination, 1495).

Mirandola and the other enemies of astrology so clouded the issue with their rhetoric that serious doubts were raised among the learned of

*An example of the use of the parts between Bonatti's time and the Renaissance is found in the delineation by the astrologer/physician Jean Ganivet of a horary figure for the Dean of Vienne, given in Chapter 8.

Europe as to the validity of astrological practice. This led to a major change in the tradition of astrological learning.

Traditionally, knowledge was transmitted primarily by oral means, from teacher to students. The teachers were thought of not as researchers or scientists but rather as enlightened spiritual masters whose words embodied great wisdom. Written material, if used at all, was only secondary to oral teaching. It was not intended to supply all the details of the skill but was simply meant as an aid to the memory. For this reason, most ancient esoteric texts, especially magical and astrological ones, were brief, cryptic, and incomplete.

The astrological tradition that had entered Europe in the twelfth century was based for the most part on these incomplete texts. There were no masters of astrology in Europe in the twelfth and thirteenth centuries as there had been at Baghdad and Damascus in the eighth and ninth centuries. Therefore, the European astrological tradition, while based on undoubtedly old written sources, was itself quite young and certainly incomplete from the point of view of a living tradition in the Renaissance. Moreover, astrological metaphysics were never totally mastered by most practitioners, owing to the tacit but powerful contradictions between Western Christian doctrine and the essentially pagan/Islamic foundation on which the art rested at that time. European astrology had in a sense sprouted from the grafting of an alien doctrine onto the Christian world view.

By attacking the Arabic sources and doctrines that had become part of astrological practice, the Renaissance Humanists succeeded in destroying the living European tradition, such as it was, in two ways. First, they cast doubt upon the validity of the art by questioning the omniscience of the masters of astrology, thus discrediting the only men who were held to be spiritually developed enough to have a right opinion in such matters. Second, the Humanists' attacks forced the astrological practitioner to also play the role of theoretician—a role that most were incapable of assuming. Moreover, these rhetorical attacks, aided by the prestige of the Humanists at court and in the universities, had the effect of forcing astrologers to prove their doctrine in the same way that the budding scientists of the seventeenth century seemed to be able to prove theirs. To make matters worse, after the mid-1600s, the astrological practitioner was expected to prove his rules in terms of the mechanistic science increasingly accepted by the scholars of Europe.

Cut off from its sources (which in any case were far removed in time and place) and forced to phrase its arguments in a language incapable of expressing them, European astrology slowly began to succumb to the cynical, atheistic, mechanistic credo that was swiftly spreading across Europe.

We must remember that astrology was originally a sacred science. Clearly, astrotheology played an important part in the Chaldean and Egyptian religions and in those of ancient India, China, and Western Europe. However, the decline of these religions resulted in the transmission, even in the Hellenistic period, of a degenerate art in which originally spiritual considerations were preserved only insofar as they led to some kind of temporal advantage. Thus, even the astrology that the Arabs inherited and passed on to the West was already shorn of its spiritual aspect. The West, in turn, further deformed this truncated astrology, beginning with the Humanist attacks.

So great was the rift caused by the Humanists that when Johann Kepler (1571-1630) attempted to provide astrological doctrine with a sound foundation, he could only come up with an unconvincing thesis based on the physical movements of the planets—and this did more to hasten the demise of the art than to shore it up. Although employed as an astrologer by King Rudolf II of Hungary, Kepler was out of touch with any true living tradition of astrology. Yet many of the modern innovations that are widely embraced today rest upon Kepler's distorted astrology.

The emphasis on a mechanistic, materialistic universe has harmed astrology certainly as much as it has the other arts and sciences. In the insistent quest for a material cause behind every phenomenon, all astrological doctrines—including the parts—that are not immediately understandable in terms of physical astronomy come under question. This present confused state of affairs stems entirely from the widespread ignorance of the traditional metaphysical foundations of astrology among Western practitioners since the Renaissance, or perhaps even since the Middle Ages.

There were, of course, sages during both the Middle Ages and the Renaissance who strove to perceive, and to state clearly and simply, the true foundations of the art. Although they did not always arrive at complete agreement with one another, and were somewhat wide of the mark on some points, still their efforts are of central importance both for what they do say and for what they imply in their writings. Careful study of their works shows that, despite differences arising from individual expression, time, place, and audience, these men shared a common vision. That they all were moved by the same Truth, the same vision of Order and Beauty, cannot be doubted for a moment.

St. Bonaventura (1221-1274), Ramón Lull (1232-c. 1312), Roger Bacon (1214?-1294?), and Marsilio Ficino (1433-1499) all called for the reappraisal of the art's practice in view of the revelation each had as to the nature of the active cause in Creation. In his *Propaedeumata aphoristica* (1558;1568), John Dee attempted to set forth simply the underlying principles of the art and in so doing utilized the work of Bacon and ultimately of al-Kindi. Dee's work shows how the foundations of astrology are clearly those of Nature itself and hence of magic and alchemy as well.

Robert Fludd's *Utriusque cosmi majoris scilicet et minoris metaphysica historia* (1617) and its associated work, the *Technica*, are an encyclopedic effort to show the relation of the seven liberal arts and several occult arts to the Metaphysics of Light. Fludd was a man of wide learning and keen insight, intellectual and subtle and industrious to a degree seldom met with. In his attempt to be accepted as part of the emerging scientism of his day, he included in his work "experiments" which, he felt, sufficiently proved his theses. Unfortunately, Fludd's experiments have not been accepted as such by the advocates of scientific theory since they frequently rest on analogy or on disputed or disproven doctrines; hence Fludd has been considered more an occultist than a scientist. To add to this, he held the geocentric view and thus has been considered obsolete. We must understand, however, that Fludd was confronted with certain facts and had to find some way to communicate them to the increasingly materialistic minds of his day. Fludd's metaphysics are sound even if his experiments are not. His vision is that of the other authors I have mentioned—all men of profound spirituality and insight.

While Dee and Fludd struggled with the metaphysical foundation of astrology, it was left to Jean Morin (1591-1659) to move from the general to the specific. This he does in *Astrologia gallica* (published in 1661) with a precision and beauty that are truly inspired. Morin's mathematical skill, combined with his sensitivity and vision, brought forth an exposition of the art from metaphysical principles which remains to this day a landmark in the field.

Despite the heroic efforts of these men, their writings failed to bring about a revival of the traditional astrology. To date, only sections of Morin's *Astrologia gallica* have been translated into modern languages, and only book 21 is available in English. (Book 22, which remains untranslated, contains Morin's references to the parts.) Dee's *Propaedeumata aphoristica* also remains untranslated, as do the bulk of Bacon's work and all of Fludd's. All seven of the magi mentioned above wrote exclusively in Latin, except for Lull, much of whose work is also in Arabic and Catalan. Thus we see once more that the materialistic technology which increasingly dominates education has cut off the serious student of the occult from important source materials—for how many today learn the classical languages? Yet learn them we must if we wish to study the principles underlying Nature. The necessary information will not easily be found in the modern languages. This work will, in a limited way, provide much of what has to date been unavailable, but it is only a beginning.

In sum, then, we have seen that as a result of the controversies of the Renaissance, astrology was dealt a severe blow and its practitioners were forced to limit their efforts to the application of those doctrines which seemed more acceptable in the new scientific context. This meant that all but those doctrines based on observable physical phenomena were tossed out of the astrologer's method closet. Among the discarded material was the doctrine of the parts, which, because of the general ignorance of its metaphysical foundation, was relegated to the dust bin. There it has remained, virtually inaccessible to the modern practitioner, until now.

Notes

1. Albumassar, *De magnis conjunctionibus annorum revolutionibus ac eorum profectionibus.* Augsburg, 1489.

2. Albiruni, *Elements of Astrology,* trans. R. Ramsey Wright (London: Luzak and Co., 1934).

3. C.H. Haskins, *The Renaissance of the Twelfth Century* (Cambridge: Harvard University Press, 1927), p. 318. Fifth printing, 1971.

2

THE METAPHYSICAL
BASIS OF THE PARTS

The proper use of the Arabic parts is impossible without a clear understanding of astrological causality. What follows is intended to fulfill this need.

Since all things flow forth from the One and since the entire art of astrology, including the parts, rests on number, we begin our discussion with the First Principle of the art: the One or Monad.*

THE FIRST PRINCIPLE

Recognized by philosophers, mystics, and saints throughout the ages, our First Principle, the Monad, has been known by many different names. Plato speaks of it as the Creature Itself; Fludd as the First Form. The German mystic Jacob Boehme sometimes calls it *flagrat,* signifying a flash or explosion of consciousness in alchemical jargon, and sometimes *lubet* or *libet,* which means in Latin "It is permitted"; for by its ceaseless and unrestricted giving, the Monad makes the Creation possible.

Some have named it Splendor, Proteus, or Phanes. Others have likened it to the Sun. Many have called it God. All agree that it is the affirmation of all-inclusive existence, the "I am."

---

*Monad: "An elementary unextended individual spiritual substance from which material properties are derived"(*Webster's Seventh New Collegiate Dictionary*). The Monad is an absolutely simple entity.

In the East, our First Principle has been known as Atman, the Supreme Spirit. The Bhagavad Gita speaks of it as the Highest Imperishable Self, whose nature is spiritual consciousness; as the Creator of all creative powers; as the Beginning, Middle, and End in Creation; as the Heat of the Sun and the Moon. Its inferior manifested nature is said to be earth, water, fire, air, ether, mind, intellect, and personality. Its superior nature is the very life which sustains the universe.

Of the secret fount from which the Monad springs, we can say nothing. We may say, however, that in its original state, it exists in an inviolable Unity, self-contained and serene, without form or attributes.

Now, the Monad wills to experience its own infinite qualities and attributes—but how can it do this in its unmanifest state of Absolute Unity? Thus, in order to manifest its latent qualities, the Monad apparently differentiates itself into three existences: Itself, the Macrocosm, and the Microscosm. This threefold existence may be represented by the following figure.

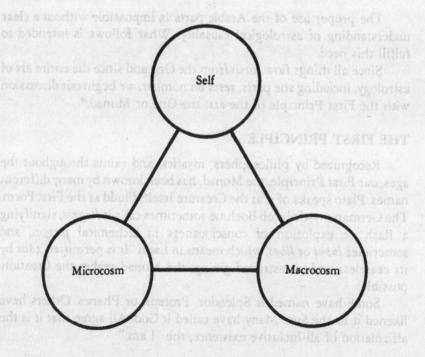

Figure 1

These three existences, having arisen from the same Source and yet contained within it, are essentially One. (I shall demonstrate this geometrically later on.) Both the Macrocosm and the Microcosm are therefore subject to the same laws and are expressions of the same elements. It follows, then, that when we study the Microcosm (as in natal astrology, or genethlialogy), we necessarily bring to light principles that are useful in understanding the Macrocosm (as in mundane astrology)—and all the while we are simultaneously studying the Monad itself.

We shall examine later how the Monad proceeds into its threefold manifestation. But first let us consider the nature of the Microcosm, or Man, and how it is related to the Monad, as well as the relationship of the Microcosm to the Macrocosm, or Creation.

ON THE NATURE OF MAN

As the sun illumines the whole earth, so the Lord illumines the whole Universe.
—Bhagavad Gita

The Light in man, which the heart of God had breathed in, signifieth or resembleth the sun which shineth in the whole deep.
—Jacob Boehme

Many philosophers, magi, and saints of the past have discoursed at length on the nature of Man. They sought to establish its characteristics and virtues and above all to discover the mysterious relationship between the Microcosm and the Macrocosm—between Man and the Creation. Again and again the works of such sages affirm the Hermetic maxim: That which is above is just like that which is below, and that which is below is like that which is above.

Bearing in mind that it is the nature of Man which defines not only the role of the parts but even the whole art of astrology, let us now hear directly from four magi-philosophers of the Renaissance who demonstrate a remarkable agreement on the subject of Man.

Henry Cornelius Agrippa (1486-1535 or 1536)

The human soul is a certain divine Light, similar to the image of the Word, the cause of causes, created of the first exemplar, the substance of God, and stamped with a sigil the character of which is the eternal Word. Moreover, the human soul is a certain divine substance, individual and whole unto itself, present in each part of the body, produced by an incorporeal author so that it *issues forth*

from the virtue of acting alone and not from the bosom of matter.
The soul is a substantial number, uniform, self-sufficient, and
rational, rising far above all bodies and matter, whose partition is
not according to matter, nor by anything inferior and gross, but
rather arising from the efficient cause. It is not so great a number,
but one which is far from all corporal laws; whence it is neither
divided nor multiplied by parts. And so the soul is a certain divine
substance emanating from divine fountains, bearing number with
itself; not indeed that divine number with which the Creator
arranged all things, but a rational number by means of which it,
having proportion with all things, is able to know all things. And
thus the human soul, according to the opinions of the Platonists,
immediately proceeding from God, is joined to this gross body by
the fitting means:* Whence indeed in that very first descent it is
involved in a celestial [i.e., sidereal] and aerial body, which some call
the ethereal vehicle of the soul. With this medium, by the decree of
God, who is the center of the world into the middle of the heart,
which is the center of the human body, it [the soul] is first poured,
and from there it is distributed through all the parts and members
of its body, where its vehicle is joined to the natural heat, through
the heat generated in the heart to the spirit. By means of this
[spirit], it immerses itself in the humors by whose office it clings to
all these, although it is poured from one to another, because the
heat of fire clings closely to air and water, although in truth, it is
carried to the water by the air. Thus it is shown how the immortal
soul is shut up in the gross and mortal body by means of an
immortal body, namely the ethereal vehicle. But when these
mediums are dissolved by sickness or some other evil, or are [in
some way] deficient, then the soul recollects itself through each of
these mediums and flows back into the heart, which was the first
receptacle of the soul. But when the spirit of the heart is deficient
and the heat extinguished, it deserts it, and the man dies, and the
soul flies forth with the ethereal vehicle, and the guardian genii and
daemons follow it and lead it to Judgment, where, their opinions
having been reported, either God conducts the good souls to Glory
or the violent daemon drags the evil souls to their punishments.[1]

Giordano Bruno (1548-1600)

...there is one thing, an efficient and formative principle from
within, from which, through which and around which the
composition [of bodies] is formed; and it is exactly like the

*Agrippa here plays on words with the phrase *"per media competentia,"* for the word *competentia,*
literally "agreeing," is commonly used to describe astrological aspects of one "star" or planet to another.
The reference is therefore to the sidereal or astral body.

helmsman on the ship, the father of the family at home, and an artisan who is not external but *fabricates from within*, tempers and preserves the edifices; and in it is the power to keep united the contrary elements, to arrange together, as if in a certain *harmony*, the discordant qualities, to keep and maintain the composition of an animal. It winds the beam, weaves the cloth, interweaves the threads, restrains tempers, gives order to and arranges and distributes the spirits, gives fibers to the flesh, extends the cartilage, strengthens the bones, ramifies the nerves, hollows out the arteries, fecundates the veins, foments the heart, gives breath to the lungs, succors all within with vital heat and radical humidity in order that the said hypostasis [union of body and soul] may be composed and the said countenance, figure, and face may appear on the outside.

Thus, the dwelling place in all things said to be animate is formed from the center of the heart, or from something proportionate to it, by its enfolding and shaping the members and conserving those which have been enfolded and shaped. Thus, necessitated by the principles of dissolution, abandoning its architecture, it [the efficient and formative principle] causes the ruin of the edifice by dissolving the contrary elements, breaking the union, removing the hypostatic composition... making its retreat from the external parts and members to the heart, and... leaves by the same door through which it was once fitting for it to enter...

[This principle is] that substance which is truly man, and not an accident which is derived from the composition. This principle is the divinity, the daemon, the particular god, the intelligence, in which, by which, and through which, just as the diverse complections and bodies are formed and form themselves, there likewise succeeds being, diverse in species, of diverse names, of diverse forms. This because it is that principle which, as regards the rational acts and appetites, moves and governs the body according to reason, is superior to it, and cannot be necessitated by it.[2]

Hermes Trismegistus*

Man is a marvel...honor and reverence to such a being! Man takes on him the attributes of a god, as though he were himself a god.... How more happily blended are the properties of man than those of other beings! He is linked to the gods, in as much as there is in him a divinity akin to theirs; he scorns that part of his own being which makes him a thing of earth; and all else with which he finds himself

---

*Hermes is the fabled author of numerous ancient astrological and other esoteric works. He is identified with the Egyptian god Thoth.

connected by heaven's ordering, he binds to himself by the tie of his affection. He raises reverent his eyes to heaven above; he tends the earth below. Blest in his intermediate station, he is so placed that he loves all below him and is loved by all above him. He has access to all; he descends to the depths of the sea by the keenness of his thought; and heaven is not found too high for him, for he measures it by his sagacity, as though it were within his reach. With his quick wit he mixes the elements; air cannot blind the intention of his soul with its thickest darkness; nor does the density of the earth impede his work, nor the profound depth of the water obstruct his downward gaze. *Man is all things; Man is everywhere.*[3]

Pico della Mirandola (1463-1494)

At last the best of artisans ordained that that creature to whom he had been able to give nothing proper to himself should have joint possession of whatever had been peculiar to each of the different kinds of being. He therefore took man as a creature of indeterminate nature and, assigning him a place *in the middle of the world*, addressed him thus: "Neither a fixed abode *nor a form that is thine alone* nor any function peculiar to thyself have we given thee, Adam, to the end that *according to thy longing and according to thy judgement* thou mayest have and possess what abode, form and what functions thou thyself shalt desire. The nature of all other beings is limited and constrained within the bonds of law prescribed by Us. *Thou, constrained by no limits, in accordance with thine own free will,* in whose hand we have placed thee, *shalt ordain for thyself the limits of thy nature.* We have set thee at the world's center that thou mayest from thence more easily observe whatever is in the world. We have made thee neither of heaven nor of earth, neither mortal nor immortal, so that with freedom of choice and with honor, as though the maker and molder of thyself, thou mayest fashion thyself in whatever shape thou shalt prefer. Thou shalt have the power to degenerate into the lower forms of life, which are brutish. Thou shalt have the power out of thy soul's judgement, to be reborn into the higher forms, which are divine."[4]

Here, then, is the answer to the question What is Man? Here also, in Agrippa's account, is the relation of the Microcosm to the Macrocosm and to the Monad; for as it is impossible for there to be more than one center of the world, it follows that if God, or the Monad, is at the center of the world, and Man is also at the center of the world—as Bruno, Hermes, and Mirandola all affirm—then God and Man must coincide. Furthermore, the locus at which they coincide must be the human heart, which all four authors have agreed is also at the center of the world.

THE METAPHYSICAL BASIS OF THE PARTS / 21

The true understanding of the coincidence of the three aspects of the First Principle as Monad, Microcosm, and Macrocosm in the center of the world, or human heart, is the key to Fate and to our art. By declaring the three in One we see that there are not three essentially separate entities but rather *essentially One* and *apparently three*. The essential Unity of the three points is the reason why the purity of the heart is emphasized in all true systems of philosophic or religious endeavor. For us as astrologers, it means that we may regard the natal figure as a diagram of the heart. Just as the heavens are in the world, or Macrocosm, and the Macrocosm is in the heart, so the figure of the heavens at the time of birth is a diagram of the heart of the native at the beginning of his or her incarnation. Moreover, these astrological figures are necessarily diagrams of the desire of the heart, be it the incarnating individual's desire or that of the Macrocosm. For the nature of our First Principle is affirmation of the desire to *be,* and this First Principle, which is the Light of Consciousness, flows forth from the Sun (or heart) and is specialized by the various powers, as will be shown.

The "stars" and "planets" employed in astrology are therefore *within*—in the heart of the world when we are dealing with mundane astrology, and in the native's heart in genethlialogy. We deal with the material globes in astrology only insofar as they are used to time the movements of the inner "planets" and "stars" that lie hidden at the center of Man's being. Herein lies the true difference between the astronomer and the astrologer, and until this is fully apprehended, the more subtle astrological doctrines, such as the parts, will remain unintelligible.

As a result of the coincidence of the center of the human self with the heart of the Creation, we find that from the seat of desire that is the heart arise both the multifarious events of the Macrocosm—that is, events political, meteorological, physical (e.g., plagues, earthquakes, birth-rate variation), and spiritual (e.g., the rise and fall of religious orders and sects)—*and* the events of the Microcosm: the course of a person's life or destiny, his health, well-being, and so on. Having arisen, these various desires in the individual and in the world become manifest in time in accordance with a fixed law that is reflected in the orderly movement of the planets around the Sun and, when we consider longer cycles, of the Sun and galaxy in the universe.

Thus the key to the unfolding of what the Hindus call karma is to be found in the study of astronomical law understood in the way explained here, and this is the true astrology and the traditional one. However, before this can be understood clearly, we must see how the various astrological causes arise in the First Principle—whether its sphere of activity is the Microcosm or the Macrocosm—and how the one is a reflection of the other.

ON THE ARCHETYPE

> The whole body of this world is as a man's body, for it is surrounded in its utmost circle with the stars and risen powers of nature; and in that body the seven spirits of nature govern and the heart of nature standeth in the midst or center.
>
> —Jacob Boehme

We should conceive of our First Principle, our Absolute, the Monad, as a thing eternally immanent, ever-present though veiled by multiplicity, yet apprehensible to a stilled mind. The Monad is different from all other numbers, as is apparent from the fact that 1×1 or $1 \div 1$ always equals One. Unity never moves away from Unity nor gives rise to anything but Unity. Hence it is stable and the self-sufficient Paradigm of the Same, as G. L. Hersey indicates.[5] Change originates with the Dyad, for all numbers after Unity, multiplied by themselves, yield something other than themselves, while the Monad remains always at rest. The Monad is like the string in a string of pearls: It ties all together, is always One, and, though it is rarely seen, is the beginning and center of every act, or pearl.

Astrology is the study of how the various forms contained within the Light of Consciousness or Monad affect the substance of Mind and cause the manifold experiences of life. It is clear from this definition that the predictive side of astrology is merely the practical application of metaphysical laws. Furthermore, since the forms referred to in the definition exist in the Divine World and are the divine or godly causes of things in this inferior world, the true study of astrology involves nothing less than the contemplation of the various angelic and divine orders and most certainly of God Himself. Since the gods, angels, and daemons are differentiations, as it were, and specializations of the Divine Unity, it is obvious, first, that any attempt to probe the nature of astrological causality which does not include the recognition of this Unity, nor continually refers to it, is at best an incomplete view and hence doomed to error; and second, that since all multiplicity flows forth from the underlying Unity, it is in number, which measures all things, that we must seek the key to the orderly unfolding of this multiplicity. For all acts which arise in the First Principle arise as an expression of the harmony of the world. Since all harmony is the loving recognition of Unity by multiplicity, and since all harmony or order is fundamentally numerical, our esoteric art is seen to rest on number.

The consideration of our First Principle as the source of number is central to an understanding of Man and Creation, astrology, and the parts. Boethius understood this when he wrote: "All things which were constructed from the First Nature of Things are seen to have been formed by reason [or by the ratio] of numbers. Indeed this was the Principle Exemplar [or archetype] in the soul of the Creator."[6] Therefore, as John Dee states: "Number hath a treble state: One, in the Creator; another in every Creature (in respect of its complete constitution); and a third in Spirituall and Angelicall Myndes and in the Soule of man. In the first and third state, Number is termed Number Numberyng. But in all Creatures, otherwise, Number is termed Number Numbered. And in our Soule, Number beareth such a swaye, and hath such an affinity therewith, that some of the old Philosophers taught Man's soule to be a Number movyng itself." Dee further states: "This discretion, in the beginnyng, produced orderly and distinctly all thinges. For His Numberyng, then, was his Creatyng all thinges. And His Continuall Numberyng of all thinges is the Conservation of them in being: And, where and when he will lacke an Unit, there and then, that particular thyng shalbe Discreated."[7]

Such, then, is the importance of number as it exists in the exemplar or archetype according to which the Creation is fashioned. And therefore number is the means of differentiation by which the Light (that is, the Light of Consciousness, not the visible light, which is only its outer aspect) becomes qualified into the planetary and stellar causes, or planets and signs.

All this is accomplished by the first nine digits and zero. These numbers represent quite fittingly the origin of Unity from the unknown, its successive differentiation, and its final return to the unknown Source. Thus the entire creative process takes place within the limits of the numbers 1 through 10. This description is not at odds with the notion that Creation manifested in nine stages, for 10 represents the reabsorption of Creation into its Source, its return to the Unmanifest.

Each of the numbers or stages of manifestation is causal of its own nature: That is, it creates a copy of itself wherever it acts. Its nature determines its operation. The number 3, for instance, not only causes all things to have a threefold character, but also, since it is the first odd number after Unity, restores all things to Unity. This is because it arises immediately after the first even number, 2—Duality, or the Dyad—and this return to oddness is like the return of Being to its origin. As there can be no variation in Unity, Duality is conceived as the negation or privation of Unity for the purpose of differentiation. For this reason the Dyad is seen as separative, the Fecund Mother as opposed to the Active

Father, the Monad. Thus all things are generated by One and Two, with Three as their Son, the Creation.

But note here that the Three contains in itself both the Monad and the Dyad and thus is thought of as the reconciliation of its parents, One and Two. Now, since all numbers are generated from the first two, all are divided into odd and even. The odd numbers generated from One are considered to be active and masculine and are associated with Reason. They are said to be in the "family" of the Same (the One). The even numbers, which depend on the Dyad for their existence (since evenness originates with the first even number) are considered feminine and passive and are associated with Desire and Matter. They are the family of the Other. Creation arises as the third point through the interaction of these first two numbers. The Three becomes the paradigm for existence, since it contains the original two elements and reconciles them in such a way that activity, the nature of Three (since it is odd) is the result. Thus, activity—that is, Creation, which is movement and change—arises from the tension between One or Same and Two or Other. The Three, or Ternary, having both the Same and Other within it, contains all the other numbers in latent form, and so Creation, held *in potentia* in the paradigm or archetype, becomes manifest through the unfolding of the first nine numbers.

We have seen that the First Principle is the same in the Microcosm and in the Macrocosm. From it arise all the experiences and events in life, all the forms and species in Nature, all the phenomena of the universe. All flow forth from Unity according to a fixed pattern. This pattern is the Word, or Name of God, which is Law for the Creation. The Word, essentially numerical, is especially hebdomadal, or sevenfold. As such it may be viewed as composed of 3 and 4, for 3 + 4 = 7.

In the East, the threefold nature of the First Principle is given greater emphasis, and there we find it represented by ꣽ. This Sanskrit mantra is usually transliterated as OM, but AUM is a more accurate rendering because the word is actually made up of three letters, or sounds. Each of these sounds stands for a primary quality of the threefold Unity. In Vedanta these three qualities (sometimes translated as "modes" or "strands") are called guna, and they are the cause of the pulsating life of the universe. They give all things a beginning, a middle, and an end; an expansion from a point (the result of two factors), and the reabsorption back to the Source (the third factor). They give to Creation a positive, a negative, and a common pole. In astrology, the three guna correspond to the cardinal, fixed, and mutable signs and to the angular, succedent, and cadent houses. There is also a connection between the generation of the planets from the primary Light and these primary qualities.

In the West, where the emphasis is somewhat different, a fourfold name has been passed down to us: the Tetragrammaton.

The Fourfold Name

The Tetragrammaton is the unpronounceable Cabbalistic Hebrew word for God, rendered in English as YHVH.* In Hebrew the letters are, reading from right to left, *yod, he, vav, he:*

יהוה

Like OM, this name represents the orderly manifestation of Creation, but in a fourfold rather than a threefold manner. We shall find the fourfold name more useful in understanding the nature of the parts; however, we shall never really be far from the threefold name, for it is inherent in the fourfold name. (Note that the Tetragrammaton is the threefold view with one element, the letter *he,* repeated.) Inevitably the practical application of the doctrine of the parts requires an understanding of both archetypes, 3 and 4. Together they give rise to the ecliptic and form the Archetypal Man, or Great Man of Heaven, whose head is in Aries and whose feet are in Pisces. This Man, who is the measure of all things, is the universal paradigm against which the individual natal figure or revolution must be judged.† Bearing this in mind, let us now analyze the Tetragrammaton.

Yod. The first letter, *yod,* י , is the First Principle. This letter has also been shown embellished with three crowns ‎ , representing the secret fountain from which the Monad issues.

In Hebrew, each letter of the alphabet has a numerical equivalent of great metaphysical significance. The *yod* is equivalent to 10, and this is of special interest because the beginning of a thing, its birth or geniture, establishes its nature and outcome, as we know from our art. Thus by necessity, the manifestation of the Creation takes place in ten stages, for the word YHVH is the name of the Creator, who acts on Himself since there is nothing outside of Him. The number 10, however, represented by 1 and 0, indicates that this activity will involve the return to the

*The pronunciation of YHVH is unknown since no vowels are indicated; however, it has been given as YAHWEH or Jehovah. Hebrew scholarship considers the latter rendering philologically impossible.

†The word "man" comes from the Sanskrit *manas* (Latin *mens*)—"he who thinks"—from the root *ma,* which also gives *matra* (measure), and *Maya* (the principle of Illusion). We also find this root in the name *Maat,* the Egyptian goddess of justice.

Source or secret fountain from whence it sprang. Thus a circulation is indicated, or two motions, if you will: out and back. This circulation is the archetype of return to the Source, of completion or perfection.

Completion of the manifesting Word, then, involves ten stages. However, there is a mystical association between the numbers or stages 1, 3, 5, 6, 7, and 10, all of which are "circular" in some sense, as we shall see. All of these must be understood by the student of astrology who wishes to penetrate to the heart of the art.

The First *He*. The second letter of the Tetragrammaton, *he,* is of great importance to this study, for it is the one that is duplicated. The first *he* follows the *yod* rather like its expression. We should think of this *he* as being breathed out or spoken by the *yod.*

The letter *he,* ה , is at once a representation of 2 and of 3. First, it is 2 because it stands on two "legs." Second, it is 3 since, composed of three strokes, it shows the descent of 2 from an overshadowing 1. It is appropriate that 2 should follow 1 and in fact flow from it. It is also appropriate that 2 should lead immediately to 3. In so doing, the 2 affirms the primacy of the One as source of all; it states that this One proceeds toward expression (the *he,* an aspirate sound, is the breathed-out Word or Logos); and at the same time it acts in a threefold way. This *he* is the first moved thing or *primum mobile.* Furthermore, the letter *he* is numerically equivalent to 5. In ancient and medieval philosophy, 5 is associated with the fifth element, ether, spiritus, which is the root of the other four elements, two of which are passive (water and earth) and two active (fire and air).[8] Five is also the number of Man, as we shall see later.

Vav and Final *He*. The letter *vav,* ו , nail-like in form, is like a link or bridge (or, in Boehme's view, a barrier) between the two *he*'s, which are likened to the waters above and below the firmament. In the Hebrew language, *vav* functions as the conjunction "and," as in Genesis 1:3:

> God said, Let there be light, *and* there was light.

Note that in this construction, the *vav,* meaning "and," acts as a kind of intermediary between the command and its fulfillment. The speech of God is creative, and so His Word is immediately followed by manifestation—through the medium of the *vav.* Similarly, in the Tetragrammaton, יהוה , *vav* comes between the first *he,* ה , and the final *he,* ה . In this way the first *he* (which is within the name, hence "inner") creates the final or "outer" *he,* and the *vav* which issues forth from the first *he* is the medium by which this is accomplished.

The numerical equivalent of *vav* is 6. *Vav*, or the area between the two *he*'s, thus represents the field of activity of the six differentiations of the primal Unity: namely, the five planets and the Moon. Add to these six planets the Sun, and we get seven planets. Thus the presence of 7 is implied within the 6. (More will be said on this later.).

Vav, then, is connected with the expansion or manifestation of the first *he*, which is then reflected in the final *he*.

The Four Worlds

The four letters *yod, he, vav, he* represent four worlds: The *yod* is the world of Emanation. The First *he* is the World of Causes, or the Angelic World. This Angelic World is objectified or embodied in the *vav*, which is the World of Formation (for us, the zodiac); and the final *he* is the Material World. Thus the creative urge, originally One, becomes successively differentiated in a measured way, and then, at the outer end of the sphere of existence, it is reflected in the physical Creation.

It should be made clear that when astrologers or Cabalists refer to "Heaven," they mean not the final or "outer" *he*, which is the astronomer's domain, but rather the first *he* and its objectification, the *vav*. The term "ether," which indicates *where* the stars are, should mean for us "space" or "sky," as well as "spirit," for Fludd derived his term for spirit—the "fiery breath"—from the Greek root *aith-* ("to burn") and *aër* ("breath"), hence *aithaër* (ether) or burning breath.[9] Our Heaven is therefore "within."

Each of the worlds is proportionately denser and darker according to how much of the creative Splendor or Light reaches it. I shall demonstrate this presently; for the moment, though, let us consider the following figure representing the four worlds. (See next page.)

Here we see the four letters of the Tetragrammaton arranged so as to resemble a human figure. This figure is the Great Man or Archetype, standing with his feet in the Material World and his head in the divine World of Emanation. The smaller figures at the right of the diagram indicate that this fourfold arrangement also exists within each of the four worlds, and this affirms the identity of the scheme as a whole with its parts (remember that "as above, so below").

The diagram shows that the expression (first *he*) of the Divine Will (*yod*) becomes differentiated and embodied in *vav*, which then descends to the second expression (final *he*) of the Will—that is, the physical world.

Vav is the locus of the zodiac, planets, and parts. It is the Subtle

Figure 2

World—the realm of Desire—emanating directly from the Causal World. For this reason, the signs of the zodiac (which means "animal-bearing circle") are represented largely by irrational beasts: the ram, bull, crab, lion, scorpion, goat, and fish. The signs indicate desires characteristic of the animals used to symbolize them. It is this realm of Desire that we deal with in astrology. It is the link between the physical realm and the higher realms of the Angelic World and the World of Emanation. In this realm are all the elements of our art, all the numbers necessary for the formation of Heaven and Earth according to the appropriate patterns.

Let us now consider how the primary astrological qualities which wield such powerful influence over the Material World arise in the Causal World. In so doing, we shall return first to the Monad and see how the multifarious forms arise from it. Next we shall look at the Dyad and Ternary and see the rise of the Quaternary and how it organizes Creation. We shall consider the Quinary briefly, see the rise of the elements from four primitive qualities, and then proceed to the relation of the Hexad to the Heptad, or Septenary. Then we can proceed through to the Dodecary. Afterward, we shall look at the generation of circular motion and of the sphere and see how number divides it into the planetary "spheres." Finally, we shall see that the Dodecary is an expression of the preceding numbers and not the reverse as affirmed by authors who have attempted to demonstrate an ascent from Earth instead of a descent from Unity. Having come this far, we will have shown the orderly progression of causes from our First Principle and established the true nature of our art.

ON NUMBER IN THE ARCHETYPE

One, Two, and Three

The First Principle, because it issues forth from the Secret Fount, the Source of all, contains within it all possibilities. But since it is One and the Same, it must undergo differentiation in order to manifest all its possibilities. Thus, in an apparent denial of its Absolute Oneness, Unity proceeds to Duality so that by the juxtaposition of Same and Other, the possibilities contained within the First Principle might become apparent.

The advent of Duality, or the Dyad, gives rise to number and measure, for as Plato and others affirm, all numbers arise as a result of the interaction of One and Two. With this rise of number is initiated an inexorable succession of permutations of the creative urge, known to astrologers as Necessity or Fate.

Since Unity is by its very nature eternal, the same, and unchanging, the juxtaposition of Same with Other, or Self with not-Self, necessarily gives rise to *Time,* in which and by which the Monad apparently undergoes the myriad changes constantly taking place in Creation. Because there is neither change nor movement in Unity, Time can only exist there as the Eternal Present. But when Unity becomes apparently divided or measured, then it seems to have a beginning, a middle, and an end. Thus arises limited duration. As the differentiation continues, various periods of time are added to or superimposed on the Present (which remains hidden within the apparent change).

In what follows, it is necessary to remember two things: First, *the world and Man are created of living substance.* Regardless of how it appears to us, there is no part of the Creation which is now, ever was, or ever will be dead. Second, *all differentiation of this living substance proceeds in a measured way according to number.* Each of the numbers that represent the stages of manifestation has a distinct subjective experience associated with it. That is, what a thing *is,* it is by virtue of its matter and its form. The matter is essentially One but appears to undergo mutation as a result of the various forms it assumes. How this occurs and how it relates to the parts I shall show presently. For now, it is important to understand that a thing, regardless of what it is, *is aware of its existence,* and that *what* it is—whether a planet, a part, or a fish hook—is determined by its *form.* As the play of forms varies, so will the experience of *what I am,* but not *that I am.* With this in mind, let us proceed.

The beginning of all things is Unity. From the One all things flow forth according to number. Unity contains all multiplicity. Without Unity, no Duality can exist. Yet Duality arises as the negation or denial of Unity and its privation. However, the condition of strife thus created cannot last. Immediately as Duality is created, there arises the Ternary, which completes the circle, reconciles the opposites, and restores Unity or wholeness.

This awesome process contains in it the paradigm of Creation and also the means of its restoration, for from the primal One arise first the opposition of Being into inner versus outer, and thence immediately the reconciling, binding, and healing Ternary. This may be demonstrated geometrically as follows.

1. Let any point, representing Unity, be posited at *A:*

.a

Figure 3

Here we have an artificial (i.e., produced by art) representation of the ineffable Unity or Monad.

2. Let any line of length *x* be drawn from *A* to any second point *B,* so that between *A* and *B* there will be one perfect opposition of 180 degrees—in other words, the perfect representation of the experience of contrariety or Otherness:

Figure 4

3. Now, regardless of the length of the line, there is some point *C* on it which is half the distance from *B* and an equal distance from *A* and *B*. This point *C* can be said to bear the same relation to *A* as to *B* and so is equal to both. Moreover, there is only one such point, since all others incline more to one term than to the other. Thus:

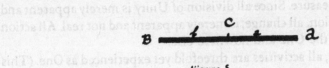

Figure 5

4. Now, if, so as to show *C* in its own integrity rather than as a mere function of *A* and *B*, we were to raise it to its own place, we would achieve the following figure:

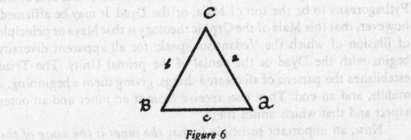

Figure 6

No other arrangement would maintain the difference inherent in Duality and at the same time preserve the Sameness inherent in Unity, for now, although *A*, *B*, and *C* are *different* and the integrity of each is maintained, they are bound by Sameness or Unity in all directions (for the lines *a*, *b*, and *c* are equal or the same). Moreover, we originally began with lines *a* and *b;* line *c* was implied when we drew Figure 6. This line *c* restored the Unity of the figure by closing the gap between *A* and *B*. Thus we now have one figure, the triangle *ABC*.

From this demonstration we must take the following principles and avoid getting caught in the diagram, for the print on the page means nothing, but the concept, everything.

1. Unity is essentially indivisible. In the diagram we are always working with one line of length *x*, which will symbolize for us the quantity of matter in the Creation. As this quantity is always constant, all experiences are permutations of the One experience which we call Affirmation of Being.

2. All subdivision of Unity is apparent and not essential. It commences with an assumed opposition or Duality.

3. Simultaneously with the assumption of Duality arises the Ternary, which reconciles the opposites, reestablishes Unity, and completes and defines the action.

4. Because this action commences with Duality, Duality is said to be the *cause* of action and measure, although Unity is the *source* of number and measure. Since all division of Unity is merely apparent and not real, all action, all change, is merely apparent and not real. All action takes place in the One and nowhere else.

5. Finally, all activities are threefold yet experienced as One. (This will be of great importance shortly.)

The consideration of this Triad is of central importance to us as astrologers, as regards both our art generally and the parts specifically. For this Triad, this threefold cause, arises from the inscrutable depths of what the Cabalists call the *Ain Soph* ("without limit"). It is said by the Pythagoreans to be the son of Maia, or the Dyad. It may be affirmed, however, that this Maia of the Orphic theology is that Maya or principle of illusion of which the Vedantists speak: for all apparent diversity begins with the Dyad or the denial of the primal Unity. The Triad establishes the pattern of all created things, giving them a beginning, a middle, and an end. They also receive from it an inner and an outer aspect and that which unites them.

Now, an important principle is that *the inner is the cause of the outer,* just as the central point of a circle is the cause of the circumference, without which there is no circle. The outer is the expression of the inner. What binds them is the mean or ratio by which they are related. This may be represented as in Figure 7.

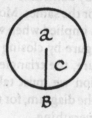

Figure 7

In this diagram I have intentionally used the same letters as before to show a relationship not otherwise apparent. *A,* the center, is the point of origin of the circle. The center, within, defines the circle. It is the inner cause of the circumference, which is the outer expression of the point. The radius *C* is the Will of the Monad or the line of attention. It is also, as in the earlier diagrams, the third point, the means or measure by which the circle is expressed. As will be explained below, the Ternary veils the Septenary and employs it in its expression. Thus the next principle is that the Ternary works through the Septenary.

Three and Four

Although the Quaternary follows the Ternary, we must not think of it as merely appended like a postscript. The Ternary and Quaternary are *coincident*. The point of their coincidence is Unity, the Monad. The coincidence of the Ternary and the Quaternary taken together is called the Septenary. It is the point of origin of the planetary powers, as will be shown in the section on the Septenary. For the moment let us recall the opinion of Plato and Pythagoras that the odd numbers flow from Unity and are causative of Sameness, which is associated with Reason, while the even numbers flow from the Dyad and are associated with Desire and Otherness. Thus we ought to consider the coincidence of the Ternary and the Quaternary as relating to the interaction of Form and Matter, of Reason and Desire.

Boehme describes the rise of the Ternary in a story that can be roughly paraphrased as follows: The tension created by the opposition of the Dyad to the Monad caused an anger or heat and an outward rush or a brilliant, shining cry to go forth from the Monad. The heat and brilliant cry are the Ternary, which is thus the vehicle for the Word. This threefold cause now manifests as a point in the deep, and owing to the brilliance of the cry, Light streaks forth from the point, chasing away the darkness and defining Creation.

From the action of the heat of the Light on the dark, watery Abyss, or first matter, arise the four worlds, each succeedingly cooler as it recedes from the Source. The four worlds arise as follows (see Figure 8).

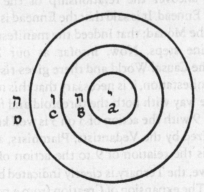

Figure 8

The threefold cause, manifesting as point *A*, acts as a Unity and polarizes the surrounding darkness, which recedes proportionately at *B*. The heat and light of the source continue to operate to *D*, where they have the least effect.

Since the effect of the heat is to rarefy the watery matter of the Abyss in direct proportion to its proximity to the central point *A*, the area from *A* to *D* is divided by the action of the Light into four regions. The area *AB* is filled with light, since it is closest to the Source. Beyond *D*, all is total darkness, the Abyss. The area *CD* is very dark, though it still contains some light. The area *BC* is a mean between areas *AB* and *CD*. We may say that *A* is to *C* as *B* is to *D*. This demonstrates the Chiasmic Proportion of Plato, who affirms that two things (e.g., *A* and *D*) may be bound together effectively by a mean *(BC)*, especially when the mean is such that it divides itself into two parts, one of which *(B)* is closer in nature to the term it adjoins *(A)* and the other *(C)* to the term it joins *(D)*. In this way, says Plato in his *Timaeus*, the Maker of the world bound together His Creation.

Thus arise the four worlds depicted in terms of the Tetragrammaton in Figure 2. Figure 8 shows the numerical foundation of the same thing. The first *he*, or the Angelic World, is at *B*, and the second *he*, the Material World, is at *D*. Between them is *vav*, the World of Formation, at *C*. It was noted before that Boehme spoke of *vav* as a "barrier." This role of the *vav* is shown clearly in the diagram, in which *vav* is the firmament separating the waters above from those below. *BC*, a realm not yet body and not yet soul but already, as it were, both, is the mean between the world of Light *(AB)* and the darker physical realm *(CD)*.

The Relation of Nine to Three and Four

Now let us uncover the relationship of the Ternary and the Quaternary to the Ennead. It is said that the Ennead is the number of the manifestation of the Monad; that indeed the manifestation of all things is achieved in nine steps. Now, insofar as our First Principle is differentiated in the Causal World and there gives rise to all the powers involved in its manifestation, it is necessary that this ninefold process be connected in some way with both the threefold and fourfold processes. The connection of 9 with the action of 3 on 3 is well known to many and has been emphasized by the Vedantists, Platonists, and Sufis. What is usually less clear is the relation of 9 to the action of 3 on 4.

As stated above, the Ternary is clearly indicated by the triangle. All acts are threefold. The expansion of Creation from a point was shown to be both threefold and fourfold. However, early on it was said that the Creation is 10 (that is, nine steps of manifestation plus a tenth step, the return to the Source). Thus a mysterious equation emerges: $3 = 4 = 10 = 9$. How may we understand this curious statement? The answer is to remember that *the whole is equal to One*. Thus $3 = 4 = 10 = 9 = 1$. We are permitted to do this because all differentiations of Unity are merely apparent, and these numbers are modes of Unity, which is never absent. Now, if we affirm all action to be threefold, we would expect the creation of each of the four worlds to be threefold, and this would give rise to 3 × 4 or 12. However, as the following figure shows, we also get 9, for the third point of each triangular activity (or world) is the first point of the next. And so our equation becomes 3 = 4 = 10 = 12 = 9 = 1.

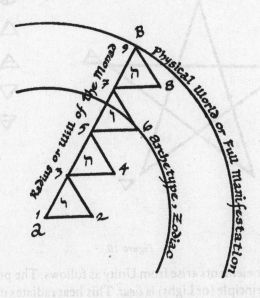

Figure 9

Figure 9 shows the connection of 3, 4, 9, and 12; for while 9 (3 × 3) is associated with complete manifestation, so is 12 (3 × 4). Also apparent in this figure is the fluid character of the interactions of these numbers. Though we are forced to speak of one number at a time to the exclusion of the others, they are in fact all present simultaneously and are acting and reacting all the time. Each maintains its own nature and at the same time interacts with the others. Hence while 3 + 4 = 7 and 3 × 4 = 12, now we find that 3 × 4 = 9! Therefore, if we are ever to reach a true understanding of this realm, we cannot afford to view number as the merchants do, but must instead consider it as a living, intelligent substance acting in harmony with itself. If we do this, we shall find that all schools agree fundamentally, and that will give us a far wider vision than we would otherwise have.

Five

Now we turn to the Quinary, the fivefold cause. Though it progresses from Unity, which it maintains uppermost (see Figure 10), from it depend four distinct qualities, the four elements, like four limbs from the same head.

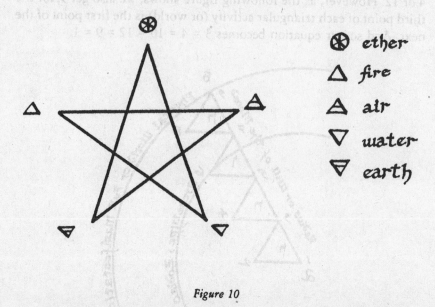

ⓧ ether

△ fire

△ air

▽ water

▽ earth

Figure 10

The four elements arise from Unity as follows. The primary quality of the First Principle (or Light) is *heat*. This heat radiates upon the Dyad (or Matter), whose primary quality is the absence or privation of heat, namely *cold*. In accordance with the Law of the Ternary, a mean arises between these two which Fludd calls *humidity*. This humidity, the offspring of the opposition of Light and Matter, finds its polar opposite in *dryness*. Thus we see how the Dyad and Ternary interact in Creation, for as soon as the Ternary (which is born of the Dyad) acts, the Dyad reacts and produces something in accordance with its own nature, which is to oppose and deny.

This reactive characteristic of the Dyad can be seen everywhere in our art. It underlies the reactive nature of the feminine signs, and so the psychology and behavior of persons in whom the feminine signs predominate are continually beset by problems arising from this very reactiveness. Thus we ought not to think that once a number has arisen, the preceding ones have disappeared. On the contrary, they are all always there, always acting in accordance with their own natures. And so we see that the Ternary produces things reflecting the threefold cause, while the Dyad immediately opposes all action with reaction, opposition, and denial.

The Quaternary is the cause of the four primitive qualities, heat, cold, dryness, and moisture (humidity), all of which are bound together in the One. Each of these primitive qualities, responding to the ordering action of the Word, containing the paradigms of Same and Other, draws near that other quality which bears more affinity with it, and opposes that quality which is other than it, as shown in Figure 11.

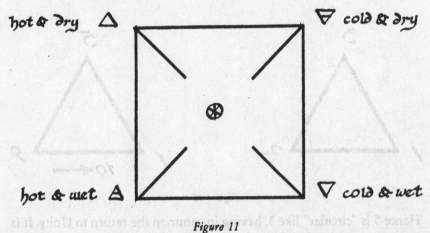

Figure 11

From this stable arrangement arise the four elements, all being subsumed in the fifth, ether. These four elements are material, having been generated by the action of the First Principle (Light) on the Dyad (Matter). For this reason they fall below the firmament. The region above the firmament is, as we have seen, one of Light, without any admixture of Matter; but below the firmament we find diverse shades of Darkness, or participation in Matter. Again, the region above the firmament is One, and the lower realms arise from succedent numbers and are for this reason inferior and posterior to the Dyad.

All this resides in the human heart, which is the center and mini-model of the world. From this center, the breath of life issues forth as from a fountain. This fountain is the locus of the horoscope, which is the diagram of the relationships of the factors in the Causal World at a given point in time. The causal factors referred to are the "numbers" from 1 to 10 considered in the most abstract sense. We may consider this fountain, the heart, from the point of view of any or all of these numbers; what we see when we do this will vary depending upon what number we are using as our viewpoint. Up to now we have considered this fountain as Unity, Dyad, Ternary, Quaternary, and Quinary. We have yet to speak of it as Hexad, Septenary, Octad, Ennead, and Decad. What must be kept in mind at all times, however, is that all these numbers are apparent manifestations of Unity and thus throughout we are really speaking of only *One*.

The Quinary has particular affinity with the Ternary, for just as the Ternary is the mean between the Monad and the Dyad, so the Quinary is the mean between the Monad and the Ennead, which is the manifestation of the Monad. As Figure 12 shows, 5 is found halfway between 1 and 10.

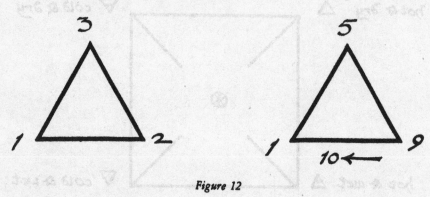

Figure 12

Hence 5 is "circular" like 3, having in common the return to Unity. It is at a point which arises from the Law of the Ternary in the same way as the Ternary itself arose. As the Ternary defines action, so the Quinary, the Divine Breath, is the first moved thing or *primum mobile.** For this reason, it, like the Ternary, is "circular." The Quinary is circular in another way, too: that is, by its own nature. For witness that 5 multiplied by itself always returns to itself: $5 \times 5 = 25$; $5 \times 5 \times 5 = 125$; $5 \times 5 \times 5 \times 5 = 625$; and so on.

Moreover, 5 is composed of the rational Ternary and the irrational Dyad. In this way it is like Man, in whom is found both rationality and irrationality, and both soul, which is threefold, and Matter, which is dualistic. The Quinary, like mankind, must decide which way it will move, for it stands at the border between the realm of Light and that of Darkness, and this consideration, as well as its circularity, is of utmost importance in the generation of the sphere, as we shall see.

Six and Seven

The Book of Genesis opens with the phrase *bereshith*, which is translated in the Vulgate as *"In principio"* and in the King James

*As stated earlier, 5 is the numerical equivalent of the Hebrew letter *he*, which was said to be the Divine Breath, spirit, and ether. In Arabic, 5 is *hamsah*. The word *hamsah* in Sanskrit means "breath" and is resolvable into *Aham sa*, meaning "I am That."

version as "In the beginning." But the word *reshith* means a principle or first thing (our First Principle) as much as "beginning." In fact, it is a beginning *because* it is the first thing and there is nothing else from which to begin. Moreover, since the Mosaic text was not pointed (no vowels were indicated), *bereshith* may also be read *barasheth*, or "He created six," as is stated in the Zohar. By combining these readings, we get the sentence "In the beginning He created six." "He" plus "the six" gives 7. This is depicted in the following figure.

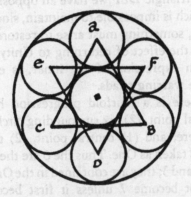

Figure 13

Here we find six circles or spheres inscribed around another and within yet another. This is a pictorial representation of our Cosmos, as composed of eight spheres.

Note that the center of the central sphere coincides with that of the outer sphere. If we let the inner sphere stand for Man, then the seven other spheres are seen to act on him from outside, the greatest being the outer sphere (the Sun), which contains all the others. If the inner and outer spheres are taken as one, the only difference being *the measure of their radii, which determine their relative size,* then we have a diagram of the First Principle (the center dot) and the Microcosm (the central sphere) within the Macrocosm (the outer sphere containing the six other spheres). This affirms the unity of the Microcosm and Macrocosm, for we could, of course, inscribe the same pattern within the inner sphere. Since the outer is the expression of the inner, we have seven spheres here, not eight, for the other six have centers that are related to the inner and outer circles but not coincident with them. However, since we affirm the identity of the inner and outer circles, we may say that the six surrounding circles are "within" the Microcosm. Thus we see the relation between the Hexad, which is the sixfold specialization of the underlying Unity, and the Septenary.

How this diversity arises should be easily seen from Figure 13, for all the circles are arranged symmetrically forming a six-pointed star. This star, however, is composed of two triangles, showing that the Hexad is the Triad reflected. Here is the relationship hinted at earlier when it was said that the Ternary manifests through the Septenary, for we have concluded that there are seven spheres in the diagram. The inner sphere represents the *yod,* which is the channel of the Will of the Absolute. This manifests threefold as an active cause, the triangle *ABC*. However, with the triangle *DEF* we have an opposition of two forces (each threefold) which is impossible to maintain, since according to the Law of the Ternary, something must arise to restore the balance. The Ternary always has the effect of returning to Unity, and so the outer sphere, which is an expression of the inner, is established as the reconciliation of the warring triads.

Notice that there is a fourfold progression here as well as a threefold: (1) central point, (2) six surrounding circles or spheres, (3) outer circle or sphere; and (1) central point, (2) triangle *ABC*, (3) triangle *DEF*, (4) all taken as One. Thus the 6 are the expression of the One acted upon by 2 and 3; they are contained in the One, hence $6 + 1 = 7$; and the One cannot become 7 unless it first becomes 3 and then progresses to 7 in 4 steps. Part of this process is the mutation of 3 into 6 by the Dyad. Now, just as the Quinary is "circular," so is the Hexad by its very nature: If 6 is multiplied by itself any number of times, it always returns to itself: $6 \times 6 = 36$; $6 \times 6 \times 6 = 216$; $6 \times 6 \times 6 \times 6 = 1296$; and so on. Moreover, all these multiplications preserve the presence of one of the odd numbers within the Decad, which indicates that the Hexad is the means by which the Same or Unity creates all things. The fact that 6 is a feminine (even) number, originally generated from the Dyad, shows *where* this activity takes place: namely, in Desire (or Appetite) or Matter, which is the Dyad. For this differentiation is a specialization— that is, a denial of Unity in preference for some limited aspect of it. This process, ruled by the Dyad, is the process of limited effects. Insofar as it is the denial of Unity and ruled by the Dyad, it is irrational. Insofar as it *seeks* a limited goal, it is "appetitive." But since the outward urge is creative, the spiritual act of reunion or return to the Source must be the reversal of the same process, a movement *against* the urge that generates form.

Remember that 6 is the numerical equivalent of *vav,* which links the two *he*'s, the inner and outer Breaths or Words, which are each numerically 5. Thus it is seen that the seven planets—the five planets plus the Moon and the Sun—operate between the Material World (final *he*) and the Causal World (first *he*) through the zodiac *(vav)*, which is the manifestation of the Great Man.* The spirit or breath (5) flows forth to the outer world (final *he*) through the center of the world, or heart (6), which contains the zodiac. Thus we see not only the relation of the Hexad to the Septenary, but also that of the Quinary to the Hexad:

$$Yod = 10$$
$$10 = 1 + 0 = 1$$
$$He = 5$$
$$Yod + he = 5 + 1 = 6 \ (vav)$$

Thus 6 rises out of 5 as *vav* out of *yod* plus *he*. The final *he* is the product of the equation.† (We shall see what this means to us as astrologers in the section on the generation of the sphere.)

Seven

Regarding the birth of the Septenary, Boehme writes:

> For so we are to consider of the creation of this world that the whole essence of eternity has moved itself in the place of this world, and the whole form was enkindled and stirred and that in the desire to manifestation: and there the generation divided itself in the flagrat of the enkindled fire into four parts, viz. fire, water, earth and the air is its moving egressive spirit....
>
> In like manner also the astrum [Zodiac] is thus generated out of the first mother [the expressive or egressive spirit]; and it all takes its rise from the inward spirit; as a hand or foot grows forth from the inward center, and has already its form in the center, viz. in the first operation, and so only grows into a form as the spirit is.
>
> The first Mother of all things, viz. the *lubet* [permissiveness] of the desire, does especially introduce itself into seven forms and yet continues steadfast in 3 only but manifests itself in 7 forms [or in a sevenfold form].[10]

Here we have an account of the manifestation of the Septenary, which I shall demonstrate numerically below. In the last paragraph of Boehme's description, we find the progression from the Monad (the "inward spirit" or the "first mother" or the *"lubet* of the Desire") to the Dyad (the "desire to manifestation"); then to the Ternary, in which it "continues steadfast"; then to the Septenary, in which it manifests itself.

---

*The *vav* or zodiac may be thought of as the "garment" of the first *he* or Causal World. In this sense the zodiac is at once part of the Subtle World and the Causal World.

†Not by ordinary arithmetic, of course, but by the working of the Name. Just as was said above, $3 = 4 = 10 = 12 = 9 = 1$, so now $10 + 5 + 6 = 5$. The first *he* produces the final *he* by reflection through the intermediary of *vav* or 6. In this sense the final *he* is "produced" by the "equation."

This description affirms that the Septenary is the means of manifestation of the Ternary; for as was said, the Ternary is the embodiment of Unity. We may symbolize this as in Figure 14.

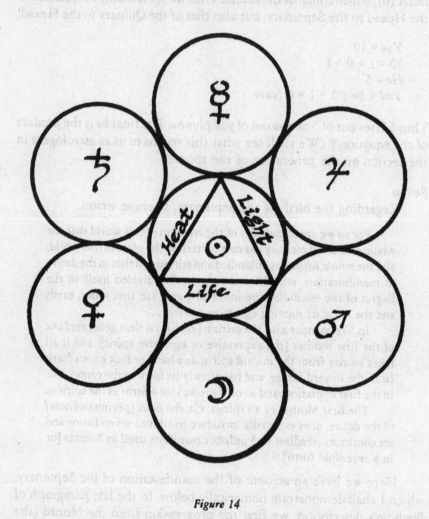

Figure 14

This is a diagram of the Causal World, the first *he* of the Tetragrammaton. It is the sevenfold manifestation of the unmanifest Ternary and the root cause of the zodiac or Dodecary.

Figure 15 shows that 7 cannot be generated from 3 by mixture as 5 may be, but rather arises directly from Unity, although it contains the Ternary and the Dyad hidden within it.

Here we see that the five elements arise "after" the three qualities,

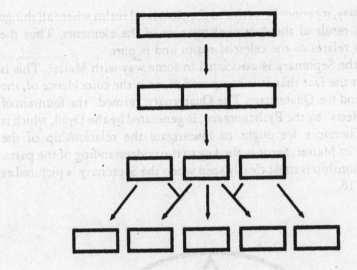

Figure 15

which arise as a result of the Law of the Ternary. But in no way is it possible to find 7 here. Nor can the Septenary be constructed in a circle geometrically, that is, with a compass and straightedge. Thus 7 is very different from 5 and arises directly from Unity. For this reason it is called Divine Virgin, for it does not descend into Matter but, being superior to Matter and maintaining union with Unity, informs the inferior elements according to its own nature.

Here it might be objected that the Quinary is coequal with the Septenary because, like the Septenary, it depends from Unity and is the origin of the elements:

But the fact that both these stars are suspended from Unity merely affirms the common origin of all things celestial and terrene. The nature of the numbers and their properties determine their employment by the Divine, and since the Septenary cannot be made by mixture as the

Quinary may, it cannot be native to the elemental realm where all things arise as a result of the continual mixture of the elements. Thus the Septenary relates to the celestial realm and is pure.

Yet the Septenary is associated in some way with Matter. This is seen from the fact that it is composed of, or is the coincidence of, the Ternary and the Quaternary. The Quaternary, termed "the fountain of natural effects" by the Pythagoreans, is generated by the Dyad, which is Matter. Therefore we ought to investigate the relationship of the Septenary to Matter, for it is the key to the understanding of the parts. This relationship is most clearly seen when the Septenary is pictured as in Figure 16.

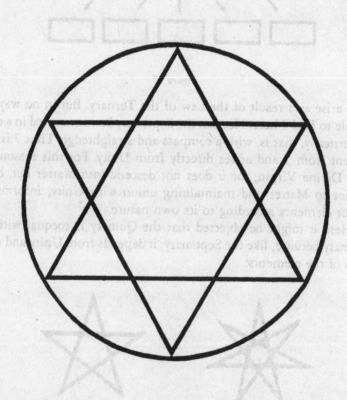

Figure 16

Here we see a central point, the Monad, from which issue forth, and around which continually shine and dance, two interlocking triads. Thus the Septenary (the outer circle) is Unity (for the outer is the expression of the inner point) binding together two hidden Ternaries. (I call them hidden because they are inner or underlying forces; I am not referring here to the six outer triads, which are also hidden in a sense.)

Now, one of these Ternaries ascends and the other descends. Since there is nowhere to ascend other than to Unity (1 and 2, Matter), the Septenary must be connected with the ascent and descent of Consciousness to and from Unity. The Ternary is particularly connected with the creative act; thus the triangle pointing upward refers to Creation, and the triangle pointing downward refers to the opposite of Creation, or Destruction. The Septenary clearly relates, then, to generation and corruption, for it contains two triads, and it is the business of 3 to act, to create. Finally, though the elements are not found in the Septenary, the Dyad (Matter) is. But this is the First Matter as Dyad, not matter as Tetrad. Since the point (the Monad) binds together the two opposing triads, the role of the Septenary is to maintain this union and to regulate it.

Herein is the key to the parts, for as we shall see, the parts, which start from the hebdomadic cause, show how the relation between these causes indicates subtle attitudes, relationships, and inclinations, all of which reflect the inner aspect of events rather than the outer aspect discoverable from the relation of planets to houses or to the Earth.

Now, we have seen that Unity proceeds through Duality to the Ternary, and that the Dyad acts on the Ternary and gives rise to the Hexad. But the Hexad is subsumed under the First Principle, the Monad, and $6 + 1 = 7$. Thus the Septenary is the means by which Matter is ordered and the rule by which mutation takes place in terrene things, for though it remains free from Matter, still it is linked to it by the One at the center, who breathes forth the five elements.

We ought not to forget that 6 is a circular number: that is, it circulates. Around what does it circulate? Around Unity, the still point that shines like the Sun in the center. The archetype of our solar system is obvious here. Thus the physical world, the final *he*, is a reflection of the Causal World, the first *he*, which is essentially numerical. This essentially numerical Causal World is the key to the parts.

Here the reader might object: "You have shown the association of the Septenary with the Monad, but your description is two-dimensional like a diagram. You have yet to convincingly show the relation of the Septenary to the Ternary and to show what makes the different planets' qualities what they are. What makes Venus Venus? What makes Mars Mars?"

In answer to this, I remind the reader that all things flow forth from One, Two, and Three. Now, the Sun sits in our solar system like the point at the center of the circle. The Sun's three primary qualities are light, heat, and Life. Life is moisture, and moisture is Love—for it is the nature of moisture or water to bind, to unite. This binding together is water materially but Love emotionally and spiritually. Therefore, since the six powers are modifications of the central One, the characteristics of the five planets and the Moon will be found to arise from the numerical permutation of these three primary qualities with the action of the Quaternary. Hence it is affirmed that the Septenary arises from the One by the interaction of Three and Four. From this interaction we get the following dispersion of the primitive qualities.

Sun	☉	heat	moisture	light
Saturn	♄	cold	dry	dark
Moon	☽	cold	moist	dark
Jupiter	♃	cold	moist	light
Venus	♀	hot	moist	dark
Mars	♂	hot	dry	dark
Mercury	☿	hot	dry	light
		cold	dry	light

Figure 17

But for completeness we must show how the Ternary is at base the cause of each of these different planetary qualities. This is done by reference to Figure 18.

This, of course, is the famous Chaldean order, starting clockwise from the Moon, listing the planets in their relative speeds as seen from the Earth, with the three inferiors separated from the three superiors by the Sun. To explain the generation of the planets by means of Figure 18, we must start from the Sun, which is the physical representation of our First Principle.

As we have seen, the Dyad follows the Monad immediately. Thus, in Figure 18, we may move away from Unity (the Sun) in two directions: one masculine, toward Saturn, and the other feminine, toward the Moon. The path toward Saturn shows the polarization of the Sun's heat, moisture (Life), and light to the cold, dryness, and darkness (Death) of

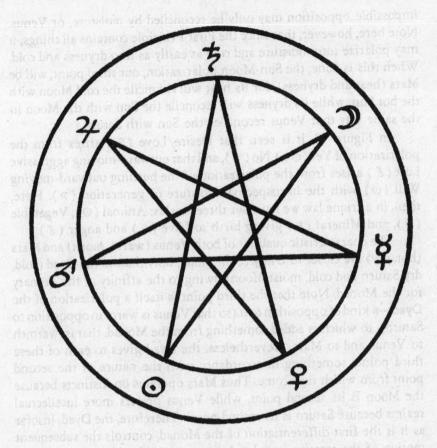

Figure 18

Saturn; this polarization is the office of the Dyad. If we take this course, we speak of the Octave: Sun, Saturn, Venus, Jupiter, Mercury, Mars, Moon, Sun. If, however, we speak of the feminine path, Sun to Moon, we then consider the Sun's polarization to moisture, cold, and activity. Hence our two choices point to two worlds: inanimate (Saturn) and animate (Moon), or outer and inner. There are various considerations to which these sequences might apply; but, having pointed this out, let us proceed with our discussion.

The Dyad therefore polarizes the Monad. Since the Dyad polarizes, it presents two possibilities between which we must choose. The Sun-Saturn path was considered in part when we spoke of the Light-Matter polarization. The third point was said to be the rise of humidity, or moisture. Humidity is here represented as Venus. The First Principle, which contains all things, is polarized by the dry, cold Saturn; this impossible opposition may only be reconciled by moisture, or Venus. Note here, however, that since the First Principle contains all things, it may polarize into moisture and cold as easily as into dryness and cold. When this is done, the Sun-Moon polarization, our third point, will be Mars (heat and dryness), for its heat will reconcile the cold Moon with the hot Sun, while its dryness will reconcile the Sun with the Moon in the same way that Venus reconciles the Sun with Saturn.

In Figure 18, it is seen that Desire/Love (♀) arises from the polarization of Yes (☉) + No (♄), and that outward-moving aggressive Lust (♂) arises from the polarization of the burning outward-moving Will (☉) with the introspective moisture of generation (☽). Here, then, in a triune law we have our three worlds: Animal (☉), Vegetable (☽), and Mineral (♄) giving birth to Love (♀) and anger (♂).

The characteristic qualities of both Venus (warm, moist) and Mars (hot, dry) are closer to Unity (Sun: moist, hot) than to the Dyad (cold, dry Saturn and cold, moist Moon) owing to the affinity of the Ternary for the Monad. Note that the third point is itself a polarization of the Dyad—a kind of opposition to it (so that Venus is warm in opposition to Saturn), to which is added something from the Monad, that is, warmth to Venus and to Mars. Nevertheless, the Dyad gives to each of these third points something in accordance with the nature of the second point from which they come. Thus Mars operates on instincts because the Moon is its second point, while Venus prefers more intellectual realms because Saturn is its second point. Therefore, the Dyad, insofar as it is the first differentiation of the Monad, controls the subsequent motion of the creative impulse. In case the reader objects that in the zodiac each of these planets, like the others, rules two signs, one masculine and one feminine, I point out that we have two sequences here, each of which will include all the planets and so account for their masculine and feminine signs.

We have now completed three stages in two modes of differentiation. Now we move to the fourth. The nature of the Quaternary requires that the fourth stage be a reflection of the second. Again, it must indicate a polarization of one quality of the preceding term. Thus our first sequence, Sun, Saturn, Venus, now brings us to Jupiter. Interestingly, this planet is symbolized by the number 4. Jupiter's nature is drier than Venus's while maintaining moisture. Therein is the polarization. Furthermore, Jupiter is a superior or heavy planet, as is Saturn, and so repeats the second term of the sequence. But we could say as well that the Law of Three is still at work here, for what we call Jupiter arises as a mean between the polarization of the moisture of Venus with the dryness of Saturn or equally of Venus's benefic nature with Saturn's malefic nature. Thus Jupiter is benefic like Venus yet heavy like Saturn.

Our other sequence, Sun, Moon, Mars, brings us to Mercury. The Dyad here causes a polarization of the Moon to Mars, and Mercury, neither male like Mars nor female like the Moon, arises as the mean. Again, Mercury is dry like Venus yet swift like the Moon and, in agreement with the Quaternary, Mercury reflects the Moon's association with measure. In fact, because of Mercury's freedom from moisture, it can emphasize measure to a degree beyond the Moon's capability.

Next the Quinary rules, and in accordance with it we find that Mercury holds the fifth position in the masculine sequence Sun, Saturn, Venus, Jupiter, Mercury; while Jupiter holds the fifth position in the feminine sequence Sun, Moon, Mars, Mercury, Jupiter. Note here that there is an interchange between the two sequences. This is why there is confusion among some authors as to the attribution of ether (5) to Jupiter or to Mercury. Mercury arises as the mean or third point between Venus and Jupiter, for both these planets are benefics, warm and moist, and their polarization must therefore be concerned with something other than these qualities. Now, Jupiter is conducive of wisdom, while Venus is conducive of pleasure, and here indeed is an opposition. Mercury has to do with neither, for it is its function to study both. Moreover, Mercury may be used for the expression of either.

Jupiter in turn arises in its sequence as a mean between the Mars-Mercury opposition. For as Mars is the epitome of aggressive, outward-moving lust and Mercury is the epitome of unpolarized, introverted purity, Jupiter must be the mean, since it is expansive, masculine, moderate, and wise.

The sixth stage of the differentiation finds us at Mars in the masculine sequence and Venus in the feminine. Mars arises as the mean between Jupiter and Mercury since Jupiter is expansive and Mercury is timid. Hence Mars as the mean between these is ambitious. Here Mars is the action reconciling religion (Jupiter) and science (Mercury). This action, however, is action under knowledge since Jupiter is the second term. Venus, on the other hand, is the mean between Mercury and Jupiter in the feminine sequence. Venus is desire and action arising from cupidity since the covetous Mercury is the second term here. This action, action under ignorance, arises by placing Mercury and not Jupiter in the critical second place, and hence desire especially venal arises. Here is Taurean Venus as opposed to Libran Venus, which we discussed above.

Finally, the seventh stage takes us to the Moon in the masculine series and to Saturn in the feminine. Thus the Moon arises as the mean between Mercury and Mars, for Mercury indicates cupidity and Mars lust, and together they give rise to the blind illusion the Moon, the mere reflection of the Glory of the Sun, which was its point of origin. The Moon is instinctual like Mars and introverted and inclined toward measure like Mercury.

Saturn, on the other hand, arises in the feminine series as the mean between Jupiter and Venus, for both these benefics, in a feminine series where the instincts prevail, incline to excess, and the result of excess is exhaustion and death.

Thus we see the members of the Septenary arising from the numerical action of 2 on 3, all within the One.

Eight

The Octad follows the Septenary as the Decad does the Ennead. In both cases we see the completion of the cycle with the return to the Source. However, since the Octad is entirely even—being divisible into two 4's and then into two 2's—its relation to the Dyad is clearly emphasized. Its cycle must therefore relate solely to the irrational or appetitive mode, while the Decad, composed of 1 and 0, illustrates the return of the whole or Unity to the Unmanifest—a most rational and unifying movement.

The eighth sphere, counting from the Earth, is the sphere of the zodiac, the animal-bearing circle, and is the orderly division of the irrational or appetitive urge which acts most powerfully on the Animal, Vegetable, and Mineral kingdoms and their corresponding realms in Man. Man contains the entire Cosmos and all the grades of being in himself. We see the mineral kingdom in the bony skeleton and in the buildup and breakdown of the various mineral deposits in the human body. We see the vegetable kingdom in the fleshy body, in which the same cycles of growth and decay operate as those observed at work in plants. The animal kingdom is seen in Man's lusts, appetites, and instincts by which he is made the most savage of beasts on earth. Above these we see that Man has a rational mind and a soul: the divine spark within him.

Neither a man's soul (the Divinity within him) nor his rational mind are subject to the compulsion of the stars, but the inferior realms of the physical and desire are. *To the degree that he increases the Animal, Vegetable, or Mineral aspects of his constitution, to that degree is he bound by fate.* Nevertheless, Fate's inexorability is mathematically precise, and an important part of this precision is the Octad. It was this association of the Octad with Fate that led the Pythagoreans to call it Justice. "As ye sow, so shall ye reap."

The Octad is composed of two Quaternaries, each of which gets equal time, so to speak: a Quaternary in the upper or Causal World and a Quaternary in the lower or Material World. Since the Quaternary is the Ternary plus one, the rise of events—which comes about through the threefold power and its reflection, all of which takes place *twice* in the Octad—is indicated by consideration of the Octad as

$$3 + 1$$
$$3 + 1$$

or the creative Hexad plus 2, namely, Creation taking place in Desire. The Octad is the only evenly even number in the Decad. This makes it entirely passive. By virtue of this passivity, the Octad may be considered to represent the Material World, the place where all the influences of the superiors are reflected. It is in this respect the very epitome of Justice, for in it is the reflection of celestial Law, mathematically precise. Hence the Octad as passive Matter is the terrestrial world, the ordinary experience. For this reason we call it Earth and place it, as will be shown, in the center of our sphere. This association of the Octad with Desire is very important to our understanding of astrological causality, as we shall see.

Nine and Twelve

Thomas Taylor relates that the Ennead was called "the horizon" by the Pythagoreans. This accords well with the assertion that the manifestation of all things takes place in nine steps, for the tenth, being the return to the Source, cannot be thought of as exceeding the Ennead; rather the Ennead must be thought of as the end result, the circumference of the circle, hence the horizon.

Taylor quotes Proclus to the effect that the Ennead was called perfector "because it gives completion to the fabrication of generation" and is associated with generation since it "proceeds from the Monad as far as to the last numbers without retrogression; and this is the peculiarity of generation."[11]

The Ennead is the base of all the Platonic and Vedic cosmic cycles, as demonstrated by the scheme below. If we add the integers of any of these periods, the result always equals 9. For instance: $1,728,000 = 1 + 7 + 2 + 8 + 0 + 0 + 0 = 18; 1 + 8 = 9.$

Mahayuga	= 4,320,000 years = 9					
Satya Yuga	= 1,728,000 years = 9		Great Year	=	25,920 years = 9
Treta Yuga	= 1,296,000 years = 9		Great Month	=	2,160 years = 9
Kali Yuga	= 432,000 years = 9		Great Week	=	540 years = 9

One degree of zodiac rises on eastern horizon at time of vernal equinox every 72 years, thus comprising one Great Day: 72 = 9.

As the Ennead is the horizon of manifestation, and the Decad the return to the source, we have completed our examination of the primary numerical building blocks of Nature. Now let us look at the Dodecary. This has been affirmed to be the product of the union of the Ternary and the Quaternary, which same coincidence gives rise to the Septenary. The coincidence of 3 and 4 producing both 7 and 12 shows that both are associated in some way. In fact, we find that they are associated in the world, for the twelve signs of the zodiac are ruled by the seven planets. Hence, as the inner rules the outer, and as planets are within the sphere of the fixed stars and signs, so the Septenary rules or gives rise to the Dodecary of the zodiac. Sequentially, 7 arises prior to 12, and posteriors are ruled by those causes which are closer to the Source, or Unity. Finally, both 7 and 12 arise from 3 and 4, and both 3 and 4 are associated with the Sun, for there are 3 aspects of the Sun's influence (heat, light, and Life) and the Sun, as the fountain of Life, is similar to the "fountain of natural effects" which is 4. So the seven planets are qualifications of the Sun's Light in the Eternal Present, while the signs, which are twelvefold differentiations of the Sun's path along the ecliptic in the course of a year, are qualifications of its influence in Time. As the Present is immanent and "inner" and gives rise to Time, so the twelve signs or temporal differentiations rooted in 3 and 4 are subsequent to the qualifications of the same source by the same numbers, resulting in 7. This is fittingly demonstrated by the following ancient figure.[12]*

Here we see the generation of 3 and 4 from the point of view of one sign; and if the pattern is repeated, be it three or four times, 12 will result. It is important to note that though the Ternary and Quaternary are here active, only 6 and not 7 points are actually manifest on the circle. The seventh, the origin, is coincident with one angle of the square. Nor ought we to forget that the Dodecary, as made up of 7 and 5, shows us its affinity both with the planets and with the elements, for by the concourse of the planets, especially the Moon, with the signs of the zodiac, the elements are arranged and excited to change.

*Students of Lull will recognize here the three elements of his art: circle, square, and triangle.

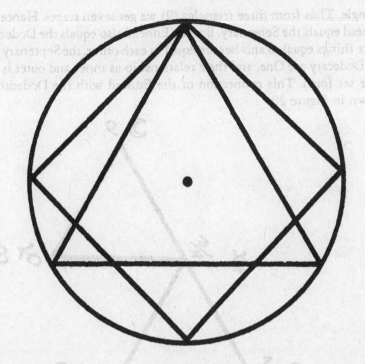

Figure 19

To be sure, both in theory and in practice, the signs and planets must be considered together as the inner and outer aspects of the One Cause, for both deal with the manifestation of this One Cause. It is important for us to maintain contact with this One Cause, the Monad or First Principle, for to lose sight of it is to lose understanding of the essential Unity of Existence and of the underlying connection of cause and effect. This means that in practice, when we see a sign affected by the presence of a planet in it other than its ruler, we must expect to find the ruler affected in conformity with the nature and zodiacal state of the planet inhabiting its sign. Thus the condition of the sign and its ruler varies as either is affected. This fact is frequently overlooked by astrologers, but it is of significance particularly when considering motivation in a natal figure or outcome in a horary figure.

Just as the Ennead and the Dodecary are the same cause manifesting differently (as shown in the section "The Relation of Nine to Three and Four"), so the Ennead bears a similar relationship to the Septenary. For while the Ennead shows the Ternary Law operating in the three worlds (causal, subtle, and gross) each of the triangles thus implied has one of its angles coincident with the apex of the next lower triangle. Thus from three triangles (9) we get seven stages. Hence the Ennead equals the Septenary. But the Ennead also equals the Dodecary. Since things equal to another are equal to each other, the Septenary and the Dodecary are One, and their relationship as inner and outer is as I have set forth. This connection of the Ennead with the Dodecary is shown in Figure 20.

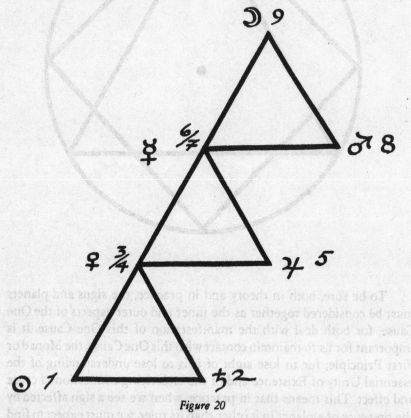

Figure 20

Here we see that both 7 and 9 are numbers of completion or manifestation. The Ennead manifests the Ternary in each of the three worlds, and the Septenary operates throughout the three worlds. Here in our Septenary scale we find our origin in the Sun (1), the Source of all, and its completion in the Moon (9), where the reflection of the solar light occurs (10).

THE GENERATION OF THE SPHERE

Now it is time to demonstrate the harmonious activity of the numerical causes. Being active, creative agents, expressions of the

Monad, these numbers establish the order of the Creation and provide the astrologer with the subject of his art. The reader should not be surprised to find that the model of the universe described here is the ancient geocentric model and not the modern heliocentric model, for our "stars," being within, are not the stars of the heliocentric model, which are merely reflections of the true stars. Moreover, as was established early in this chapter, the subject of our art resides at the center of the Creation and this coincides with the heart of Man, who is a terrestrial creature; thus how else ought we to expect these causes to be arranged to show their influence on the subject? Our art relates to the manifestation of events in this world, and so we place the Earth at the center of the world near the heart and operate from that point. Our model is not based on physical phenomena; rather, physical phenomena and the illusory events of life are determined by our model.[13] The numerical causes act on the intelligent matter of the Causal World in such a way that whenever and however they inform it, there is created thereby an intelligent creature, independent from all other creatures by virtue of its proper form yet united to the same single Source, the Monad, and hence One with all other creatures. Therefore I ask the reader to consider that fluid mental relationships or proportions which are at the same time mathematically precise in their form and effects are the causes of the sphere and its divisions, of the planets acting within it, and finally of those hidden points, the parts. For unless I had shown that the entire art is founded on the action of the inner qualities of number, how could I expect that the parts (which are only this) might be accepted as efficacious?

But now behold: There arises in the Abyss a point which determines the threefold nature of existence. This point, the Monad, polarized to itself, produces a line which streams forth from the point to the measure (which no man yet knows) and thus constitutes itself under the action of the Dyad as a ray or radius. Immediately therefrom springs the Ternary, causing the radius (2) emanating from the still point (1) to describe a circular plane (3) and then a sphere of light (4) which is the perfect embodiment of the creativity and Universal Affirmation of Being of the Three-in-One nature and the field of manifestation of the Word. All specific effects, all limited experience, all natural phenomena find expression within this context as a result of the interaction of 1, 2, and 3 manifesting as the limitation of this Infinite Creativity by a mathematically precise form acting on a suitably disposed matter. The first stage of this process is the archetypal organization of existence according to the numerical principles, as follows.

This sphere is animated by the threefold nature traveling down the radius (the Dyad) to the outer term of the radius. There, as 5 or the Divine Breath, it acts according to its nature, which is circular, and causes the sphere to revolve from east to west (east being by definition the direction from which the Breath moves). Hence the celestial equator is produced by 5, the Quinary or *primum mobile* (see Figure 21).

Now, in the course of the revolution of the celestial equator—the movement which causes day and night and is called the first motion—there arise two other movements. These motions each participate* 2 and 3 like the first motion from which they arise, although each participates* *differently* owing to the action of the Dyad. Thus the first motion, which is rational by reason of its primacy, is opposed by an irrational movement arising from the action of the Dyad. This opposing motion is that of the ecliptic, which Plato calls the Circle of the *Other*, while the equator is the Circle of the *Same*. But since the movement of the ecliptic is Other and thus ruled by Duality, it divides itself into two parts. One of these is visible and one invisible, and these two circles are the circles of the signs of the zodiac and of the constellations. Now, while the first motion is exceedingly swift, the second, in order to be different, must be slower. Again, in order for the third circle to be different still, it must be even slower than the second. Thus the three major celestial movements of our art are accounted for and can be seen to arise as a result of number, particularly 2 and 3.

Because these circles are generated by the Dyad and Ternary, which are the sources of measure and division, it follows that they will exhibit the activity of measure and division in accordance with these causes. Thus all three circles are divided in the same way into 360 degrees. The number 360 tells us what the causes are which generated these circles and what kinds of effects will arise from them. Just looking at the figure 360, we see the Ternary, the Hexad, and the circle itself. This tells us that the circle itself arises from the action of the Ternary and the Hexad. This would seem to differ from what I have set forth above until it is

---

*As the activity of the numerical causes proceeds to multiplicity, we begin to see not one number only at work at a given stage of this process, but numbers working together simultaneously with each other. In the process described above, that of the generation of the sphere, we do not have a sequence 1, 2, 3, or point, radius, circumference so much as a single complex activity in which the affirmation of the point, as the expression of the Monad; the extension of the radius by virtue of the Ternary; and the describing of the circumference which is the activity of the Dyad all occur simultaneously. The entire process exhibits all three numbers in one activity. To speak of this simultaneous activity of more than one numerical cause, I use the word "participate." I say that the above process "participates" 1, 2, and 3. Later on, when we consider the astrological houses, we shall see that the seventh house "participates" the Dyad through its being opposed to the first. The seventh house thus exhibits both the Septenary and the Dyad.

remembered that the Hexad is twice the Ternary. Hence we ought to read this number as a kind of sentence or equation which would tell us that *The circle, the embodiment of the Monad, is measured first by the Ternary and then by the Ternary acting with the Dyad to give rise to the Hexad.* Again, 3 + 6 + 0 = 9, and the Ennead is the measure of the full manifestation of all things.

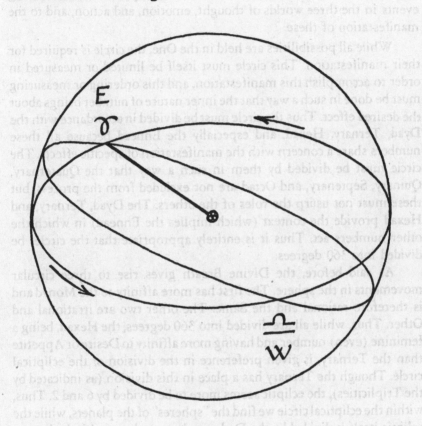

Figure 21

From these two considerations alone, we should know that the circles of our art are considered with the manifestation of the potential of the Monad, for the circle is the embodiment of the Monad and the representation of Universal Affirmation of Being. Note that the return to the Source is not indicated as within the range of astrological causality since here, at the very beginning of our art, the measuring of the circles, the Decad does not appear. Thus, while astrology may be of service in this spiritual endeavor of return, it is only so by virtue of the fact that such returns are of necessity by the same path as the one taken on the outward movement.

But to return to the circles: In considering the number 360 we also see that we are dealing with an art that is concerned with the events (3) arising in or created by the appetites (6), which are of a cyclic nature (0). Finally, we see that the art must deal with the appetites and recurring events in the three worlds of thought, emotion, and action, and to the manifestation of these.

While all possibilities are held in the One, the circle is required for their manifestation. This circle must itself be limited or measured in order to accomplish this manifestation, and this ordering or measuring must be done in such a way that the inner nature of number brings about the desired effect. Thus the circle must be divided in accordance with the Dyad, Ternary, Hexad, and especially the Ennead because all these numbers share a concern with the manifestation of specific effects. The circle must be divided by them in such a way that the Quaternary, Quinary, Septenary, and Octad are not excluded from the process, but these must not usurp the roles of the others. The Dyad, Ternary, and Hexad provide the context (which implies the Ennead) in which the other numbers act. Thus it is entirely appropriate that the circles be divided into 360 degrees.

As said before, the Divine Breath gives rise to three circular movements in the sphere. The first has more affinity to the Monad and is therefore rational and the Same. The other two are irrational and Other. Thus, while all are divided into 360 degrees, the Hexad, being a feminine (even) number and having more affinity to Desire or Appetite than the Ternary, is given preference in the division of the ecliptical circle. Though the Ternary has a place in this division (as indicated by the Triplicities), the ecliptic seems more to be divided by 6 and 2. Thus, within the ecliptical circle we find the "spheres" of the planets, while the ecliptic itself is divided by the Dodecary in accordance with the law set forth at the end of the section "Nine and Twelve."

Both the equator and the ecliptic arise as a result of the Divine Breath, which is the Prime Mover, the first *he*. Both these circles revolve or circulate because of the nature of their numerical causes. But they do not move in the same plane nor in parallel because to do so would make them too much alike and because having arisen from the same cause (the Divine Breath), they must have something in common. This common point is the vernal point. It is the point on the surface of the sphere where the Divine Breath gives rise to the two circles in question. The autumnal point rises in opposition to this, and in accordance with the

Ternary, the point of the summer solstice arises. This is opposed by the point of the winter solstice, and the cardinal cross is thereby completed by the fourfold archetype.

The ecliptic is the path of the Sun, which is the source of the threefold Light of our world. The Sun moves steadily through each of the signs of the irrational or animal-bearing circle, and its light is changed by each in accordance with its nature. Thus in Aries, the beginning point, the power of the Sun as pertains to its vivifying capacity is the strongest, since here the Sun's own nature coincides with the outflow of life from the Source of all. The opposite point, 0 degree of Libra, is the beginning of the weakening of the Sun's effects because the autumnal point arises as a denial of or opposition to the vernal point and is therefore determined to the opposite effect. Thus with the other points mentioned above.

Since the ecliptic is the path of the Sun, and since the several "spheres" of the planets are the sevenfold differentiation of the Sun's Light, it is easily seen that the spheres are "within" the "sphere" of the ecliptic as the Sun is, as shown in the section "Nine and Twelve."

As the Septenary is entirely active and involved with Matter only insofar as it informs it, so Matter is entirely passive and inactive. Thus the active planetary causes are 7, and that upon which they act is 8. Since 8 is the only evenly even number in the Decad, it is the most passive thing in the Decad and must be the thing which is informed by the active causes. It is therefore by definition Matter and properly placed at the center of our model where the surrounding "Heaven" can inform it. But if 8 is Matter, the Ennead is the finished product or that which has been produced in matter by the operation of the superiors. Finally, the Ennead, the Ternary times itself, indicates the activity of the threefold cause of events at work in each of the three worlds, bringing to complete manifestation the possibilities of the World of Causes.

THE ACTIVITY OF THE CAUSAL FACTORS OR PLANETS IN THE COMPLETED MODEL

In the foregoing we have seen the generation of our model of Existence from the inner nature of numbers operating in the light of our First Principle. We have emphasized that number must be considered both as inner and outer, for herein lies the "cause"-and-"effect" relationship. Again, since Unity is undifferentiated Being affirming itself, our entire model, which arises from the apparent division of Unity, is alive and intelligent. Indeed, our sky, our ecliptic, is 6—that is, Desire (2) and Action (3)—so there should be no wonder that it desires to act to express itself. Thus we find that the astrological causes of our actions are due to this and nothing else: namely, that the differentiation of rational Sameness (5) occurs at 6 as the desire to act out or manifest as Other. Here is the compulsion of Fate. Here act the three gunas and two genders, and although these are present in 5, the Divine Breath, they remain *in potentia* there because of the ruling Sameness of 5, and they are not separated until 6, where the desire for Otherness or separate existence becomes manifest. Here begins incessant motion for new experiences. Here also is the Fall of Man from the Garden of Eden (5) and the beginning of his labor (6). Finally, it is here, in the zodiac (6), that the causal factors (the planets) which existed *in potentia* in 5 find manifestation as superior causes on the inferior elements. Man at 5, before the Fall, was coequal with the gods and therefore above the compulsion of the cosmocrators or planets, but after the Fall at 6, he submits to their rule.

Now, the fatal operation of the planets or causal agents is in concert with the sky or ecliptic (6). Here we have two factors. But the arising of events requires three factors, for actions or events are ruled by the Ternary. Thus something else is required, namely a place or subject in which the action must take place. This we find ready at hand in the Earth (8). But here, too, the events that will arise through the action of the causal factors (the planets and sky) will not be specifically defined unless the subject Earth is in some way determined or specialized toward some specific object or event. This is accomplished by the houses, which permit the determination of the passive Earth toward specific areas of life or categories of experience.

The houses arise in the Earth (8) as a reflection of the twelvefold division of the archetypal circle or Causal World. The particular affairs of the houses are attributed to them through the affinities which the inner nature of the numbers have to particular kinds of experiences and also through the interrelationships of these numbers to each other. Thus, while the first house is given to the native because we desire that he be our point of reference, the tenth, which is nine houses away from the first, will indicate his actions considered as manifestations or realizations of his inner nature. The seventh house will represent the partner and all those opposed openly to the native because it participates the Dyad. The interrelations of the houses considered from the numerical point of view will elucidate the reason why so many apparently unrelated things are included within the attributions of the houses.

Thus we have all we need to find an event, for we have three factors which will be embodied in a fourth: that is, (1) the Ternary Law, (2) the effective causes, (3) the passive subject properly disposed toward some area of life by the houses, and (4) the event which embodies the previous three factors and which *must* arise under the proper circumstances.

This last point is very important and seems not to be understood by most psychologists or astrologers. We can say that the event *must* arise because the nature of the Heaven is the Divine Breath which moves out. Its nature is that it seeks expression, and as was said, the sphere is the perfect expression of the Universal Affirmation of Being. However, to give rise to limited experiences—that is, anything less than the sphere—requires the limiting or measuring of this Affirmation of Being to less-than-universal proportions. In other words, the "I am" must become "I am... something." This is accomplished at stages 6 through 9, with 6 providing the desire for less than Infinity or the sphere, and 9 being the final manifestation of the limited existence. In the Macrocosm this means that Infinity must be realized in Time, for at no one time can all possibilities be expressed. In the Microcosm it means a limited personality with specific talents, abilities, likes, dislikes, and so on, in each of the three worlds (causal, subtle, gross) and the corresponding limitations. All of this is the expression of the Divine Unity modified by superimposed limitations maintained by the desire for separateness (2). The arising of some expression, however, must occur by the very nature of the sphere, i.e., Desire (2) and Action (3). This we should always keep in mind both theory and in practice. Our problem is to be able to foretell the precise form this expression will take, and in the fulfilling of this task we must draw on the rules of our art, our theoretical understanding, and our practical experience.

It is therefore clear that the production of events in the model occurs by the concourse of causal factors within 6 operating on 8 in conformity with the Ternary and Quaternary laws. More simply stated, the events of our lives arise as a result of the action of Heaven upon Earth. The Ternary shows how; the Quaternary embodies the activity. The Septenary and the Dodecary give variety to the effects.

That this is in fact the law underlying the operation of astrological causality is seen from consideration of the judgment of planetary effects, for we find that always there is our circle, the Heaven; our planet, the Earth; and its houses. These three factors must always be present for us to predict the fourth factor—the event—which incorporates the three factors as a threefold cause.

Thus all events arising either in the life of the Microcosm or in the history of the Macrocosm arise from number acting on number (or

"Number Numbering," as Dee put it) in accordance with this law, which I shall henceforth refer to as the Astrological Law of Manifestation or, more simply, as the Law of Manifestation.

THE NUMERCIAL BASIS FOR THE EXALTATIONS OF THE PLANETS

The attribution of the exaltations of the planets has long been a matter of consternation and embarrassment to astrologers, for it seemed there were none who could convincingly show how the signs designated as the exaltations of the planets were arrived at. It has been held that this information was lost along with much else with the fall of the Egyptian and Babylonian priesthoods and the general decay of astrological tradition. However, I can now show, thanks to a suggestion from the Egyptologist Bika Reed, that the basis of the exaltation of the planets is a numerical order indicating the stages of the refinement of a particular emotion or planetary cause within the Dodecary. By so doing, I hope to make it apparent that the reason the exaltations are not understood by modern astrologers is that they persist in regarding as the foundation of their art the movements of the physical bodies of heaven which somehow bring to pass events on earth.

The planets ought to be considered as modifications or limitations of the Universal Affirmation of Being; as living intelligent "states of consciousness" and modes of action; as causes; as gods. These planetary causes, the abstraction of desires, apparently submit themselves to further modification by their interaction with the sign they are in, where the elemental nature and gender of the sign as well as its cardinality, fixity, or mutability, etc., must be weighed, and by "relationships" such as aspects, orientality, and occidentality. However, the exaltation of a planetary quality is a somewhat different matter, as it relates more to the "superrefinement" of a given quality to a degree rarely met with. This process is essentially alchemical, although it does occur in Nature accidentally, as it were. And we must remember that art is Nature prodded by the artist under knowledge. Nevertheless, there is something *un*natural about the exalted planets, for they indicate a degree of refinement which begins to bring in qualities that are somewhat uncharacteristic of the planetary quality under any other circumstances. For example: The Sun exalted in Aries brings to the native a self-satisfaction and a directness better referred to as a nobility or simplicity not characteristic of the Sun in Leo or any other sign. In Aries the Sun loses its overweening egocentricity and conceit and becomes far more idealistic and "other-oriented." Thus while the Sun remains the Sun, the negative qualities seem to be greatly mitigated and spiritualized, and the native is likely to have abilities and desires far beyond the average person. So also with Mars in its exaltation. We find that the Mars-in-Capricorn person no longer feels the need to wield Mars so openly and aggressively (assuming a satisfactory condition of Saturn, Mars's dispositor).

Now, these considerations point, as has often been said by many authors, to the assumption that the exaltations have to do with the purification of a quality in nature to the extent that it acts as a bridge to a higher existence, that is, an extranatural condition or spiritualization of a quality. Thus we find that the person whose natal figure can bear the high energy of several exalted planets is someone with extraordinary abilities deriving from extraordinary refinement of being. Usually one finds great idealism and faith, fearlessness, and very wide-ranging vision. The virtues seem clearly to be connected with these exaltations. The marked rises and falls of such persons, quite apart from arguing against the above interpretation, point convincingly to the interaction of the ambient (or influences acting on the world at a given time) and the natal figure as the cause of such variations, where the ambient for practical purposes must be considered the variable and the natal (directions, revolutions, and transits notwithstanding) as constant. In politics the ambient is most clearly reflected in the people (the ascendent of the mundane figure), and as the condition (i.e., desires) of the people vary, so do their leaders. Thus, for instance, one can find the meteoric rise to fame of a Napoleon followed by a dramatic fall.

The highly charged nature of exalted planets can cause very great problems where the figure cannot properly channel the energy. Here one can find split personalities, demonically intense and destructive drives, and the like. Therefore it is always well to remember two things: (1) Insofar as the exaltation of a quality is extraordinary, work must have been done to prepare the individual for the appearance of the energy, or it will be destructive rather than constructive. If such work has gone on in the past, it will be reflected in the figure. If not, judge the worst. (2) The exaltation of all planets is in their own terms. This means that just as the effect of an exalted Mars is different from that of an exalted Jupiter, so we can expect the process of the exaltation to differ as well as the effect, although the numbers underlying the process will sometimes be the same. The Moon will always be the Moon; Mars, Mars, and Jupiter, Jupiter. Therefore, since some planets are malefic and naturally destructive and others benefic and naturally constructive, their essential nature does not entirely change with their exaltation. This must be kept in mind in considering the "processes of exaltation" given below.

There are two directions in which a planetary quality may be perfected. Remember that the Septenary is the differentiation of the Monad, whose nature is Universal Affirmation. Through polarization, this Universal Affirmation, embodied as the Sun, becomes modified into the Septenary. The two paths by which this can occur are (1) toward density and stillness (Sun to Saturn) and (2) toward movement as a reflection of the active creative nature of the One (Sun to Moon). This may be illustrated as follows.

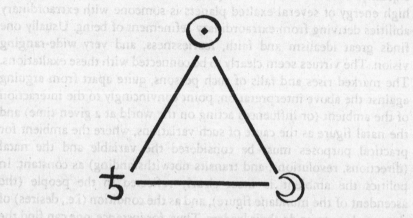

This paradigm clearly indicates the threefold cause or Ternary at work again and indicates the common origin (Sun) of the inner (Moon) and outer (Saturn). Now, the movement from refinement and life (Sun) to grossness and death (Saturn) is the ordinary movement of Creation, the movement "in the order of the signs," the movement of habit. Opposing this, so as to balance it and to provide a way back to Unity in accordance with the nature of the Ternary, is the Sun-Moon sequence, which moves from refinement and life (Sun) to its reflection (Moon). Therefore, in any considerations of number as involved with sequences of one sort or the other, we must always be clear about which of these great movements our sequence pertains to, for just as the Dyad determines the direction of the creative urge (since it is the first polarization of the urge), so it casts its character on the subsequent modifications of the urge and thence its outcome.

Now, the consideration of the exaltations involves just this: sequences of modifications of a particular planetary quality in one of two possible "directions," either Sun to Saturn or Sun to Moon. Thus the exaltation or supernatural perfection of a particular planetary emotion always begins at purity, that is, in one of the houses which the planet rules, where its nature and the nature of the sign coincide. This is a state of Unity and exists because of the essential identity of the Septenary (planets) with the Dodecary (signs).

In esoteric astrology we deal with two movements along the ecliptic: (1) counterclockwise in the order of the signs and (2) clockwise, against the order of the signs. (See Figure 22.) By the first is indicated the soul's involution into matter and by the second the escape of the soul from bondage. Spiritual work, insofar as it brings about escape from the compulsion of Fate, is "unnatural," requiring effort against appetite, instinct, and habit. Here we speak of the first motion as Sun to Saturn, since the Sun moves toward crystallization in Capricorn; and the second as Sun to Moon, since the Sun moves toward the inner or lunar world in Cancer.

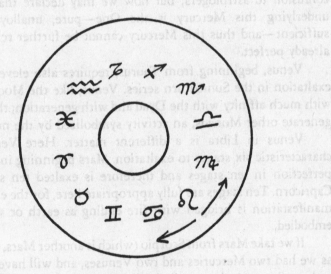

Figure 22

In the outer or Sun-Saturn sequence, the number of stages required for the exaltation of a particular differentiation of the Monad is determined by the nature of the planet, the "direction" the exaltation takes, and the starting point, that is, the sign ruled by the planet which is the beginning of the operation.

As each planet of the Septenary rules two signs, one diurnal and one nocturnal (with the exception of the luminaries, which are the causes of diurnality and nocturnality and which rule only one sign each, the Sun diurnal Leo and the Moon nocturnal Cancer), the planets may be represented by two numbers, each giving the stages in the exaltation of the diurnal or nocturnal aspects of the planetary quality. (The Sun and Moon each have but one such number, since they each rule but one sign.)

Thus the Sun, which is the heart of the world, the embodiment of the Monad, the author of Life and Light and the "fountain of all natural effects," manifests its exaltation in nine stages as we would expect. Since we are here considering the outward thrust, we count nine signs inclusively counterclockwise from Leo ruled by the Sun and come to Aries (see Figure 22).

The Moon, the lesser light, which is the immediate cause of motion in sublunary things and the embodiment of the Dyad or Other, achieves exaltation in eleven stages. Mercury beginning in Gemini achieves exaltation in four stages, while when beginning in Virgo it requires no work. This Mercury exaltation in Virgo has been a matter of great confusion to astrologers; but now we may declare that the number underlying this Mercury is the One—pure, unalloyed, and self-sufficient—and thus this Mercury cannot be further refined, for it is already perfect.

Venus, beginning from Taurus, requires also eleven steps to its exaltation in the Sun-Saturn series. Venus, like the Moon, is a planet with much affinity with the Dyad and with generation; therefore, both generate other Monads, an activity symbolized by the number 11.

Venus in Libra is a different matter. Here Venus takes its characteristic six stages to exaltation. Mars beginning in Aries attains perfection in ten stages and therefore is exalted ten signs away in Capricorn. Ten stages are fully appropriate here, for the entire range of manifestation is bridged with fire ending as earth or with the Will embodied.

If we take Mars from Scorpio (which is another Mars, of course, just as we had two Mercuries and two Venuses, and will have two Jupiters and two Saturns), then we find a shorter path to exaltaion, namely three stages. This path is particularly of note, for while it is a worldly path, the Scorpio Mars attains perfection through Sagittarius—that is, through the sacrifice to higher values—while the diurnal Mars struggles through the entire gamut of ten signs.

Jupiter in Sagittarius attains perfection in eight stages. Jupiter in Pisces attains perfection in five stages. Thus the Sagittarian Jupiter materializes by eight while the Piscean Jupiter must achieve exaltation by transcending the elements (5).

Saturn in Capricorn is exalted after as lengthy a struggle as Mars in

Aries, namely ten stages to Libra. Saturn in Aquarius repeats the same number of stages, nine, as the Sun, being exalted in Libra.

This, then, is the outward thrust; the numbers give the sign of exaltation's distance from the house ruled by the planet. One may say that the number of stages is thus a function of the arrangement of the signs in the zodiac. But the arrangement of the signs is fixed by the archetypes 3 and 4, and thus the numbers given above are both effects of the arrangement and causes insofar as they determine the number of steps from one state or quality to another.

Moreover, the numbers involved all indicate by their own inner qualities the nature of the exaltation of that planetary quality. We must not put the cart before the horse as we so often do. That we find these numerical relationships present in the archetype is not without importance. These numbers are descriptive because they are causal. Exaltation of a planetary quality cannot occur without them, and if exaltation has occured, it is testimony to the fact that the number is fulfilled.

We should not fail to note that the exaltation of a particular quality is not necessarily desirable. This is especially so with those planets whose exaltation requires eleven stages in either sequence, for 11, the Undecad, is considered by Cabalists to be a number of evil signification in that it indicates by its very form a lie, that is, two Monads. This clear impossibility can only be the result of an illusion based on reflection, which is an indication that Desire, the Dyad, is behind the process. Thus, to say that the temporal process of exaltation of the Moon takes place in eleven stages is to say that the process of the exaltation of Desire is involved with or causes the *apparent* duplication of Divinity. I emphasize "apparent" here because this condition is clearly an illusion. According to W. Wynn Wescott, 11 is also called the Number of "Sins" and is the "essence of all that is sinful, harmful and imperfect."[14] So it is clear that the temporal exaltation of the Moon or Venus, whose temporal exaltation occurs in eleven steps, and also the esoteric or spiritual exaltation of Mars are all matters of great danger and most unfortunate.

The overall effect of the outward sequence must be to crystallize and fix a particular quality since the movement is from Sun to Saturn. However, the effect of the Sun-Moon sequence, which is more an "inner" sequence, is rather different. Here the effect is to refine the quality and spiritualize it.

Thus in the Sun-Moon series (clockwise in Figure 22), the Sun reaches its exaltation in five stages; the Moon in three; Mercury in

Virgo is still again; Mercury in Gemini, ten; Venus in Taurus, three; Venus in Libra, eight. Mars reaches exaltation from Aries in four stages; from Scorpio in eleven. Jupiter reaches Cancer, its exaltation, in six steps from Sagittarius and nine from Pisces. Saturn requires four steps from Capricorn and five from Aquarius.

For the sake of clarity and easy reference, this information has been put in tabular form, as follows.

Planet	rules sign	exalted in	⊙/♄ Sequence	⊙/☽ Sequence
☉	♌	♈	9	5
☽	♋	♉	11	3
☿	♍	♍	0	0
☿	♊	♍	4	10
♀	♉	♓	11	3
♀	♎	♓	6	8
♂	♈	♑	10	4
♂	♏	♑	3	11
♃	♐	♋	8	6
♃	♓	♋	5	9
♄	♑	♎	10	4
♄	♒	♎	9	5

It will be seen that these sequences are related to each other: Thus the Sun's pattern or sequence is the same as that for Saturn in Libra and opposite that for Jupiter in Pisces. Venus in Taurus and the Moon share the same sequence and are both contrary to Mars in Scorpio in the Sun-Moon sequence. This is of interest for it indicates that difficulties may arise in the ordinary existence (Sun-Saturn) through the abuses arising from the exaltation of the Moon and Venus, while these give aid in the spiritual direction (Sun-Moon), for in the outer their sequence is 11 while in the spiritual it is 3. However, just the opposite occurs with Mars, for in the temporal a strong Mars is a great good thing (3), but in spiritual activity it brings sin (11). Other such relationships exist which readers can easily see for themselves.

In conclusion, let me state that the numbers which form the basis for the system of exaltation arise from two causes: first, the Septenary acting in the Dodecary—that is, the archetypes of 3 and 4 in their various modes of action—and second, the nature of the planetary quality itself. This second cause determines in fact the number of stages involved in its exaltation, although it cannot do this outside of the arrangement of the signs and their rulers, since these causal factors are all there in Creation: There is nowhere else for them to act. Moreover, they all arise from the Ternary and Quaternary and thus cooperate with them.

From what has been given in this section and what was said before, it should now be clear that the exaltations of the planets in the signs constitute an essentially numerical consideration depending on the nature of the planetary quality to be exalted and its sign of origin.

NUMERICAL RELATIONSHIPS AND THE PARTS

Events and inner qualities, such as opinions, do not arise merely by the influences of one planet operating in one sign and affecting one house of the figure. Events and less well defined phenomena such as opinions or inclinations also arise from more complex considerations which may be collectively referred to as "relationships" between the various factors of the Causal World (the planets and signs). That is, just as numbers are considered both independently and as modifying the significations of other numbers by their relationships to them and to the things associated with them,* so also do the planets act independently and secondarily by virtue of their "relationships." The independent action of a number or of a planet is, of course, straightforward and simple, and in such cases the operation of the Law of Manifestation is exemplary. The action of a planet in relation to other planets is secondary to its independent action according to position, but not less important. Indeed, the experience of life proves that rarely do simple, straightforward events manifest. More often the event affects several areas of life at once and involves several emotional qualities, thus indicating the involvement of several planets. Such events are produced by planets in "relationship" to other planets in the figure.

Relationships between planets or between a planet and the cusp of a house are essentially numerical and serve to modify the effect of the planet on the Earth in accordance with the nature and state of the other planet. The most evident of these "relationships" (in terms of the clarity of the events produced by them) are the aspects of the planets. When two or more planets are in aspect, the effect of the relationship is judged not only according to the nature, state, and determination of the aspected planet and those aspecting, but also with due consideration to the nature of the aspect itself. This active nature of the aspect is derived from the inner nature of the number underlying the geometrical form of

*As for instance, when considering the seventh house as the completion of the native's life (from the fact that all things are completed in seven stages) and also as the house of open enemies, since, being opposed to the first house, it participates the Dyad, whose nature is denial and animosity.

the aspect. Hence the sextile (6) is the aspect of desire, love, and union and is given to Venus. The opposition (2) is the aspect of denial and hatred and is given to Saturn. The trine (3) is the aspect of "perfect friendship," according to Morin, and we can see why: The trine is founded in the Ternary, which always restores Unity, ends the discord of the Dyad, and reminds one of the One Truth. It is appropriately given to Jupiter. The square (4), on the other hand, is the opposition opposed to itself. It is therefore the intensification of animosity or conflict and thus belongs to Mars.

Other relationships include considerations of orientality, occidentality, elevation, depression, antiscia, midpoints, and such considerations as when a planet is twelve signs away from its own sign, or four away so that it squares itself. Similar to this last category are those of detriment and fall, which occur to a planet when it is in the signs opposite its domicile and exaltation. Such signs participate the Dyad in the same way the seventh house does in relation to the first.

These relationships have all been recognized by astrologers for some time. Most of them are discussed by Ptolemy. However, what has not been recognized or fully understood is the numerical foundation on which they rest. Kepler and others, recognizing that the major aspects could not possibly be the entire story with regard to this matter, attempted to increase the number of aspects by introducing several minor aspects, such as the semisextile, the quincunx, and the quintile. But while there may be value in such aspects, the result is still limited, for we now know that the entire sphere is creative, being the manifestation of the Divine Breath, and especially the ecliptic (6), which is the path of the Sun. However, while some have recognized vaguely that this was so and have attempted to make practical use of this recognition by attributing specific characteristics to each degree, no one to my knowledge has yet effectively and convincingly found a way to employ this knowledge in the judgment of the figure. Nor has anyone who has tried to do so published any clear statement of the principles upon which he based his judgment.

This situation exists solely because the metaphysical tradition which formed the underlying foundation of the art was allowed to lapse as described in Chapter 1. A doctrine contingent upon this metaphysical tradition was the doctrine of the parts, which relied heavily on a numerical interpretation of natural phenomena both "outer" (as in purely physical phenomena) and "inner" (as in psychological and spiritual phenomena). Properly understood in terms of the numerical philosophy as expressed in this chapter, the doctrine permits us to expand our judgment of a figure by making available to us specific significations not indicated by the physical position of the planets or by any of the presently recognized "relationships" of the planets to each other or to the ecliptic. It does this by expressing the angular relationship, whatever it is, be it 2 or 200 degrees between the planets considered as universal significators, hence as factors in the Causal World, in a "proportional, therefore numerical, relationship" with a house cusp, usually the ascendant. In so doing, this doctrine recognizes that all parts of the ecliptic (or the Coelum, as Morin calls it) are creative and are determined toward some particular aspect of life, whether they appear to be according to the present standard methods of delineation or not.

Since the parts are generated by the discovery of the distances between the planets considered as universal significators, they represent shadowy reflections of the "relationship" between these factors expressed in terms of zodiacal longitude. Hence their significations must be considered as secondary or ancillary to the actual significations of the planets as indicated by position, rulership, and state.

That the parts have real existence, but as "proportional relationships" between causal factors and hence as an expression of the active causal nature of number underlying the art, was perceived by Morin, who supported the use of the part of fortune and in so doing gave tacit approval to the entire doctrine. On the part of fortune, Morin states that its power "is not present in it insofar as it is considered as a point absolutely or as the beginning part of the heaven pertaining to the figure [as the ascendant is], but insofar as it is the *proportional connection of the Sun and the Moon with the ascendant:* by which reason it is able to have power or insofar as it is a point of the heaven determined in a particular way by the Sun and the Moon."[15] To the objection that it is unreasonable that the part of fortune is considered as associated with riches regardless of its house position and the state, determination, and nature of its dispositor, Morin replies:

> I respond that even though the Sun and the Moon are determined as other planets are to the significations of the house in which they are and that which they rule, nevertheless, because they are the primary planets—indeed by universal agreement, the parents of the Universal Causes of all sublunary effects; to which the conditions of orientality and occidentality of the other planets ought to be observed for their particular effects—it seems that it ought to be conceded in every way that there is a certain transcendental power of good present in the Sun and the Moon

merely by their own virtue alone [i.e., as universal significators] on account of which the part of fortune, transcendentally determined by them or to their nature may be allotted a transcendental determination of utility or harm according to the essential significations of the house to which it is particularly determined by its position and according to the nature and determination of its lord. [16]

That Morin, whose *Astrologia gallica* was intended to establish sound astrological doctrine and method after a century and a half of severe attacks by critics, should include this reference in his work speaks well for the soundness of the doctrine of the parts. Morin was a keen observer of astrological phenomena and of human behavior. He openly attacked doctrines he considered spurious and excised them from his practice. That the use of the part of fortune survived his knife is an indication of its value.

Morin is noticeably cautious in the above passage regarding the precise nature of the cause involved. This caution, I believe, stems from his recognition that open declaration of the numerical foundation of the entire art in his time would have smacked too much of "occultism" and not enough of "science." Throughout the *Astrologia gallica* Morin maintains a strictly mathematical and scientific tone to his work. His use of the term "transcendental" is atypical of the rest of the work. Nevertheless, at various points—especially at the preface to his work, in his treatment of the houses, and in his treatment of Light—he clearly relies on Cabalistic, mystical, and even alchemical concepts. We must remember that Morin was both a mathematician and an astrologer of considerable spirituality and sensitivity. Thus, that he would perceive that the inner nature of number was at base the active cause of the parts, indeed of all astrology, is not particularly unusual. Further, that he would hesitate to openly declare the fact strikes me simply as good politics, in an age already succumbing to atheistic materialism following the initial advances of the scientific revolution in physics, astronomy, and chemistry.

Kepler had challenged the Pythagorean and Platonic interpretation of music and of nature and contended with Fludd, whose Rosicrucianism required that he accept the numerical philosophy. Descartes's, Galileo's, and even Kepler's mathematical theories had more affinity with a mechanistic interpretation of Creation. The older "Platonic" view of the Renaissance was embroiled in controversy. The learned world was at a turning point, and Morin judiciously played down what he saw to be the true nature of the parts.

Morin, reputedly Richelieu's astrologer, rightly saw beneath the surface to the foundations of the parts and thus with Guido Bonatti, Frederick II's astrologer, embraced a doctrine of unknown antiquity which permits considerable extension of the astrologer's vision in a number of areas.

Thus, having shown that the foundation of our art is number; having established that the active cause behind the parts is number or "numerical relationship"; having declared our First Principle and its relation to the Macrocosm and Microcosm and generated our model from the very building blocks of existence, I shall now proceed to the mundane business of the practical application of this knowledge in our art.

Notes

1. Henry Cornelius Agrippa, *De occulta philosophia,* Book 3, chap. 37. Emphasis added.

2. Giordano Bruno, *Expulsion of the Triumphant Beast,* trans. and ed. by Arthur D. Imerti (New Brunswick, N.J.: Rutgers University Press, 1968), p. 77. Emphasis added.

3. Hermes Trismegistus, *Asclepius,* in *Hermetica,* trans. Walter Scott (London: Dawson's, 1968), I, p. 295. Emphasis added.

4. Pico della Mirandola, *Oration on the Dignity of Man,* trans. Elizabeth Livermore Forbes, in *The Renaissance Philosophy of Man,* ed. by Cassirer, Kristeller, and Randall (Chicago: University of Chicago Press, 1948), pp. 224-225. Emphasis added.

5. G.L. Hersey, *Pythagorean Palaces* (Ithaca, N.Y.: Cornell University Press, 1976).

6. Anicius Manilius Torquatus Severinus Boethius, *De institutione arithmetica libri duo. De institutione musica libri quinque. Accedit Geometria quae fertur Boetii,* ed. G. Friedlein (Lipsiae, 1867).

7. John Dee, *Mathematicall Praeface* (New York: Neale Watson Academic Publishers, 1975 [1570]).

8. For more on the relation of the elements, breath, OM, and the guna, see Sankaracarya, *Pancikaranam,* 2nd rev. ed. (Calcutta: Advaita Ashrama, 1972).

9. Robert Fludd, *Utriusque cosmi majoris scilicet et minoris, metaphysica, physica atque technica historia* (Oppenheim Impensis Johannis Theodori de Bry. Typis Hieronymi Galleri, 1618), p. 56.

10. Jacob Boehme, *The Signature of All Things* (Cambridge, England: James Clarke and Co., 1969), chap. 4, p. 32.

11. Thomas Taylor, *The Theoretic Arithmetic of the Pythogoreans* (New York: Samuel Weiser, 1972), p. 204.

12. Titus Burckhardt, *Mystical Astrology of Ibn Arabi,* trans. Bulent Rauf (Aldsworth, Gloucestershire, England: Beshara Publications, 1977), p. 19.

13. The reader desiring to know more about the doctrine of representation employed here should refer to the work of Schopenhauer, especially *The World as Will and Representation;* René Guenon, *The Symbolism of the Cross* and *The Reign of Quantity;* and Titus Burckhardt, *Mystical Astrology of Ibn Arabi* (see note 12), especially pp. 11-22.

14. W. Wynn Wescott, *Number: Their Occult Power and Mystic Virtues,* (New York: Allied Publications, n.d.), p. 100.

15. Jean Baptist Morin de Villefranche, *Astrologia gallica* (Paris, 1661), Book 22, Section 11, chap. VI.

16. Ibid.

PART II

THE DOCTRINE OF THE PARTS

3

HOW TO USE THE PARTS

Bonatti, in his exposition of the doctrine of parts (the translation of which is given in Chapter 4), reports that basically three things are required for the "projection" of the parts: (1) two "fixed" significators, usually two planets or the luminaries, chosen because of their affinity, considered from their universal significatorship, with the matter under consideration; (2) the distance between them measured in zodiacal longitude in the order of the signs, which constitutes what was referred to in Chapter 2 as their numerical relationship; and (3) a "movable" significator such as a house cusp (usually the ascendant) or its ruler, from which the "projection of degrees" is made on the ecliptic in the order of the signs.

The "fixed" significators are considered as such relative to the "movable" significators. That is, since the diurnal motion of the heaven, caused by the rotation of the Earth on its axis, is the swiftest, the planetary positions seem to vary little over short periods of time and thus appear to be "fixed," while the degree of the sign on the eastern horizon and that of the zenith and hence the houses change quickly.

The longitudinal distance between the "fixed" significators is projected from the movable significator in the order of the signs, and the place where this distance ends is the sought-for "part."

Since the part is first of all determined by the numerical relationship between two of the causal factors of the Septenary (within which we shall include the so-called modern planets), these "fixed" terms are, as it were, the parents of the part. As their zodiacal condition varies, so will the signification of the part. Here I emphasize that as the part is an expression of the interrelation of the Septenary and the

Duodenary, so its signification must be in terms of this interrelation indicated by the zodiacal condition of the "fixed" significators and dependent thereon.

It is for this reason that the use of the parts must be restricted to that of a secondary consideration in the judgment of a figure. We ought not to proceed with the projection and judgment of the parts until after we have established the nature of the figure as a whole clearly in our mind. Even then we ought not to base our judgment merely on the house position and sign in which the part falls, but must consider carefully the nature and state of those planets connected with the part.

Therefore, in any consideration of parts, the first matter of importance after the selection of the appropriate planets or "fixed significators" is the analysis of their zodiacal condition. To overlook this, as do many astrologers who chase after aspects without any regard to the planet's relation to the sign in which it is placed, is to lose precision in judgments and to condemn oneself to shallow interpretations.

Next, consideration ought to be made of the part's dispositor in the same way as we consider the "fixed significators." Lastly, any aspects to the part itself are to be considered from several points of view. The first consideration is the benefic or malefic nature of the aspecting planet. This is of some importance, as today an increasing number of astrologers and "astrophiles" ignore this essential classification of planets. Malefics categorically destroy life and benefics increase life except when either may accidentally do its opposite. This, however, happens only under specific astrological conditions—namely, when the malefic's zodiacal condition is exceptionally good and it is well disposed (for instance, when Mars is in Capricorn and its dispositor, Saturn, is in Virgo and trine to Mars) or when the benefic is in exceptionally poor zodiacal state and badly disposed (as when Venus is in Scorpio and Mars opposes Venus from Taurus). In the first case Mars may lay aside its destructive heat especially if a good Venus favorably aspects it. In this situation Mars may cause increase. In the second, Venus loses its purity and destroys through a lack of measure or by adulteration, especially when afflicted by Saturn. In almost all other circumstances benefics will be of very good influence, while malefics will produce notable evil. Nowhere is this more clearly evident than in judgments of parts associated with the cycle of production and the growth cycle. This will be seen very clearly in sections 17 and 18 of the translation, in which Bonatti discusses parts for determining the variations in commodities.

The excising of "benefic" and "malefic" from the astrologer's vocabulary may have value when it comes to dealing with clients. Here consideration ought to be the rule, and the melodramatic abuse of such terms is of course to be avoided. However, in astrological thinking and in judgment these differentiations are critical, and to avoid them or make believe they don't exist is to indulge in destructive delusion motivated by the relativistic nonsense that gained acceptance in the psychedelic sixties and is now obsolete.

The second consideration of aspects is the zodiacal state of the aspecting planet. This will give an understanding of how much aid or harm is to be expected from the planet and in what way. For instance, Saturn in Pisces afflicting the part of fortune with a square, the latter being in Sagittarius, will be less of a worry than if Saturn were afflicting the same part from Virgo. For Saturn is less able to exert its cold and dry nature in Pisces than in Virgo, and in considerations of life and health the quality of moisture is of importance.

Third, how strong by quantity is the aspecting planet? Angular planets affect strongly; succedent planets half as much; cadent planets a quarter as much as an angular planet.

Fourth, we must consider if the planet aspecting the part is one of the "fixed" significators or the dispositor of the part, for in either case it can markedly aid or impede the signification of the part as it aspects it favorably or unfavorably.

As Bonatti relates, and as I shall show in Part III, the parts may be projected for solar revolutions* of nativities and for ingresses of the Sun into the cardinal signs. In the former case the significations of the parts must of course be subordinate not only to the planetary significations of the revolutional figure, but also to those of the natal. The parts of the natal will give broader signification than those of the revolution and relate more to the outline of the native's life than to the particular year of the revolution as would be expected. In the latter case—that is, mundane revolutions or ingresses—the parts will give valuable information relating to mundane considerations, such as politics and the health of a nation, and are particularly useful in considerations associated with productivity in agriculture and industry. This is to be expected considering the "lunar" or "inner" nature of the parts. What has been said regarding the use of the parts for solar revolutions applies as well to lunar revolutions* provided the limitations appropriate to lunar revolutions are observed.

Since the parts represent less obvious relationships between the several factors of the Septenary, there is no reason why they cannot be

---

*Solar and lunar revolutions or returns are predictive figures erected for the time of the return of the respective luminary to the position it held in the natal figure.

applied to questions and elections with as much propriety as to nativities and revolutions. This application was common in both Europe and the Middle East before 1700 and was considered sound astrological practice. In Part III you will find an example of such usage: a decumbiture from Jean Ganivet's *Amicus medicorum,* a fifteenth-century medical work.

It is in horary work that the astrologer is in many ways most tempted to permit flights of fancy and speculation to influence his judgment. Here the constraints of the natal figure and other practical, immediate familiar problems such as economics, class, and family, which tend to keep judgment within reasonable boundaries, seem more distant. Here one is confronted either with a temporary panic as to what the horary figure might portend or the temptation to jump to conclusions not strictly based on logic and the rules of judgment. It is for this reason that the use of the parts must be very judiciously and conservatively applied in horary concerns. To do otherwise is to multiply the number of considerations exponentially and either to completely confound one's ability to judge the figure or, worse, to indulge in empty fantasy, thus misleading the client and destroying one's credibility.

It is no doubt in horary matters that the greatest use of the parts was made by the Arabs and others, and it is probably here that the proliferation of the parts which al-Biruni decried took place. Therefore, be disinclined to rely too much on them here, as their signification can only be to flesh out a judgment based upon the structure of the figure as indicated by the planets, houses, and signs. If these considerations are kept in mind and the judgment of the parts is made *after* the judgment of the figure, as an ancillary method, there should not be any difficulty or error in the judgment.

These things having been stated, we may now proceed to Bonatti's exposition and then to the practical illustrations of the use of the parts.

4

BONATTI'S TREATISE ON THE PARTS

A NOTE ON THE TRANSLATION

Following is my translation of Bonatti's treatise on the parts, which originally formed a portion of his *Liber astronomiae*.* It consists of nineteen chapters, which I shall refer to as "sections" in order to avoid confusion with the chapters of this book.

Bonatti's style is frequently rambling and, at the beginning, a bit disjointed. In his time there was little editing as we know it today, and this is evident in the translation, especially in the beginning, where Bonatti juxtaposes his own commentaries on the parts with those of Albumassar, and at the end, where he does the same with the opinions of Alchabitius. The work appears to have been dictated to Bonatti's students or at least written as though it were delivered at a series of lectures. This was not uncommon in the Middle Ages. However, though it requires the full attention of the reader, I thought it important to edit the material as little as possible so that it would reflect as accurately as possible the thinking and practice of the medieval astrologer. In Part III

*I used the 1550 Basel edition, *Guidonis Bonati Forliviensis Mathematici de Astronomia Tractatus X universum quod iudiciariam rationem nativitatum, aeris tempestatum attinet, comprehendentes*. The translation is of the second part of his treatment of Revolutions of the Years of the World, which is the fourth part of the work and covers columns 616 to 664.

I give a number of examples in which the instructions given by Bonatti are interpreted and applied with sufficiently full explanations that readers who have even a modicum of astrological experience will have no trouble understanding and employing the parts themselves. It is best that readers study Chapters 3 and 4 and the examples in Part III step by step before attempting to employ the parts in their own astrological work, because there is considerable misunderstanding at present as to the proper use of the parts and such a procedure will make it possible to avoid this error.

1. ON THE PROJECTION OF THE PARTS AND ON THEIR SIGNIFICATIONS

Some things relating to the entire work to be considered first:

The ancients considered the extraction of parts a matter at once useful, fitting, and extremely opportune; dealing with subjects which are dealt with in the revolutions of years. These things occur often in astronomical work, and the industrious artist will receive very great utility from them.

Albumassar said that the extraction of parts is done for two reasons.[1] One is when one planet is joined to another or when it is separated from it by a perceivable distance. Such a planet acquires a signification of good or evil because a planet signifies one thing when it applies, another when it is with the other planet, and yet another when it departs and is separated from it. The planets signify certain things by their nature, certain things by accident, certain things according to more, certain things according to less, and certain things according to equally.[2] Now, if two planets have signification over one and the same thing, that one is allowed as stronger which is stronger in nature, power, or dignity; or if it is diurnal and the other nocturnal; or is Almutem [ruler] over that part or is the planet signifying the beginning, while the other signifies the end; or if it is stronger in any way or more dignified, it is to be preferred as you see in the extraction of the part of the father, whom the Sun and Saturn each signify equally.[3] However, we begin from the Sun by day because it is stronger than Saturn is by day. Indeed, the Sun signifies clarity and splendor and rejoices in [these] things. But Saturn signifies obscurity and darkness and rejoices in those things which are contrary to the aforesaid. Understand likewise concerning the other matters as is discussed in their own time and place

There is a second way[4] in which the extraction of parts may be made. If there are two or three significators which signify one matter and if each is of equal virtue, or if one is more worthy or stronger than the other, Albumassar said that there will be a "similitude" in the signification, and in order to resolve the matter[5] the extraction of parts is necessary.

Definition of the Term "Extraction of Parts"

The extraction of the parts is the knowledge of the longitude which is between two significators who [both] naturally signify one thing. But the effect of the part would not be well known unless a third [significator] is brought in, that is, one which also naturally signifies the thing for which the part is extracted.

The planet from which it is begun is called the first significator of the thing. The other is called the second, and these two are called immovable.[6] The third significator is called "he from whom the projection of degrees of distance which is between the first natural significators is begun," and this third significator maybe the lord of the ascendant or the lord of another house [or house cusp] from which the projection of the degrees of distance begins and is movable, as will be explained below in the appropriate place. And because of this it is said, "Take what is between this and that planet and add it to the degree of the ascendant and project from the ascendant, or from such and such a place into another place or from one planet to another, giving to each sign 30 degrees according to equal degrees, and wherever the number [arrived at by the above addition] comes to will be the place of that part."

Why the Parts Are Extracted

This was done in two ways and for three reasons [sic].[7] The first reason was so that it might be known what ought to be judged regarding good or evil. This would be signified by the lord of the sign in which the part falls, whether from the ascendant or from another place from which the part is projected.

The second reason is because the ascendant signifies the bodies and beginnings of all things, although [sometimes] the projection is from one or another of the planets or from other places because that house or planet is of the same nature or complexion with the place of the part.[8]

Albumassar said that because the ascendant or other house of the circle (from which the longitude which is between the two natural significators is projected) changes every hour, the third significator is called movable with regard to its signification. Furthermore, equal degrees[9] are used with the parts, because the parts are moved according to the axis of the ecliptic, and the ascendant is considered according to the degree of the circle of the ecliptic, and the degrees of the ecliptic are equal. Albumassar said, "Therefore a planet is in such and such a sign and such and such a degree and the ascendant is this or that degree of this or that sign." He also said that the whole is spoken of according to equal degrees of the ecliptic. He said that the degrees of ascension are from the degrees of the circle dividing and surrounding[10] the ecliptic and that this right circle moves the ecliptic and the other circles.[11]

Albumassar also said that the ancient Babylonians and Egyptians and some others used ninety-seven parts, as is reported in their books.[12]

Three Methods of Projecting of Parts

There are three methods of projecting the parts. The first of these is the projection of the seven parts of the seven planets. The second consists of the parts of the twelve houses. The third consists of parts of other things concerning which no mention or commentary is made in the twelve houses, yet which are necessary in certain places, both in revolutions and in nativities. There are seven sections to the first method; the second has twelve sections, and the third, ten. But first the parts of the seven planets ought to be discussed.

Notes for Section 1

1. "two reasons": *duobus modis.*

2. In these categories we see the influence of Aristotle's *Physics and Metaphysics* on the medieval European and Arab astrologer. What Bonatti is attempting to do in this section is to show that parts are sometimes used in questions, elections, and nativities where very subtle astrological indicators require resolution in order for a satisfactory judgment to be made. What follows, however, is much more straightforward and simple.

3. The Sun and Saturn signify the father as general significators, just as the Moon and Venus signify the mother. I have left out a line (italicized below) here which is redundant: sicut vides in extractione partis patris, quam significat Sol et Saturnus aequaliter: *quoniam uterque eorum habet significare patres.* See section 7, pages 231-232, for the extraction of the part of the father which Bonatti refers to.

4. "way": *modo.*

5. "In order to resolve the matter": This sounds as though the system of parts was developed to aid the astrologer in judging.

6. The immovable or "immobile" significators are the first and second significators. The third is called the movable or "mobile" significator. Bonatti explains this in the following text.

7. Bonatti actually gives two reasons *(causae)* and three methods *(modi)*, as is seen in what follows.

8. It is this second category with which this treatise is primarily concerned.

9. "equal degrees": or degrees of longitude of the ecliptic *(secundum axem circuli signorum).*

10. "dividing and surrounding": *circumdantis.* Both "dividing" and "surrounding" are acceptable translations of *circumdantis.* The right circle or equator is conceived as surrounding the ecliptic as well as dividing it at the equinox.

11. Cf. Plato's *Timaeus,* trans. Benjamin Jowett. *The Dialogues of Plato,* vol. 2, pp. 17-20.

12. These books have not survived.

2. ON THE PARTS OF THE SEVEN PLANETS AND THE PARTICULAR SIGNIFICATIONS OF THEM, AND FIRST CONCERNING THE PART OF THE MOON, WHICH IS CALLED THE PARS FORTUNAE

Albumassar said, "Know that a part is not extracted unless from two significators, naturally signifying the matter for which the extraction is made." For when two planets naturally signify one thing and agree in duration of effect or in other qualities, the extraction of the part ought to be begun from the stronger planet, as has been said regarding the Sun and Saturn, who are equal in the signification of the father and in duration.[1] However, the extraction of the part of the father is begun from the Sun because it is stronger on account of the reason assigned above.[2] And if they were equal in signification just as was said, and one was diurnal and the other nocturnal,[3] the extraction of the part is begun in a diurnal figure from the diurnal planet because the day then prevails over the night and ought to be preferred to it. But at night it is begun from the nocturnal planet because of its equality in signification with the diurnal planet. For example, the extraction of the *pars fortunae* is extracted from the luminaries, which, as the ancients said, are of equal strength for good. But because the Sun is the diurnal benefic, it begins from the Sun in the day, and because the Moon is the nocturnal benefic, it is begun from the Moon at night. And this part is preferred above all the other parts in the same way as the luminaries are preferred to all the other stars. And this part contains all the other parts[4] just as the luminaries contain all the other stars. Similarly the Sun is more splendid than all the other stars and is called the diurnal luminary because day occurs by his rising and is removed and made night by his setting. The Sun signifies the natural life and the other things which have been discussed in the chapter on his significations, and the Moon is the luminary of the night and the benefic significatrix of bodies and of all things, just as was said elsewhere in her chapter.

I shall give you an example of the extraction of the *pars fortunae* [see Figure 23]. Let it be posited that the Sun is in the 12th degree of Taurus and in the 5th minute and that the Moon is in the 12th degree of Virgo and in the 5th minute, and let the matter on account of which you desire to extract the *pars fortunae* be in the day. Now you have to take the place of the Sun from the place of the Moon and there will remain four signs.[5] And let there be 5 degrees and 5 minutes of the sign ascending. Begin to project from the beginning of the same sign (by equal degrees) giving 30 degrees to each sign, and wherever the number ends, there will be the place of this part.[6] On the other hand, at night [i.e., in a nocturnal figure], you take the place of the Moon from the place of the Sun and add it to the degree of the sign of the ascendant and project[7] this from the ascendant, and wherever the number ends, there will be the *pars fortunae*. However, if both luminaries are in the same degree, the *pars fortunae* will be in the degree and minute of the ascendant.

This part signifies the life, the body, and also its soul, its strength, fortune, substance, and profit, i.e., wealth and poverty, gold and silver, heaviness or lightness of things bought in the marketplace, praise and good reputation, and honors and recognition, good and evil, present and future, hidden and manifest; and it has signification over everything. It serves more for rich men and magnates than for others. Nevertheless, it signifies for every man according to the condition[8] of each of those things. And if this part and the luminaries are well disposed in nativities or revolutions, it will be notably good. This part is called the part of the Moon or the ascendant of the Moon, and it signifies good fortune.

Albumassar said that when that which has passed of the hours of the day is

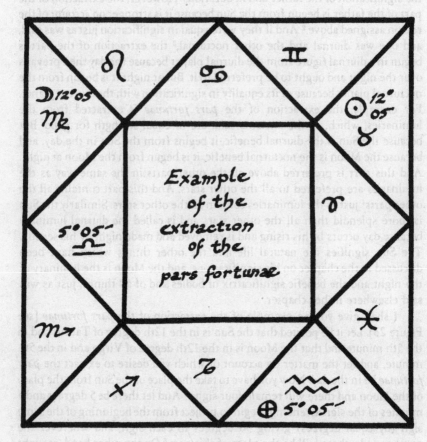

Figure 23

multiplied by the parts of the hours of the day and the product is projected from the place of the Moon according to equal degrees, it falls with the *pars fortunae* or close by it.[9]

And if one significator is stronger than the other in the place of the part,[10] the part will begin from the stronger either by day or by night. If, however, the signification is from the sign and its lord, this will begin rather from the lord of the sign to the degree of the sign because the signification of the sign is strengthened by the signification of the planet. And if it happens that the sign is stronger in signification, it will begin from the sign and the ascendant, or some other place of the circle to which it was advanced will be a participant with it.[11] And this will be discussed more widely, openly, and clearly below in the course of the tract concerning the parts of the twelve houses and of produce[12] as they happen to each of those parts when we will discourse concerning them, if God permits.

On the Pars Futurorum [Part of Things to Come], Which Is Called the Pars Solis [Part of the Sun]

After the part of fortune, which exceeds all the other parts in strength and fortune, the part of things to come or *pars futurorum*, which is called the *pars solis*, ought to be spoken of. This, immediately after the part of fortune, exceeds and is more worthy than all the other parts, although some astrologers seem to care little about it; but it does not seem consistent to me since it is reputed by the wise to be extremely useful for this work. This part is extracted in a way contrary to that in which the *pars fortunae* is extracted: i.e., by day from the Sun to the Moon; by night, from the Moon to the Sun; so the *pars futurorum* is extracted by day from the Moon to the Sun and at night from the Sun to the Moon, and this is added to that which ascends of the rising sign and is projected from the beginning of the sign of the ascendant, giving 30 equal degrees to each sign. And wherever the number ends is where the part will be.

The parts of the luminaries precede the parts of the other planets. All things arise from generation and corruption. The interaction of the Sun and Moon cause generation.[13] Corruption happens by the motion of the planets; nevertheless, the operations which are caused by the other planets do not appear so manifestly, nor do they appear so similar as those which are caused by the luminaries.

The *pars futurorum* signifies the soul and the body after the *pars fortunae* and the quality[14] of these, and faith, prophecy, religion, and the culture of God and secrets, cogitations, intentions, hidden things and everything which is absent, and courtesy and liberality, praise, good reputation, heat, and cold. And Albumassar said that the significations of the *pars fortunae* and *pars futurorum* appear more over things both absent and future than that which is present. They make known more regarding beginnings of works and of the revolutions of years both of the world and of nativities. And he said that the significations of the *pars fortunae* appear more during the day than the significations of the *pars futororum*, and the significations of the *pars futurorum* appear more at night than the significations of the *pars fortunae*. And although mutations and alterations happen in their times by the mutation of the planets from sign to sign and they cause generations and corruptions and life occurs in animals and other vegetable things and by the same reason they destroy[15] and corrupt generated things; nevertheless, the luminaries operate on these [sublunary, generating things] more manifestely and more sensibly than all the other planets, and so these two parts work above all others both for good and for evil. And their significations are similar to the significations of the luminaries.

On the Heavy Part Which Is Called the Pars Saturni [Part of Saturn]

The *pars Saturni*, which the wise called the heavy part on account of the serious and weighty matters which are signified by it, is taken in the day from Saturn to the part of fortune and at night in the opposite direction, and is projected from the ascendant, giving to each sign 30 equal degrees, and where the number of its degrees and minutes fall, that is where the part will be.

These are its significations: It signifies memory and profundity of mind and counsel; faith and religion and moderation in those things and constancy and durability. It signifies a matter which has perished or been lost or which was stolen or which fled or was submerged in the sea or a river or fell into a well or into a similar place, or was killed, and it signifies the condition[8] of the dead, that is, by what death the native may die or will die. It signifies the condition[8] of the lands and the condition[8] of the harvests of other lands and of the growing things of the earth, and it signifies heredities, especially those which are bought. It signifies heavy buildings and especially those which do not rise high above the earth, and diggings and accumulations of lands and the transportation of them on high and the productions of the waters and the like. Indeed it signifies avarice and punishment of miserable men to pity the living, and it signifies praise and disgrace. It signifies old age and time causing one to grow old, and everything conquered, incarcerated, or placed in a jail and the liberation from the jail or from confinement.

On the Part of Jupiter or Pars Iovis, Which Is Called the Part of Happiness

The part of Jupiter, which the philosophers call the part of happiness and of assistance, is taken by day from the *pars futurorum*, which signifies fortune, to Jupiter, which signifies happiness and assistance, and by night the reverse, and it is projected from the ascendant. And its signification is concerning honor and the attainments of things, victory and assistance and happiness and goodness. Also the laudable end of things and the petition of faith or the attainment of it and what the nature[16] of this is and belief in God, and the zeal in every good work, and the choosing of it or of justice and of just judgments between men. Also buildings for the purpose of prayer, and it signifies wisdom and the wise and the sublimity of wisdom. Also trust, faith, and all good things which men enjoy and the mutual participation of the good.

On the Part of Mars or Pars Martis, Which Is Called the Part of Daring

The *pars Martis*, which the ancients call the part of daring, is taken by day from Mars to the *pars fortunae* and by night the reverse, and this is projected from the ascendant. Its significations are these: the disposition of armies, of wars and battles, and the worth and sharpness of the soul, also resolution, anticipation, and greatness of heart with impulse and haste; it also signifies lascivious incest from cunning and seductions.

On the Part of Venus or Pars Veneris,
Which Is Called the Part of Love and Concord

The *pars Veneris*, which is called the part of love and concord, is taken by day from the *pars fortunae* to the *pars futurorum* and at night the reverse, and is projected from the ascendant. Its significations are these: It signifies pleasures, desires, and wants in venereal things and in the culture of them both licit and illicit, and the things which venereal people love and in which they delight and which the soul desires, unions and all things which pertain to the inclination to coitus and pleasure from games and joys and delights.

On the Part of Mercury or Pars Mercurii, Which Is Called the Part of Poverty and Ordinary Intellect

The *pars Mercurii*, which is called the part of poverty or of ordinary intellect, is taken by day from the *pars futurorum* to the *pars fortunae* and at night the reverse, and it is projected from the ascendant. It signifies poverty and meanness of intelligence and intellect, and it signifies war, fear, hatred, contentions, injuries, and anger in the hour of injuries and enemies. It signifies negotiation, buying and selling, also cogitations and intelligence, cunning and writings, numbers and the pursuit of astronomy and of diverse sciences.

This is the method of extracting the parts of the seven planets, and the things mentioned above are their significations. Whence if you ever extract a part concerning any of the aforesaid significators and you project it in any figure, judge its good or evil signification according to its conjunction or that of its lord with the planets or their aspects. Nor do I wish to introduce you to the diversities of opinions of the ancients because this way is more correct than those preserved by our most reverend predecessors Hermes, Guellius, and Albumassar, who were the flowers of the Latins,[17] although they and likewise their followers studied in Athens where the study then flourished. But the other significations of the parts are discussed below in the appropriate places and chapters, if God permits.

Notes for Section 2

1. Bonatti had discussed the part of the father earlier in the work from which this is taken. For an analysis of his method of using the part of the father for determining the length of the father's life and the native's life, see Appendix D.

2. "above": The section referred to appears in this work in Appendix D.

3. The diurnal planets are Saturn and Jupiter, and the Sun by definition. The nocturnal planets are Mars and Venus, and the Moon. A figure is diurnal when the Sun at the time of birth is above the horizon; nocturnal when it is below.

4. Compare this with what is said on page 94 on the *pars hyleg*.

5. The distance in longitude between the place of the Sun and the place of the Moon is 120 degrees, or four signs.

6. As shown in the figure, this comes to 5 Aquarius.

7. This "projecting" and adding are actually the same act, not two acts as the phrasing of the sentence suggests. See the figure on page 86.

8. "condition": *esse*.

9. I don't know what Bonatti is referring to in this paragraph, which he has interjected into his discussion.

10. "Place of the part" here may mean the area of life, hence the house to which the consideration belongs. This is the way Bonatti has catalogued the parts. The other interpretation, "place of the part" as "the place where the part falls" is not relevant since

the author is discussing a way of determining which of two "immovable" significators is the one from which to begin to measure the distance to the other. The "place in which the part falls" has not yet been found. This section is confusing, however.

11. Bonatti is obscure here. He becomes clearer in his examples and refers us to section 17.

12. See section 17.

13. Bonatti is intentionally confusing in the original Latin: Licet generentur per corruptionem generanda et corrumpantur corrumpenda. He doesn't want us to get too easily the idea that the planets' modification of the soli-luna generation is corruption. Nevertheless, this understanding is embodied in the doctrine of the parts.

14. "quality": esse.

15. "destroy": Bonatti uses deficio, which astronomically can mean "to be eclipsed." This might be a reference to the occultations of the planets.

16. "nature": esse.

17. "the flowers of the Latins": This phrase seems to imply that Bonatti knew of the three authors Hermes, Guellius, and Albumassar from Latin translation.

3. ON THE SIGNIFICATION OF THE PARTS OF THE TWELVE HOUSES

The signification of the seven parts of the planets and their significations and extraction having been discussed, the parts of the twelve houses ought to be discussed next.[1] The parts extracted above are in themselves more useful and necessary. And when it is said regarding the place of any part, "Take from such and such a planet to such and such a planet or from such and such a place to some other place, and project from the ascendant," I say that you always add the distance between both places to that which is from the beginning of the sign from which you project [to the degree from which you project], as was said regarding the extraction of the part of fortune, and the others are extracted in the same way.[2]

Nor does it seem to me that diversities of opinions ought to be recited here[3] but only to apply the mind with greater diligence. The limits of all the things which are signified by each of the houses are not the same but diverse, although some may have their beginning or origin from the same house and certain others from others. For example, regarding the significations of death, the limit of its significations will not [always] be the same. However, they all signify death. For some men die in their beds or elsewhere from infirmities, some from short illnesses, others from long ones, some die suddenly, some by the sword, others by fire, others are suffocated, some are hung. Men as it were die in innumerable ways. And although the deaths are not all of the same kind, nevertheless each is a death. And so, too, regarding the profession which is signified by the tenth house, because a magistrate is one thing, a kingship another, a commander another, a duke another, a count another, and another is some kind of artisan or the like. And although they may not all be the same, nevertheless they all have their origin from a thing signifying honor and dignity. And so all the significations of any house are each according to its own quality[4] and according to the nature of the house whose signification it is necessary to know.

Many other parts will be discovered which would be too long to narrate. You, however, will consider them as you come across them by your own industry; nor will you be grieved by what I say to you and if all the things which are signified by the houses cannot be made manifest at the same time and immediately. Otherwise, such and so many things are set forth as to suffice for the extraction of all the parts of the houses, from which anyone who is worthy will see that the part of the significators of anything is signified by one of the houses of the circle, and he will be able by his own industry to comprehend clearly enough things which have not yet been explained to him.

Notes for Section 3

1. "the parts of the twelve houses ought to be discussed next": Nevertheless, Bonatti chooses to digress briefly here.

2. Bonatti is expressly trying to set straight the procedure of projecting the parts here. Apparently the language of other manuals dealing with the parts led the student to project from the beginning of the sign of the ascendant and not from the degree of the ascendant itself. Thus, in the example of the part of fortune, where the ascendant was 5 Aries, one might have projected from 0 degrees Aries instead of 5 Aries, and this would be wrong.

3. On other matters, such as the discovery of the hyleg, the various opinions of the ancients as well as his own were discussed at length by Bonatti, but to do so here would not be helpful.

4. "quality": *esse*.

4. ON THE PARTS OF THE FIRST HOUSE— THAT IS, THE ASCENDANT—AND ON THEIR EXTRACTION AND SIGNIFICATION

Now concerning the extraction of twelve houses and first concerning the first house or ascendant and the significations of these parts and their extraction. As was said in the chapter on the twelve houses, the first house signifies the natural life. I say "natural" for this reason; because very often the relative strength of the nature causes death or some kind of accident, as was said above in another chapter. And therefore, for this reason the part of life or *pars vitae* and its extraction ought to be considered, for by this the quality of the life of the native is determined and what kind of existence[1] he will have. It is extracted from Jupiter and Saturn on account of their altitude and their great distance from the Earth and on account of their movement, which is slower than that of the other planets, and for this reason rulership[2] has been given to them over things the length and durability of which we aspire to. And for the reason given above the ascendant participates with them. This part is taken by the day from Jupiter to Saturn and by night the reverse, and it is projected from the ascendant.

This part is the significatrix of the natural life and signifies the condition[3] of the body and its sustenance. If it is well disposed, it signifies length of life and its continuity, the safety of the body, and the vitality of the soul. If, however, it is impeded, it signifies paucity of life and the shortness of it and its evil quality with a multitude of diverse infirmities and with sorrow of soul and the sadness of it. This, therefore, will signify the quality of men in revolutions of the years both in nativities and in the world.

We have discussed the first part of the ascendant, which is the *pars vitae*; next the second part of the ascendant ought to be discussed. This is the part of durability and stability or *pars durabilitatis*. It is the part of the security of the ascendant or *pars fiduciae ascendentis*. Thus, since it is more noble and more worthy an accident than may be in this world, it was necessary that it should be perfected by something more noble in durability and stability; and it was fitting for that to be by the union or completion of the soul and the body, and this was not able to happen unless by the stronger of the supercelestials; and these are the luminaries whose parts are stronger and are found to be more fortunate than others, and in the same way as the luminaries are stronger benefics than the other benefics, accordingly their effects are perceived to be stronger and more apparent than the effects of the other planets, and so their parts signify the body and soul just as the luminaries signify them.

Nor can durability happen or last in living things without the union of the body and the soul. Just as living things are caused and last in accordance with the complexion or union of these [i.e., soul and body], so they are corrupted by their dissolution or separation. And this is the cause which moved the wise of the ancients to extracting this part. They counted it from the *pars fortunae* as if from something more worthy in this way: The *pars fiduciae ascendentis* is taken by day from the *pars fortunae* to the *pars futurorum* and by night the reverse, and it is projected from the ascendant.

Albumassar said that this part coincides with the *pars Veneris* and certain things are allotted to it which are not given to the other parts.[4] It signifies the beauty of the native and his deformity. Likewise it signifies his similitude to his parents.

When this part or its lord is well disposed in a nativity, the native will be physically beautiful, having a beautiful face and surrounded everywhere with beauty in all his parts, and this will be extended to his offspring, and this will last until one of the malefics hinders and impedes them. The native will abound in good things and the more so if the *pars fortunae* and *pars futurorum* are well disposed, and again more if their lords were fortunate. Then indeed he will have that which he desires from everyone. He will have very great profit both on journeys and wanderings and in other places. However, if this part is impeded, it signifies the native's deformity and ugliness and the badly complexioned condition of his body, accompanied by infirmities. He will be unfortunate, and all the good things mentioned above will fall into their contrary according to the place and disposition of the aforementioned part and significators. And this will very likely be extended to his descendants all the way until one of the benefics will discover their significators in a nativity of either of them.

Albumassar said that if it inclines to the significator of the mother, the native will be like the mother and will stay at home with her. And he said, if you desire to know the durability of anything, for instance the life of the native, from a question or a revolution or from whatever other method you desire to know his durability or death, whether the matter is known or unknown, manifest or occult, look to this part. If it is aspected by the lord of the house or exaltation or of the two other dignities of the sign in which it is, or if it is with the lord of the ascendant of that year or is with one of the lords of the angles and is in an angle, it signifies stability and durability of the matter and all the more strongly and firmly when it is in the first or the tenth house. But if it is cadent, it signifies his removal and destruction. However, if it is succedent and even more so if it is in the second or eighth, it signifies that the durability of the matter is always uncertain and in doubt. But if it is impeded in an angle, it signifies durability with sadness and terror. But if a benefic is with it or aspects it by a trine or sextile aspect or indeed by a square with reception, and the benefic is not impeded, there will be durability in the home, although with fear or suspicion. And Albumassar said, if it is fortunate in its own debility, the native will enjoy a fortune in accordance with the degree of its debility.[5] However, if it is impeded, it will be evil and horrible in accordance with the degree of its debility. And if it is in a revolution of someone's nativity, the significations will be more than they are accustomed to be and they will be more stable, more constant, and more firm than usual.

The first and second parts of the ascendant having been discussed, now we ought to discourse on the third part, which is the part of reason and sense or *pars rationis et sensus*. And since man is not able to be truly without reason and sense, the wise considered whence they were able to extract the *pars rationis et sensus*. And since they saw that Mercury was naturally the significator of both and also of imagination[6] and speech and understanding, and that Mars was the significator of heat and motion, they extracted the part from these two and called it the *pars rationis et sensus*. In fact, this part could also be called the part of imagination and speech. It is taken by day from Mercury to Mars and by night in the opposite direction, and it is projected from the ascendant. And they said that this part signifies sense and reason and science and imagination and understanding and speech. But if this part is well disposed in anyone's nativity and it is with the lord of the ascendant or with the lord of the house in which it is posited, or if the lord of the ascendant [being] in his own dignity aspects the lord of the house [7] and at the same time Mercury aspects both the part and the lord of the ascendant or the lord of the part, by trine or sextile aspect or even a square with reception, and if Mercury is fortunate and strong and not impeded—then the native will be rational, knowing, speaking, thinking, and understanding; and if at the same time Mars should aspect the ascendant or its lord or the lord of the part, the native will be wise, as I said, and he will be of sharp mind, learning easily and retaining well and not forgetting those things which he has learned.

We have discussed the first, second, and third parts of the first house. It remains for us to discuss the fourth part, which is called the part of the hyleg or *pars hyleg*. The ancients did not care to say much regarding this part because it is so involved with other things. But none of them are able to exist without it. But this part is able to exist without them. It is to these things as matter is to form. The ancients would have been able to set forth the doctrine on this if they had so desired, but they set it aside for the reason stated above. This part is the root of the others[8] and is taken by day or night from the degree of the conjunction or prevention which preceded the nativity or the question or the revolution, to the degree of the Moon, and this is then projected from the ascendant. And this part is called the *radix vitae* [root of life] because it comprehends entirely the whole being[9] of the native or querent or even the revolution, and if it is well disposed, it signifies universally the good "being"[9] of the native and of other matters. However, if it is evilly disposed, it signifies the contrary of the aforesaid.[10]

Notes for Section 4

1. "existence": *esse*.
2. "rulership": *virtus*.
3. "condition": *esse*.
4. "certain things are allotted to it which are not given to the other parts": The *pars durabilitatis* seems to be of special importance from a metaphysical point of view.
5. A benefic "fortunate in its debility" is an apparent contradiction. To be so it would have to be well disposed and favorably aspected by a benefic.
6. "imagination": *cogitationes*. This could perhaps also be translated as "thought."
7. "Lord of the house": *eum* (literally "him"). Grammatically, the *eum* must refer to the lord of the house since it requires a masculine antecedent and the part is feminine.
8. Compare with the example of the *pars fortunae* on page 85. The part of the hyleg is discussed again in section 16.
9. "being": *esse*.
10. Compare this with what is said of the *pars fortunae* on page 85.

5. ON THE PARTS OF THE SECOND HOUSE AND THEIR EXTRACTION AND SIGNIFICATION

Having spoken above on the parts of the first house, we ought next to discuss the parts of the second house, which is called the house of substance because the first thing which man requires after birth, aside from life, is substance. It was for this reason that the signification of substance was given to the second house.

The first part of the second house is called the part of substance or *pars substantiae*, which is taken by day or night from the lord of the house of substance to the degree of the house of substance and is projected from the ascendant. And this part signifies the maintenance of the life of men and their profit and other things which are used by men for their sustenance. If it is well disposed and located, it signifies the good condition[1] of the native or querent both in food and in money and the like. If, however, it is impeded, it signifies the contrary of those things which have been said. And Albumassar said that the other significators of substance and fortune signify the other visible species of substance, that is, the kind which are hoarded and saved. The same happens in revolutions. And the part of poverty is one of the parts of Mercury.[2]

The part of moneylenders or *pars foeneratorum* is taken by day or night from Saturn to Mercury and projected from the ascendant. If it is fortunate and well disposed, it signifies money and the increase of substance because of usury and moneylenders. However, if it is impeded and the lord of substance[3] is also impeded, it signifies that the native will lose the greatest part of his own substance by usury and moneylenders and the like. And likewise with the querent. The same thing happens in revolutions. Men's means are disposed according to the disposition of the aforesaid part.

The part of happiness or *pars beatitudinis*, which is elsewhere called the *pars Jovis* and the *pars triumphi et victoriae*, is taken by day from Saturn to Jupiter and at night in the reverse direction, and it is projected from the ascendant.

The fourth part of the second house is called the part of collection or *pars collectionis*. It is taken by day from Mercury to Venus and by night in the reverse direction, and it is projected from the ascendant. And this part signifies abandoned things or semi-scattered things which someone discovers at some time or other in his journeys on the roads, in fields, on the seashore or on riverbanks, in the mountains or by digging or in some way not planned, or it is a thing which had fallen or had fled from some place or had been forgotten or in some similiar fashion had been separated from its lord or had gone out from his hands. If this part is in an angle or if any of the lords of any of the dignities of the sign in which the part is, or either of the luminaries, is joined[4] to it (unless it is combust) or if the luminary aspects the part with a trine or a sextile aspect, the things mentioned above will come into the native's hands and he will be fortunate in them and he will rediscover any of his own things he may have lost or misplaced or if he left them for some reason as was said regarding others. And if the significators of the part are in good condition,[1] in the places in which they are and in the radix of the nativity, he who discovers or rediscovers a thing will have good, profit, vitality, and good luck and will be successful concerning the things which were thus discovered. If, however, the aforesaid significators are evilly disposed, the native will not discover anything or grow rich, but rather things will turn out contrary to this and be damaged. The same happens to men in revolutions when the aforesaid part or significators are disposed in this way.

Notes for Section 5

1. "condition": *esse.*
2. "one of the parts of Mercury": The part of poverty is the only part that Bonatti gives.
3. "lord of substance": presumably the lord of the second house.
4. "joined": For Bonatti, as with the ancients generally, "conjunction" may be corporal or aspectual. Thus two planets at 3 degrees Libra are in corporal conjunction, while one planet at 3 degrees Libra and another planet at 3 degrees Cancer would be in aspectual conjunction. Today we would say of the latter case that they are in aspect.

6. ON THE PARTS OF THE THIRD HOUSE AND THEIR EXTRACTION AND SIGNIFICATION

The third house has three parts. The first is the part of brothers or *pars fratrum* and is taken in the day and night from Saturn to Jupiter and projected from the ascendant. The lord of the house [i.e., sign] of this part signifies the condition of the brothers and their agreement. And if this falls in a sign of many brothers,[1] there will be many brothers. The number of brothers is known by the number which is between that part and the lord of the sign, giving one brother to each sign.

The second part, concerning the number of brothers or *pars de numero fratrum,* is taken from Mercury to Saturn and is joined to and projected from the ascendant, and if it falls in a sign of many children[2] there will be many brothers and sisters according to the number of the signs or planets, and perhaps the number equals the quantity of years of the planets, either the mean or greater,[3] and if there are any aspecting planets, they increase the years. And if this part falls in a sign of few children, there will be few.

The third part is the part of the death of the brothers and sisters or *pars mortis fratrum et sororum.* It is taken by day from the Sun to the degree of the Medium Coeli and is added to and projected from the ascendant. It signifies the cause of death of brothers and sisters. When this part comes to the significators of the brothers or sisters, or they to it, by profection[4] or direction of degrees, they will have evil.

Notes for Section 6

1. The "Signs of many brothers" are Gemini, Virgo, Sagittarius, and Pisces.
2. "signs of many children": fertile signs.
3. The years of the planets referred to are as follows.

	least	mean	greater	greatest
♄	30	43½	57	256
♃	12	45½	79	427
♂	15	40½	66	284
☉	19	39½	120	1461
♀	8	49	82	1151
☿	20	48	76	461
☽	25	39½	108	520

It is not likely that anyone in the United States would have a family anywhere near the sizes stated in the table, although for a powerful person such as a medieval king (or his equivalent in the medieval Islamic world at the time Bonatti's source material was written), such things were not unheard of. Of course, 1,000 or more children would have been a prodigious effort even in those times of mythological exaggeration. We can, I assume, consider that the "greatest" number would rarely have been realized. Even the optimistic Bonatti does not mention the "greatest" number—only "perhaps...the mean or greater." At any rate, if there is any value in this method of reckoning offspring and siblings, the matter will have to be considered in light of the realities of our less prolific times. The years of the signs are the least years of the planets which rule them.

4. "by profection": This is a predictive technique not much in vogue among present-day Western astrologers because of its purely symbolic nature. For a discussion of this method, see Appendix C.

7. ON THE PARTS OF THE FOURTH HOUSE AND THEIR EXTRACTION AND SIGNIFICATION

Now we shall speak on the parts of the fourth house and first on the part of the father or *pars patris*, which is taken by day from the Sun to Saturn and by night in the reverse direction, and is projected from the ascendant. This part is taken from those two planets because Saturn signifies antiquity and masculinity and the Sun signifies the natural heat which is the cause of the life of animals, and fathers are more ancient than sons and are the cause of the sons. However, if it happens that Saturn is under the Sun's beams, then the *pars patris* is taken from the Sun by day to Jupiter and by night the reverse, and it is projected from the ascendant.

Albumassar said that the lord of the part signifies the fortune of the father and his substance and labors. If the part is of good quality, the father will be noble. And if its lord is of good quality, he will be fortunate and of long life. However, if it is impeded or evilly located, he will be laborious, unfortunate, and of short life. And he said that its lord signifies the place of origin of the native and his honors and fortitudes.

The second part of the fourth house is called the part of the death of the father. It is taken by day from Saturn to Jupiter and at night in the reverse direction, and it is projected from the ascendant. This part signifies the cause of the father's death. As many times as the profection of the year comes to this part or to its lord, it signifies the father's danger and misfortune. Likewise when any of them[1] come to the significators of the father.

The third part of the fourth house is called the part of grandfathers or *pars avorum*. It is taken by day from the lord of the house of the Sun to Saturn and at night in the opposite direction, and it is projected from the ascendant. If the Sun is in Leo, it is taken by day from the first degree of Leo to Saturn and by night from Saturn to the first degree of Leo and is projected from the ascendant. If the Sun is in Capricorn or Aquarius, it is taken by day from the Sun to Saturn and by night the contrary, and it is projected from the ascendant. Nor will you then care whether Saturn is under the Sun's rays or not. This part signifies the things of the grandfathers. Whence whenever it is joined to the benefics, the grandfathers come upon something good.

The fourth part of the fourth house is called the part of the ancestors or *pars parentelae* or of understanding or of generosity. It is taken by day from Saturn to Mars and by night in the opposite direction and is projected from the ascendant. To this is added the number of degrees which Saturn has completed in the sign in which he is, and it is projected from the beginning of the same sign, and where it falls is the place of the part.[2]

Albumassar said, after this, see if this part is in an angle and whether any of the lords of the dignities of the sign in which it is aspect it, or the Sun or the lord of the tenth or any of the lords of the angles with an aspect of friendship. If so, the native will be of noble progeny and of honest ancestors. However, if the part is cadent and joined to the malefics or if none of the lords of the dignities of the sign in which it is or the lords of the angles aspect it, the native or querent will be of low-quality parents or of low-quality understanding or generosity.

The fifth part of the fourth house is called the part of inheritances or possessions or *pars haereditatum vel possessionum*. It is taken by day or night from Saturn to the Moon and projected from the ascendant. Albumassar said that this part coincides with the part of the king and kingdom or *pars regi et regni*, or what kind of work the native will be employed with.[3] When it is of good condition[4] and well located and likewise its lord, the native will be fortunate because of inheritances or because of the cultivation of the earth or planting, and he will acquire substance. But if it is of evil condition[4] it signifies sorrows and sadness and dejections or something evil and horrible because of the aforesaid.

There is another part of inheritances according to the wise of the Persians, and it is the sixth part of the fourth house. This part is taken by day from Mercury to Jupiter and by night in the opposite direction, and it is projected from the ascendant. This part is not considered in the kingdom, nor in the profession nor in the cultivation of the earth nor in seeds, but only in things which are called inheritances.

The seventh part of the fourth house is called the part of the cultivation of the earth or *pars cultus terrae*. It is taken by day and by night from Venus to

Saturn and is projected from the ascendant. If it is fortunate and its lord is fortunate, the native or querent will be successful in the cultivation of the earth in planting and sowing and he will be fortunate in those things. It happens likewise for all men in revolutions of the world and for natives in the revolutions of their nativities, if the aforesaid are so disposed.

The eighth part of the fourth house according to Alchabitius is called the part of the nobility of the native or *pars nobilitatis nati* and "of him regarding whom there is doubt as to whether he is the son of his father or of another." By day it is taken from the degree of the Sun to the degree of its exaltation and is projected from the ascendant.

The ninth part of the fourth house is called the part of the ends of things or *pars finium rerum* and is taken by day from Saturn to the lord of the sign of the conjunction if the figure is conjunctional[5] or to the lord of the sign of the prevention if the figure is prevential,[6] and it is projected from the ascendant. And Albumassar said that if this part and its lord are in signs of short ascension[7] or are otherwise fortunate, the end of the businesses of the native or querent will be good or their nature laudable. However, if they are in tortuous signs or are impeded, their ends will be bad. And if one of them is in a direct sign and the other in a tortuous sign, their ends will be complicated, neither entirely good nor entirely bad. And Albumassar said, "After this the thing reverts to that which will be signified by the sign in which the lord of the part is."

Notes for Section 7

1. "any of them": *aliquis eorum;* malefics, presumably.

2. This section mentions two places from which one ought to project. One must be a mistake. In section II, "On the Parts of the Eighth House," Bonatti quotes Albumassar as saying that the *pars loci ponderosi* is similar to the *pars parentelae.* In the former the distance between Saturn and Mars is added to the number of degrees that Mercury has completed in the sign in which it is, and this sum is projected from the beginning of the same sign. Thus, in the directions above, the phrase "and is projected from the ascendant" is probably an error.

3. Actually, this part coincides with the *pars regum et quid operis agat natus.* It is the eighth part of the tenth house and is covered in section 13.

4. "condition": *esse.*

5. "if the figure is conjunctional": that is, if the figure is after a New Moon.

6. "if the figure is prevential": that is, if the figure is after a Full Moon.

7. "short ascension": *directae ascensionis.*

8. ON THE PARTS OF THE FIFTH HOUSE AND THEIR EXTRACTION AND SIGNIFICATION

We ought now to speak on the parts of the fifth house and first concerning the part of children or *pars filiorum.* This is taken by day from Jupiter to Saturn and by night from Saturn to Jupiter and is projected from the ascendant. By this part it is signified whether the native or querent will have any children or not.

Albumassar said that if this part or its lord is in a sign of many children, the native will have many children. However, if it is in a sign of few children, he will have few, and if it is in a sterile sign, he will not have any. If the part signifies children, and it is fortunate and of good condition,[1] the children live. However, if it is impeded, it signifies that they will not live. And he said that it signifies the entire being[1] of the children, and the way it holds itself to the significators of the father will determine to what degree one loves the other. And he said that the distance in longitude, between the part and its lord, is taken and one child is given to each sign which may be between them.[2] However, if there is a common sign between them, the number of the same sign will be multiplied because he will then have two children, whereas the first condition indicated only one. And he said that if there is a planet between them, it will be counted as one child for him, just as was said concerning brothers above. The second part of the fifth house or *pars masculorum vel foeminarum*, which signifies the hour in which the child will be born, and the number of children and whether they are masculine or feminine, is taken by day or night from Mars to Jupiter and is projected from the ascendant. This is because the effect of children is signified by Jupiter on account of his temperate hot and moist nature and because he is the cause of increase.[3] And because of the signification of Mars over heat and because of his motion and his delighting and hungering for natural coitus or because he predominates more in men. And because a child is not able to be unless by the coitus of men and women and by the natural heat and humidity connecting them. This is the reason this part is extracted from these significators. And Hermes said that if the first part and other significators of children signify that the native or querent will have children, this part will give the number of them, and this when Jupiter arrives to this part by body or by a trine or sextile aspect, and so much more so if it is with reception. If coitus occurs at this time, then it signifies that it generates a child in the same hour if his age permits. And Albumassar said that if it is in a masculine sign, many of his children will be masculine; if in a feminine sign, then many will be feminine. And he said if the significators signify a multitude of children for the native or querent, look to this part and its lord and see in what sign it may be; because this signifies that the number of sons he will have will be according to the number of the minor years of the lord of the part or the mean or the greater.[4] And he said that it is very likely that aspecting planets will increase the number according to the number of their years.

The third part of the fifth house, which signifies masculine children or *pars filiorum masculorum*, is taken by day and night from the Moon to Jupiter and is projected from the ascendant. Alchabitius said that it is then taken by day from the lord of the Moon to the Moon and by night in the opposite direction, and it is projected from the ascendant. This part is extracted in this way because the Moon signifies youth and the younger age during which generation occurs, which is stronger for procreating than old age or even advanced age, and the operations of nature will be more excellent or more potent at that age than in others because of its nearness to its nativity.[5] Moreover, to generate masculine children is more noble than to generate feminine ones because masculinity is acting while femininity is passive, and action is more noble and more worthy than passivity. Jupiter is the significator of the effect of children and of creation and the increase of them and especially of masculine children; for this reason the wise take this part from him.

Theophilus and certain other wise men of the Persians seemed to wish to say something else. But Albumassar held the dictum of Hermes as closer to the original.

They also said that this part aided the fortune of the native in the same way as the part of fortune, and this is not denied by the wise of that time.

The fourth part of the fifth house signifies the being[1] of the daughters or *pars esse filiarum*. According to Alchabitius it is taken by day and night from the Moon to Venus and is projected from the ascendant.

The fifth part of the fifth house, by which it is known whether a conception is masculine or feminine, or *pars de conceptione*, is taken by day from the lord of the house of the Moon[6] and in the night the reverse, and it is projected from the ascendant. And if it falls in a masculine sign, then the native or the one whom it is asked about will be masculine, but if in a feminine sign, feminine.

Notes for Section 8

1. "condition," "being": *esse*.

2. Therefore, if the part is at 10 Sagittarius, and Jupiter, its lord, is at 10 Aquarius, then two signs fall in the distance between, which would indicate two children.

3. According to the Hindus, Jupiter predominates in the guna known as *sattwa* (spiritus or ether), whose quality is to convey consciousness. Fecundity, in Man as well as in the world, is determined by both the quality and the quantity of the conscious/creative energy available to him. Therefore, it is appropriate that Jupiter should be chosen for this part. Rajasic Mars, on the other hand, is impulsive, impetuous, and outward-moving, as is the instinctual sexual desire, and hence Mars, too, is appropriately chosen for this part.

4. See note 3 for section 6 (pages 96-97), where these years are given.

5. A creature is fuller of consciousness, hence more able to procreate, at the beginning of its existence because it is closer to its Source, provided of course that the body has had time to develop. The outward movement of generation from the Source, which is Life and Being, to its opposite, or death, is the creature's expenditure of the quantum of energy allotted to it.

6. The text is incomplete, for no second significator is given. However, we may surmise that the second significator is the lord of the house of the Sun.

9. ON THE PARTS OF THE SIXTH HOUSE AND THEIR EXTRACTION AND SIGNIFICATIONS

The narration of the parts of the sixth house, and first concerning the part of infirmities and accidents and of inseparable vices or *pars infirmitatum*. This is taken by day from Saturn to Mars and by night the reverse and is projected from the ascendant.

The second part of the sixth house, called the part of infirmities both separable and inseparable, is taken by day and by night from Mercury to Mars and is projected from the ascendant.

The third part of the sixth house is called the part of servants according to Alchabitius, and according to Theophilus it is taken by day from Mercury to the Moon and the reverse at night and it is projected from the ascendant. But according to Hermes, whose opinion was considered as closer to the original by the wise, it is taken by day or night from Mercury to the Moon, and it is projected from the ascendant. This because Hermes and the wise in those times considered servants both male and female (as many servants and handmaids and messengers are) to be unfaithful and readily changeable, and this in order to be contrary to their lords rather than their own profit, and therefore they attributed all these things and other quickly changing things to the lighter planets. And so they extracted this part from them. If the part is fortunate and of good condition[1] and likewise its lord, it signifies that the native or the querent will have good from the aforementioned significations of the part. However, if it is impeded, it signifies the contrary. And if the part is of good condition and its lord impeded, or vice versa, it signifies that the native will have good from them first, followed by its contrary from them. And if this part is in a sign of many children, it signifies that the native or querent will have many manservants, handmaids, or other servants. If it is in a sign of few children, he will have few servants. If it is in a sterile sign, he will lack them completely. And the same thing happens in revolutions concerning the aforesaid parts for those who have them.

Theophilus and certain others said that this part is taken from Mercury to the *pars fortunae*. Albumassar approves more the dictum of Hermes.

The fourth part of the sixth house, which is called the part of captives and the conquered or *pars captivorum et vinctorum*, is taken by day from the lord of the house of the Sun to the Sun and by night from the lord of the house of the Moon to the Moon, and it is projected from the ascendant. If it falls in a good place from the ascendant and is with any of the benefics, the querent or captive will be liberated from that captivity. But if it falls in an evil place and is with the malefics, it signifies for the captive evil and misery and it may signify the death of the captive especially if the lord of the tenth aspects it. And Albumassar said if the Sun is in its own house by day, or the Moon by night, one of these will be the signification. And he said, after this look to that one of these [i.e., the Sun or the Moon] which is the significator, in what place of the circle it is and from which planet it is separated or to which it is joined, and work according to this. Understand the same in revolutions.

Note for Section 9

·1. "condition": *esse*.

10. ON THE PARTS OF THE SEVENTH HOUSE AND THEIR EXTRACTION AND SIGNIFICATION

The discourse on the parts of the seventh house, and first regarding the part of men's marriages or *pars coniugii virorum secundum Hermetem*. This part is taken by day or night from Saturn to Venus, and it is projected from the ascendant. Hermes and the other wise men extract it from these two planets because Saturn signifies antiquity and things which are long-lasting, and marriage ought to be long-lasting. Moreover, Saturn has signification over masculinity and Venus has signification over feminity, and masculinity ought to precede feminity by the nature of masculinity and action. If this part is of good condition[1] and well disposed, it signifies that the marriage is appropriate and of good fortune and that the native or querent profits from it and that good follows from that marriage, and it signifies indeed that the native contracts a marriage with a beautiful and decent woman. But if it is impeded, it signifies that the marriage will be bad and harmful and that damage and danger and disturbance with adversities will follow from it. See if Jupiter comes to the part or aspects it with a fortunate aspect, because then the marriage will be fortunate if it was consummated in that hour.

And Albumassar said that when this part is with the lord of the sign in which it is posited or the Sun aspects it and the Moon and its lord with a strong and favorable aspect, it signifies that the native is joined with one of his own parents.[2] Understand the same thing regarding weddings which are made in revolutions when the aforesaid part and its lord are thus disposed, as has been said.[3]

And Albumassar said there is a second part of men's marriages which Vellius relates which is taken by day and night from the Sun to Venus and is projected from the ascendant.

The third part of the seventh house is the part of cunning and of craftiness[4] of men toward women or *pars calliditatis et ingenii virorum erga mulieres*, and it is similar to the *pars coniugii virorum* according to Vellius.

The fourth part of the seventh house is the part of coitus of men with women or *pars coitus virorum cum mulieribus*, and it is similar to the *pars coniugii virorum* of Vellius.

The fifth part of the seventh house is called the part of luxury and fornication of men or *pars luxuriae atque fornicationis virorum*, and it is taken by day and night from Venus to Saturn and it is projected from the ascendant. If it is in a good place, there will be a laudable union and the man will succeed in what he wants from women. However, if it is evilly located, the union will be disgraceful, nor will he be able to succeed with women. And Albumassar said that if it is in a sign signifying impeded coitus, the man will be of frequent coitus, lascivious, and a fornicator. However, if it is fortunate, the man will be of frequent coitus and the coitus will be at least partly laudable. And he said that on the signification of this part, if the lord of the part which Hermes calls the part of the wedding of men or *pars nuptiarum virorum*,[5] falls with Vellius' part[6] or if the lord of this part [i.e., *pars luxuriae atque fornicationis virorum*] is aspecting the *pars nuptiarum virorum,* the native or querent will fornicate with the woman before he is joined to her by marriage, and afterward make the fact known publicly.

The sixth part of the seventh house is called the part of marriage of women or *pars coniugii mulierum.* Hermes said that it is similar to the cause of the marriage of men, and it is taken in both day and night from Venus to Saturn and is projected from the ascendant.

Albumassar said that this part coincides with the *pars cultus terrae.* Vellius took it by day and by night from the Sun to Mars, and projected it from the ascendant. Hermes, however, was closer to the original intent than he. If this part and its lord are well disposed and of good condition,[1] it signifies the fortune of women by marriage. But if it is impeded, it will signify sorrows and sadness and afflictions or tribulations which the native or querent will discover as a result of the marriage, and the wife will be lustful. Again, Vellius took it in another and better way; he took it by day and night from the Moon to Mars and projected it from the ascendant, and this method pleased Albumassar more. This is the seventh part.

The eighth part of the seventh house is called the part of cunning and craftiness[7] of women toward men. Hermes said that this is similar to the *pars coniugii mulierum.*

The ninth part of the seventh house is called the part of pleasure and amusements or *pars voluptatis et delectationis.* It is taken by day or night from Venus to the degree and minute of the seventh house and is projected from the ascendant.

The tenth part of the seventh house is called the part of lascivious women and their foulness or *pars lasciviae mulierum et turpitudinis earum.* Vellius said that it is similar to the *pars coniugii mulierum.* It is taken by day from Venus to Saturn and projected from the ascendant. When it is of good condition[1] and well disposed, the woman will be pleased with her marriage and will praise it. But if it is of evil condition or evilly disposed, her marriage will displease her and she will blaspheme it and she will be sorry and suffer because of it and strive in treachery and deception of the mind of men. And if this part is of good condition[1] and well placed or in signs of cunning and craft such as Leo, Sagittarius, Capricorn, and Pisces, the woman seduces whatever man she wishes. But if it is outside of these signs or otherwise evilly located, she will not be able to seduce anyone.

On the signification of the part of conjunction and their coitus: If it is in a sign signifying impeded coitus, she will be a foul fornicatrix, an evil, lascivious woman. But if it is fortunate in a sign signifying coitus, she will be full of desire in coitus, partly, however, in an appropriate way.[8]

And on the signification of the *pars lasciviae mulierum et turpitudinis earum:* Albumassar said that if the *pars conjugii mulierum* which Hermes mentions is with the part of the same name which Vellius mentions, and if the lord of this part is with the *pars conjugii,* she will fornicate with a man and later be married to him.

The eleventh part of the seventh house is called the part of religion and of the honesty of the woman or *pars religionis et honestatis mulieris.* It is taken by day and night from the Moon to Venus and is projected from the ascendant. And he[9] said that this part is also the part of daughters. If it is in a fixed sign or in the aspect of any of the lords of the dignities of the sign in which it is [placed] or of any benefic, the woman will be honest and religious even if she may be longing for coitus. But if the malefics aspect it without reception and it is in a mobile sign, the woman will be excessive in her desire for coitus, giving herself to men and inviting them to coitus for a cheap price, and she will be in every way a fornicatrix.

The twelfth part of the seventh house is called the part of marriage of men and women according to Hermes or *pars conjugii virorum et mulierum secundum Hermetem.*[10] It is taken from Venus to the degree and minute of the angle of weddings, that is, of the seventh, and is projected from the ascendant. If it is joined to the benefics, the woman marries and it is said of her marriage that it is good. However, if it is of evil "condition"[1] and evilly located and joined to the malefics or if they aspect it without a perfect reception, her marriage will be scandalous and it falls into the reproach of the public. But if the lord of the sign in which the part is, is itself in an evil place and Venus is under the Sun's rays or impeded by Saturn, the woman will not marry forever but leads her own life in a foul way.

The thirteenth part of the seventh house is called the part of the hour of marriage and it is taken by day or night from the Sun to the Moon and is projected from the ascendant.[11] If Jupiter aspects it with a favorable aspect or is joined to it corporally and they are of good condition[1] and the figure is for a man, the man will be married to a beautiful, honest, easily appeased, and desirable woman. And Albumassar said that this part is found in this way because when the nativity of a man signifies that he will marry, the cause of the matter will be that one luminary is hot and masculine and the other is humid and feminine, and because all generation in this world is caused by the conjunction of heat and masculinity with humidity and feminity, and it was for this reason that this part was named.

The fourteenth part of the seventh house is called the part of intelligence and ease of marriage or *pars ingenii et facilitatis conjugii.* It is taken by day or night from the Sun to the Moon, and it is projected from the degree and minute of Venus. If it falls in a sign of cunning and is of good condition,[1] fortunate and strong and well disposed, it signifies that he who aspires to marriage will attain it with ease as he planned. If, however, it is impeded and of evil condition,[1] his marriage will be attended by severity and affliction and he will hardly ever be able to attain that which he intended.

The fifteenth part of the seventh house is called the part of fathers-in-law. It is taken by day and by night from Saturn to Venus, and it is projected from the ascendant. And Albumassar said that this part coincides with the *pars conjugii virorum secundum Hermetem.*[12] If it is fortunate, strong, and well disposed and agrees with the lord of the house in which it is, the native will agree with and be good to his wife's parents and relatives even more than to his own. But if it is impeded, he will be an enemy to them.

The sixteenth part of the seventh house is called the part of contenders and of contentions or *pars contendentium et contentionum.* It is taken by day from Mars to Jupiter and from Jupiter to Mars at night, and it is projected from the ascendant. And Albumassar said that if this part is in the ascendant or with its lord in any of the angles, the native will be given to much fighting. If this part is fortunate, evil follows from contention.[13] But if the part falls with the lord of the seventh in the ascendant, the native will be one of those who contends before kings and judges.

Notes for Section 10

1. "condition": *esse.*

2. "parents": *parentelae,* possibly for *parentelia. Parentelae* literally means dead ancestors.

3. See Bonatti's report on the fifth part of the seventh house.

4. "craftiness": *ingenii.*

5. *"Pars nuptiarum virorum"* refers to the first part discussed in this section, the *pars coniugii virorum secundum Hermetem.*

6. Vellius' part is the second part of men's marriages referred to earlier in this section.

7. "craftiness": *calliditatis.*

8. This paragraph and the following were inserted by Bonatti for comparison with what has already been said. Unfortunately, the extraction of the part of conjunction and their coitus (*pars coniunctionis et coitus earum*) is omitted.

9. The text does not indicate which author this is attributed to.

10. The *pars conjugii virorum et mulierum secundum Hermetem* is not to be confused with the *pars coniugii virorum secundum Hermetem,* which is the first part of the seventh house; or the part of the same name according to Vellius, which is the second part of the seventh house; or the *pars conjugii mulierum secundum Hermetem,* the sixth part of the seventh house; or the part of marriage of women according to Vellius, the seventh part of the seventh house; or the eighth part of the seventh house, which Hermes says is similar to the part of marriage of women (*pars conjugii mulierum*) but which is properly called the *pars ingenii atque calliditatis mulierum erga viros;* or finally the tenth part of the seventh house, called the *pars lasciviae mulierum et turpitudinis earum,* by which he means that part listed here as the sixth part of the seventh house.

11. Although Bonatti makes no mention of the fact, the thirteenth part of the seventh house coincides with the *pars fortunae* in a diurnal figure.

12. The *pars conjugii virorum secundum Hermetem* is the first part of the seventh house.

13. This is the opposite of what we would expect.

11. ON THE PARTS OF THE EIGHTH HOUSE AND THEIR EXTRACTION AND SIGNIFICATION

Now in this chapter, we ought to discuss the parts of the eighth house, which are five, and first concerning the part of death or *pars mortis*. This is taken by day or night from the Moon to the degree of the eighth house. To this is added the distance which Saturn has completed in the sign in which it is, and this sum is projected from the beginning of the same sign.[1] It is extracted in this way because the Moon is the significatrix of the body, and the eighth house is the significatrix of death, which is the destruction of the body, and Saturn has signification over the ends of things and other sorrows and sadnesses and lamentations and difficulties and dissolution and destruction, all of which follow from death. This is the reason why the signification over the fact of death was given to these three significators. But if this part and its lord are free and of good nature[2] or well disposed or located, the native will die in his own bed by a natural death. If, however, they are impeded and the benefics do not aspect them or at least one of them, the native will die a most disgraceful death. But if the said significators in any revolution are thus evilly disposed, as has been said, the native will die by such a death in that revolution.

The second part of the eighth house, called the part of the killing planet or *pars interficiendis planetae*, is taken by day from the lord of the ascendant to the Moon and by night the reverse, and it is projected from the ascendant. This part is extracted like this because the lord of the ascendant signifies the soul and the Moon signifies the body, although sometimes it is posited as the other way around. While the soul is enfolded in the body, it signifies the temperament, and they remain thus so long as they are in agreement. However, when they are diverse, the body will die, although the soul still remains. For this reason this part was extracted in this way by the wise.

Albumassar said that if the Moon alone aspects the part and she[3] is impeded in a sign of the members of the abscissors[4] or if the lord of the sign in which the part is or the lords of the signs in which they are impede each other, the native or querent dies with suffering. If, however, they[5] were not impeded nor impede each other in turn, the native will be mutilated in the member assigned to the sign in which the Moon is at the time but will not die from this.

The third part of the eighth house is called the part of the year in which death, affliction, destruction, impediment, or heavy affliction is feared for the native or *pars anni in quo timetur nato*. It is taken by day from Saturn to the lord of the house of conjunction or prevention which preceded the nativity, question, or revolution, and it is projected from the ascendant. And this part is extracted in this way for the following reason. Saturn is the significator of cold and death and the end, and of afflictions which make for destruction. The degree of the conjunction or prevention likewise. Therefore they counted this part from these two places. And Albumassar said that this part coincides with the *pars finium rerum*. And he said that when this part and its lord are with the lord of the ascendant and impeded, the native will be of many infirmities and afflictions in body and substance, and frequently he will approach physical danger and loss of substance. And whenever a year arrives to this part—whether the part arrives by profections, by which one year is given to each sign, or by direction, which is made by degrees of ascension to the ascendant or its lord—the native will discover danger in the body or his members from infirmities, and he will discover difficulties and horrible things in his substance. And death will be feared from diverse parts.

The fourth part of the eighth house is called the part of the heavy place or *pars loci ponderosi*, and it is taken by day from Saturn to Mars and at night in the opposite direction. This distance is added to the distance Mercury has completed in the sign in which it is, and it is projected from the beginning of the same sign.

Albumassar said that this part is similar to the *pars parentelae*. And he said that if this part and the lord of the ascendant are impeded in someone's nativity, he will have the incurable illness called azemena[6] in the member assigned to the sign in which the part is, and he will be unfortunate in all his businesses and will be occupied and troubling himself with them and will never be able to bring them to a good end, nor to complete any matter whether for good or ill. Things will move very slowly and he will hardly ever be able to finish them.

And Albumassar said that when the year reaches from the ascendant to this part or from the part to the ascendant, or to its lord by profections (by which one sign is given to each year) or by the direction of significators, the native will be involved with his businesses in that year and they will delay the realization of whatever he had hoped for from them, and as a result of these things he will suffer sorrows, sadness, and afflictions. He will begin nothing that year which will be successfully completed by him; rather he will suffer loss. He will discover infirmities in the member assigned to the sign in which the year of the revolution reaches this part. And if the malefics aspect it, he will find difficulties and destruction.

The fifth part of the eighth house is called the part of occupation, severity, and destruction or *pars occupationis, gravitatis, et destructionis*. It is taken by day from Saturn to Mercury and by night the reverse, and it is projected from the ascendant. And if it happens that the lord of the ascendant is with the part and impeded in the radix of the nativity, it signifies that the native will be in evil and trouble all the days of his life. And if he were ever to do anything from which he expects good or benefit, he will get trouble and evil from it, and what he intended will not follow. And if at any time the year comes to either or both of them by profections [i.e., the year which is obtained by giving to each sign one year according to the succession of the signs] or by directions of degrees, just as is said in the tractate in nativities. When a degree is directed by terms to any place and the direction arrives to the part, the native will find evil from which he will not be liberated in that revolution. And if he was liberated from it, he will fall into another, perhaps more severe. And if the benefics aspect the place [of the part] from strong places, they will alleviate the evil but not do away with it entirely.

Notes for Section 11

1. This amounts to taking the distance between the Moon and the eighth house and projecting it from Saturn's position.

2. "nature": *esse*. Here the part should be in the sign of a benefic and well disposed.

3. "she": *ipsa*, which could indicate either the Moon or the part.

4. "abscissors": killing planets.

5. "they," i.e., the Moon's dispositor and the ruler of the part as I read it.

6. Bonatti in *Tractatus secundus pars secunda* (chapter XXVI) tells us that Ptolemy, Alchabitius, and others said that there are certain degrees of certain signs which are called azemene because they are associated with an incurable disease called azemena. Just what the association is is not made clear, but we may assume that when the ruler of the ascendant, the ascendant itself, or either of the luminaries is placed in these degrees the native will be born with the infirmity. Bonatti tells us that the term means literally "maiming" (*debilitatio*). The infirmity is usually gotten "in the mother's womb" and once contracted "the native will always have it with him as long as he lives." "It is an incurable illness such as blindness from birth, deafness from birth, limping [or lameness], a hunched condition from birth and similar things." (Est aegritudo inseparabilis a corpore nati sicut est naturalis caecitas; naturalis surditas; claudicatio, naturalis gibbositas, et similia.) The azemene degrees are:

♈	0	0	0	0	0
♉	6	7	8	9	10
♊	0	0	0	0	0
♋	9	10	11	12	13
♌	18	27	28		
♍	0	0			
♎	0	0			
♏	19	28		18	19
♐	1	7	8	18	19
♑	26	27	28	29	
♒	18	19			
♓	0				

12. ON THE PARTS OF THE NINTH HOUSE AND THEIR EXTRACTION AND SIGNIFICATION

In this chapter we shall discuss the parts of the ninth house, which are seven. The first is called the part of travel or *pars peregrinationis*. It is taken by day and night from the lord of the ninth sign to the degree of the ninth house, and this is projected from the ascendant. This part and its lord signify the native's or querent's travel. If it is of good condition and well disposed, it signifies that his travels are useful and profitable. Understand likewise in revolutions of years. However, if [they are disposed and conditioned] evilly, say the contrary.

The second part of the ninth house is called the part of the journey or travel on water or *pars itineris ac peregrinationis in aqua*. It is taken by day from Saturn to the 15th degree of Cancer, and by night in the reverse direction, and is projected from the ascendant. If this part falls in watery signs with the benefics, the native will see good, utility, and profit, also money and health, from journeys at sea and the conducting of them. And certain of the ancients said that if Saturn is in the 15th degree of Cancer and that degree is rising, with Saturn in it, they will then be the significators. Then look at them and their condition,[1] also the aspect of the planets, and judge[2] according to them.

The third part of the ninth house is called the part of religion or *pars religionis*. It is taken by day from the Moon to Mercury and by night in the opposite direction and is projected from the ascendant. And if this part and its lord fall in the ascendant or with the lord of the ascendant or with the Almutem[3] over it, the native will be religious; also if the significators of the part or the lord of the ascendant aspect the part. If, however, the part is impeded, none of the aforesaid occur, but rather the contrary.

The fourth part of the ninth house is called the part of oration and profundity of counsel or *pars orationis atque profunditatis consilii*. It is taken by day from Saturn to the Moon and at night in the opposite direction and is projected from the ascendant. The part signifies reason, consideration of profound things; also the profundity of praiseworthy counsels and invention and wisdom, even more so if Saturn is above the Earth by day and again more if he is oriental aspecting the part and receiving it, or if the Moon aspects it from a very good place[4] from the ascendant.

The fifth part of the ninth house is called the part of wisdom and patience or *pars sapientiae*. It is taken by day from Saturn to Jupiter and by night in the reverse direction, and it is projected from Mercury. And it is taken in this way because while Saturn signifies stability, philosophy, and profundity in things and close attention to speech and prolixity of cogitations, Jupiter signifies wisdom and patience and reason, and Mercury signifies writings and wisdom and experiments of things, so it was extracted from these. If Saturn and Jupiter aspect it or are joined to it and if both or one of them receives it,[5] the native will be wise, patient, and rational. And if Mercury aspects it or is joined to it, he will be wise, of acute and profound mind, the greatest expert or investigator of profound things, and he will be swift in the discovery of all things able to be discovered.[6]

The sixth part of the ninth house is called the part of histories and of science or rumors and fables or *pars historiarum et scientiae*, etc. It is taken by day from the Sun to Jupiter and by night in the reverse direction and is projected from the ascendant.

And Albumassar said that this part coincides with the *pars patris*. And he said that when Saturn is under the Sun's rays, if this part falls in an angle in the aspect of Mercury and Venus and the lord of the ascendant aspects the part, the native retains ancient histories and rumors of men and will be an inventor of fables and beautiful stories by which the listeners are delighted and they laugh and enjoy them. And Albumassar said that if, however, it was otherwise, it will be the contrary.

The seventh part of the ninth house is called the part of rumors whether they be true or false, or *pars rumorum, utrum sint veri vel falsi*. It is taken by day or night from Mercury to the Moon and projected from the ascendant. Albumassar said that this part is similar to the *pars sevorum*. If it is in an angle or in a fixed sign or a sign of direct ascension, the rumors will be true, and even more surely if the Moon is joined to a true planet,[7] and truer yet if with this a true planet is in the first, second, fifth, or ninth. But if it is otherwise, it will be the contrary.

Notes for Section 12

1. "condition": *esse*.
2. "judge": *operare*.
3. The Almutem of any place is that planet which has the greatest number of honors in that place. This planet may not be the ruler of the ascendant.
4. "from a very good place": *ex optimo loco*.
5. "if both or one of them receives it": It is impossible for *both* Saturn and Jupiter to receive any part or planet.
6. With this difference: that Jupiter and Saturn incline to religion and philosophy and a metaphysics that is more religious than scientific, while Mercury produces minds more inclined to precision, logic, and systematization and more mundane in their application of theory then Jupiter and Saturn.
7. "true planet": *planetae veridico*.

13. ON THE PARTS OF THE TENTH HOUSE AND THEIR EXTRACTION AND SIGNIFICATION

In this chapter will be given the discourse on the parts of the tenth house. First concerning the part of nobility or *pars nobilitatis*, which is taken by day from the Sun to the 19th degree of Aries, which is the degree of its exaltation, and by night from the Moon to the 3rd degree of Taurus, which is the degree of its exaltation, and is projected from the ascendant. And it is extracted in this way because the Sun, who is the luminary of the day, is the significator by day of the native's life and its duration, and it signifies the soul and honor and his degree of elevation, also kingdom and victory; and the Moon is the luminary of the night and by night it signifies that which the Sun signifies by day. And it was called the *pars nobilitatis* for this reason, because it is extracted from the luminaries which are the more noble bodies and from the degrees of their exaltation. By means of this part are known the nobility or generosity of the native and whether or not he is the son of the man whose son he is said to be, and by this part his honor and exaltation or his kingdom, success, and victory are known. If it falls in a good place, such as the tenth house, and is with benefics which are well located and of good condition,[1] it signifies that the native will attain to honor, nobility, advancement, riches, and the publication of his good reputation, each according to his own degree, so that if the native were one of those fit to be king, he will attain to honors and dignities appropriate for him.[2] The same thing happens if this part is so disposed in someone's nativity.

But if this part falls in the aforesaid degrees and the nativity is diurnal, Albumassar says that the signification of those degrees will be the same as the signification of the degree of the ascendant. But if the significators of this part aspect it and they are in good connection with it, the native will be the son of him to whom he is attributed. If, however, it is otherwise, he will not be his.

The second part of the tenth house is called the part of kingship or *pars regni*. It is taken by day from Mars to the Moon and by night in the opposite direction, and it is projected from the ascendant. And Albumassar said that if this part and its lord are of good condition[1] and they are connected with the lord of the tenth and the lord of the ascendant, the native will be king or duke and he will be with rich men, who receive his words and heed them.

The third part of the tenth house is called the part of kingship and of kings and of dispositors or *pars regni, regum, et dispositorum*. It is taken by day from Mercury to Mars and by night in the opposite direction, and it is projected from the ascendant. This part is extracted from these significators because the signification for giving, receiving, writing, prohibiting a matter from reaching the consulate, for writing letters, sending them, and receiving the Mass, counting money, and clarity of mind has been given to Mercury. And signification of fear and terror is given to Mars, and therefore this part was counted from these planets. When the part and its lord are well disposed and of good condition[1] or well located with the lord of the ascendant, the native will be of good mind, easily instructed, and rational, and he will attain the consulship if he is fit for it. He will be a scribe of kings or a collector or a custodian of their census or of the substances of greater kings. And if he is fit for kingship or empire, he will attain that and his reputation will surpass his status, and it will extend all the way to the borders of the lands and he will raise up certain men and will elevate them beyond measure and depose certain powerful men and subjugate them, and soldiers will run freely about and the affairs of men will be according to his hand.

The fourth part of the tenth house is called the part of kingship and victory and assistance. It is taken by day from the Sun to Saturn and by night the reverse, and it is projected from the ascendant. And Albumassar said that this part coincides with the *pars patrum* when Saturn is under the rays of the Sun. When it is well disposed or of good condition and especially when with the lord of the tenth house and with the lord of the ascendant, it signifies kingship for the native. If he is one of those who are fit for kingship, it signifies honor and exaltation for each according to his being,[1] and further, he will be extended and preferred and prevail over those of his own kind. Albumassar said if it is in a sign in which the lord of the ascendant or the lord of the tenth has dignity, it will signify victory for the native over those who contend with him. The same thing happens in revolutions, if this part is so disposed.

The fifth part of the tenth house is called the part of those who are suddenly elevated or *pars illorum qui repente sublimantur*. It is taken by day from Saturn to the *pars fortunae* and by night the reverse, and it is projected from the ascendant. And Albumassar said that this part is similar to the *pars Saturni*. If in anyone's nativity or question it is in some very good place from the ascendant and from the benefics, he will be suddenly elevated. And if the lord of the ascendant is with the part or aspects it with an aspect of friendship or from a good place and is well disposed, his elevation will be increased unexpectedly, and he will attain kingship very quickly and in the shortest time, so that men will wonder because of it. And Albumassar said, look to this part when you know that the man will be elevated[3] and will acquire kingship and honor. But he said that if this part is impeded, the native or querent will find evil and impediment and danger and sudden fall from power. Understand the same in revolutions, because if the part is of good condition[1] and well disposed, the native and others will acquire good suddenly in that revolution, and if it is impeded, he will be impeded to the same degree.

The sixth part of the tenth house is called the part of nobles and of those who are known among men or of honored men, or *pars nobilium*. It is taken by day and night from Mercury to the Sun and projected from the ascendant. When it and its lord are of good condition[1] and well disposed, the native will be noble and honored among kings and the wealthy and powerful. And Albumassar said that if it is with a planet which has great dignity in the Medium Coeli, the native will have an eminence by which he will be counted, as a tribe of a city is counted among its citizens.[4] However, if it is otherwise, the contrary will happen. Understand the same in revolutions.

The seventh part of the tenth house is called the part of soldiers and ministers or *pars militum et ministrorum*. Albumassar said that it is taken by day from Mars to Saturn and by night in the opposite direction, and it is projected from the ascendant. And he said that if this part and its lord are commixed with the lord of the ascendant, the native will be a follower of the king or one of his soldiers or ministers.

The eighth part of the tenth house is called the part of kings and what kind of work the native does, or *pars regum et quid operis agat natus*. It is taken by day or night from Saturn to the Moon and is projected from the ascendant. This because Saturn signifies labor, adversity, necessity, poverty, and all laborious works such as superintendents of houses, of diggings, operations of iron and its extraction from the ore, and other odious and tedious works, because Saturn is the significator of labor and affliction and he is the significator of riches which are heavy and ponderous. And the Moon signifies labors and quickness in things because of the speed of her motion and she is the significatrix of the common people, and therefore the wise counted this part from these significators.

Albumassar said that this part signifies kings, honor, and magnificence and what kind of work the native does which he does for its own sake and what profession he will practice and whether he profits from his profession or not.

And he said that if this part is in Gemini or Virgo or in signs of art or instruction, he will be elevated by works of his hands which are necessaries for the ornamentation of the rich, and he will be with rich men and magnates because of his skill and his talent. And if the part is commixed with significators of substance, the native acquires a great quantity of substance from his profession. And he said that if the contrary, he will be a pauper and unfortunate in his profession, barely able to get his daily sustenance; nor will he be able to be wearied of it, and if he is not wearied of it, he will die of hunger—no one will offer him sustenance. The same thing happens in revolutions: There are sometimes years in which fortunate men do not gain anything, and that is when that part is evilly disposed in a revolution. And there are sometimes years in which unfortunate men acquire something, and that is when the part is well disposed.

The ninth part of the tenth house is called the part of tradesmen and those who work with their hands or *pars negociatorum et operantium manibus suis.* It is taken by day from Mercury to Venus and by night the reverse, and it is projected from the ascendant. Albumassar said that this part is similar to the *pars collectionis.* This part signifies ingenious men, artisans in venusian and mercurial professions such as those who know how to work gold, silver, precious stones, and the like; and those who know how to do business, that is, to buy and sell precious and choice merchandise such as pearls, rings, and the like; and those who know how to make beautiful clothes which pertain to women, and how to paint and write and to make stamps[5] and to sculpt sigils and the like, which pertain to the nature of Mercury and Venus.

If this part and its lord are of good condition[1] and well disposed and they are commixed with the lord of the ascendant by conjunction, trine, or sextile aspect, the native or querent will be elevated because of his works or the skills of his hands. He will make beautiful instruments and beautiful works by hand which become nobles and rich men and magnates. However, if the contrary, he is not introduced into the employ of these since the opposite to these things will occur to him. If this part and its lord are well disposed in someone's revolution, or in a revolution of the world, the aforementioned artisans will gain from their trades. If, however, the contrary, the contrary comes about.

The tenth part of the tenth house is called the part of trade of buying and selling or *pars negotii emendi atque vendendi.* It is taken by day from the *pars futurorum* to the part of fortune and by night in the reverse direction, and it is projected from the ascendant. And Albumassar said that this part is similar to the part of Mercury. And he said that when these parts which are of trade are received in the aspects of Mercury, the native will be an expert in trades and he will have the science of buying and selling. And if they are well disposed, they will profit him and he will gain from them and because of them. If, however, they are of evil condition[1] and evilly disposed, although he may know them, he will not introduce himself into their employ because it will be in its contrary. It ought to be understood to be the same in revolutions both of the world and of nativities.

The eleventh part of the tenth house is called the part of work and of a thing which must happen necessarily and absolutely must occur, or *pars operis et reique necesse est ut omnino fiat*. It is taken by day from the Sun to Jupiter and by night in the opposite direction and is projected from the ascendant. And Albumassar said that when Saturn is under the Sun's rays, this part is similar to the part of the father. And he said that when this part is with the lord of the ascendant, the native will be outstanding in his works. He will know his business better than anyone else. He will struggle and be anxious about everything which he desires to do. He hopes to complete everything hastily and will always doubt whether a thing will be completed until he sees it complete. Hence when someone wants to make something, and he wants to know what is going to happen from it, look to this part. If it is of good condition[1] and especially if it is with the benefics, it will profit him to make the thing, and especially if he hurries to make it. However, if it is with the malefics or otherwise impeded, he will find evil, detriment, and trouble, if he makes it for this reason, and the more he hastens to make it, the worse and more horrible the results of it are for him.

This holds not only in nativities, but also in questions and revolutions both of the world and of nativities.

The twelfth part of the tenth house is called the part of mothers or *pars matrum*. It is taken by day from Venus to the Moon and by night the reverse and is projected from the ascendant. This part signifies the being[1] of mothers. If it is of good condition[1] and well disposed, it signifies that the mother's being[1] is good. In a nativity, if it is in trine or sextile aspect to the lord of the ascendant, it signifies that the mother loves her son, the native. If the lord of the tenth receives the lord of the ascendant and the lord of the ascendant does not receive the lord of the tenth or the Moon, it signifies that the mother loves the son; however, he does not love her. And if the lord of the ascendant receives the lord of the tenth and the lord of the tenth does not receive him or the Moon, it signifies that the son loves the mother more than she him. If each receives the other, both love the other; if neither receives the other, neither loves the other. The same ought to be said in questions, revolution, and nativities. And the wise posited that the part of the mother is in the tenth because it is opposite the fourth, which signifies the father.

The thirteenth part of the tenth house is called the part signifying whether the cause of the kingdom may or not be. It is taken by day and night from the Sun to the degree of the Medium Coeli and is projected from the degree of Jupiter.

The fourteenth part of the tenth house is called the part of death of the mother. It is taken by day from Venus to Saturn and at night the reverse, and it is projected from the ascendant.

Notes for Section 13

1. "condition," "being": *esse*.
2. The degree of rise in social status that the native is likely to enjoy depends upon

three factors: (1) the natal horoscope, the rules for the delineation of which in this matter are given by Ptolemy in his *Tetrabiblos*, book 4, chap. 3; (2) the native's economic class; (3) the status of the ethnic group to which the native belongs, as Ibn Ezra affirms in his *Liber nativitatum* in *Abrahe Avenaris judei astrologi peritissimi in re iudiciali opera: ab excellentissimo philosopho Petro de Abano post accuratam castigationem in latinum traducta* (Venice, 1507).

3. "when you know that the man will be elevated": That is, the natal horoscope must first indicate this; then the part may be considered.

4. One large ethnic constituency may wield great influence in the politics of a city such that it has more impact as a group than an individual or other less influential groups might. Such would be the degree of influence of a man whose *pars nobilium* was disposed as above.

5. "stamps": *movetas;* also translates as "money."

14. ON THE PARTS OF THE ELEVENTH HOUSE AND THEIR EXTRACTION AND SIGNIFICATION

In this chapter we shall discuss the parts of the eleventh house. First, concerning the part of excellence and nobility or *pars excellentiae atque nobilitatis*, Albumassar said that it is taken by day from the *pars fortunae* to the *pars futurorum* and by night the contrary and is projected from the ascendant. And he said that this part is similar to the *pars stabilitatis et durabilitatis* and to the *pars Veneris*. This part is extracted in this way: Since it is more noble, more stable, and far more useful, it was fitting that it be extracted from the two parts which are more noble and excellent than the others, and these are the *pars fortunae* and the *pars futurorum*.

When this part is of good condition[1] or well disposed, and is with the benefics well located, and the better if it is in the tenth or eleventh house and none of the malefics impede it, the native will be one who excels other men and is both noble and fortunate, and his fortune will last, and he will be one of those whom men seek out on account of his good luck and whom men will revere, and he will be like a prince among the tribes. And his name will remain through the ages for many years, and he will see good and joy and what pleases him from every work which he does. However, if it is the contrary, the opposite will happen to him. Understand the same thing in general questions,[2] and it is able to have a place in other things, likewise in revolutions. When this part is so disposed, good or evil happens to each according to his own being.

The second part of the eleventh house is called the part signifiying how the native or querent is loved by men or how they hate him, or *pars significans qualiter diligetur natus*. Albumassar said that is is taken by day from the *pars fortunae* to the *pars futurorum* and at night the reverse, and it is projected from the ascendant. And he said that this part is similar to the *pars Veneris*.[3] If it falls in the house, exaltation, or triplicity of any benefic, and if that benefic aspects the part and is not impeded by any of the malefics, the native will be beloved of men and lovable to them and sweet and pleasing in their eyes. But if the part falls with the malefics or in their aspects, they do not desire to see him and he frequently does and says things displeasing to men, even when saying and doing good.

The third part of the eleventh house is called the part of the native among men and of an honored man among them and by which of them a business or activities are perfected, or *pars nati inter homines*. It is taken by day from the part of fortune to the Sun and by night the reverse, and it is projected from the ascendant. If it is well located and received by the Sun, Jupiter, or with Venus, while Mercury and the Moon are in benefic condition or aspecting the part and the lord of the ascendant with a trine or sextile aspect, the native or querent will be honored both by the powerful and by the common people, and they will love him and return to him because of his deeds, and they will give to him many things and many business deals for perfecting or for the purpose of defining their terms, and they will have especially great faith in him.

The fourth part of the eleventh house is called the part of felicity and profit or *pars felicitatis et profectus*. It is taken by day from the part of fortune to Jupiter and by night in the opposite direction, and it is projected from the ascendant.

If it is with the lord of the ascendant or if the latter aspects the part by a trine or sextile aspect or even by a square with reception, and if it is not otherwise afflicted, it signifies that the native will be fortunate and profiting in all things and he will acquire all the temporal things which are necessary to him, and not only his businesses but even the businesses of others are perfected by his hand according to what he desires. But if with this, the benefics aspect the part, he will acquire whatever he desires with ease so that it will seem as if none of those things he desires is lacking to him. Albumassar said that he might even acquire something more than that which he desired easily. But if it is not with the lord of the ascendant and if the lord of the ascendant does not aspect it and the malefics aspect it, it will be the reverse. The same thing happens in questions and in revolutions.

The fifth part of the eleventh house is called the part of concupiscence and zeal or appetite for love of secular and temporal things, or *pars concupiscentiae*. It is taken by day from the *pars fortunae* to the *pars futurorum* and by night in the opposite direction, and it is projected from the ascendant. Albumassar said this part is similar to the part of Venus. If it is in a very good place in a nativity, question, or revolution, he subdues his own sensual instincts and his desires. And he said if it is in an evil place, his instincts conquer him and he will be striving and hungering after the world and its pleasure, and he will lose whatever he has in it.

The sixth part of the eleventh house is called the part of faith and hope. It is taken by day from Saturn to Venus and by night in the opposite direction, and it is projected from the ascendant. If in anyone's nativity or interrogation it and its lord are in a very good place, fortunate and strong, the native or querent will acquire everything he hoped for and in which he had hope. However, if they are of evil condition[1] and evilly located, he will not acquire any of what he had hoped for, although he may profit himself to some degree. The same happens in revolutions. For if they are of good condition[1] and evilly located, men acquire enough of those things which they desire in that revolution; however, if it is impeded, the contrary.

The seventh part of the eleventh house is called the part of friends or *pars amicorum*. It is taken by day and by night from the Moon to Mercury and is projected from the ascendant. This part is taken in this way because Mercury is of changed appearance and of varied signification, at certain times signifying masculinity and at others femininity, and so at certain times speed, at others slowness, at certain times heat, at others cold, at certain times good fortune, at others bad fortune, and he is always inclined to the nature of that planet to whom he is joined. Likewise the Moon does that same thing on account of the speed of her motion, and is quickly changeable, for which reason the wills of men are quickly changed with friends nor do they remain long in the same condition,[1] and therefore the wise extracted the part of friends from these two planets because they are swifter and more changeable than the others.

If it is of good condition[1] and well disposed and its lord well disposed and in mobile signs, the native or querent will have many friends. But if they are fortunate, his friends profit him and he them, and they each enjoy good things. If they are received, he will be considered praiseworthy among them and beloved by them. But if it is the contrary, judge accordingly.

The eighth part of the eleventh house is called the part of the agreement of friends and of husbands and wives and their discord, or *pars concordiae amicorum*, etc. It is taken by day and night from the *pars futurorum* to Mercury and it is projected from the ascendant. This part is one of the more difficult to employ of all the parts because it is necessary to know the nativity of the native *and* of those who are posited as his friends, or of the man and the wife, and to see if the part falls in the ascendant of the nativity of the native or with its lord without the impediment of the malefics, or if it is in the sign which ascends in their nativity or is in the eleventh or joined to his lord or joined with the lord of the ascendant and the latter is of good condition[1] and well disposed and in the aspect of the benefics in a good place from the ascendant and is not impeded by any of the malefics or if it is in the exaltation of any of the planets or, as Albumassar said, if it is in agreeing signs, because if it is thus, each will love the other with his friends and his wife. But if it is in a sign of descension[4] of any of those or in a sign of its fall or in opposition to the ascendant or in argumentative[5] signs, they will be each other's enemies.

The ninth part of the eleventh house is called the part of fertility and abundance of good in the home or *pars fertilitatis et abundantiae boni in domo*. It is taken by day or night from the Moon to Mercury and is projected from the ascendant. Albumassar said that this part is similar to the *pars amicorum*. He said that if this part and its lord are in good connection[6] with the *pars fortunae* and with the lord of the ascendant, the native or querent will be bountiful in the home with every fertility, and if it is otherwise, he will be the contrary. But if it is thus disposed in a revolution, the same thing happens.

The tenth part of the eleventh house is called the part of the goodness of the soul or *pars probitas animi*. It is taken by day from Mercury to the Sun and by night the reverse, and it is projected from the ascendant. If it falls in a good place with any of the benefics and especially with Jupiter or if the Sun aspects it with a trine or a sextile aspect, the native or querent will be sweet and light and patient of soul. And Albumassar said that if this part and its lord are in signs of goodness, the native will be of good soul, and if it falls with the malefics or in signs contrary to goodness, it will be the contrary. Understand the same in revolutions.

The eleventh part of the eleventh house is called the part of praise and of gratitude or *pars laudis et gratitudinis*. It is taken by day from Jupiter to Venus and by night in the opposite direction, and it is projected from the ascendant. Whence if the part and its lord are of good condition[1] and well disposed and the benefics aspect them or are joined to them, and especially Jupiter, the native or querent will be praiseworthy, deserving thanks above all in that for which purpose it is posited. And he will be praised for all his works, and he will benefit from them. However, if it is evilly disposed or the malefics aspect it, he will not be praised because of his works, nor because of his services, and moreover, he will not be praised for nor benefited by the services he does nor even receive thanks for them, and it will be possible that in place of financial reward for the services he does, he will receive vituperation and malevolence for them. The same thing happens to men in revolutions, if this part and its lord are thus well disposed as was said.

The twelfth part of the eleventh house is called the part of necessity and of the selection of things or *pars necessitatis et dilectionis rerum*. According to the Persians, it is taken by day and night from Venus to the house of brothers [the third house], and it is projected from the ascendant. But according to the Egyptians, it is taken by day from Mars to the house of the brothers and is projected from the ascendant.

Notes for Section 14

1. "condition": *esse*.

2. "in general questions": *in quaestionibus generalibus*. This may be a reference to Albumassar's universal question, or the means of establishing a natal figure when the birth time is unknown.

3. It is also similar, I might add, to the first part discussed in this section, the *pars excellentiae atque nobilitatis*, and thus to the *pars stabilitatis et durabilitatis*.

4. "in a sign of descension": that is, in a sign of detriment.

5. "in argumentative signs": *in signis contrariis*.

6. "connection": *complexione*.

15. ON THE PARTS OF THE TWELFTH HOUSE AND THEIR EXTRACTION AND SIGNIFICATION

Mention ought to be made in this chapter concerning the parts of the twelfth house, and first concerning the part of secret enemies or *pars inimicorum*. This is taken by day and night from Saturn to Mars and is projected from the ascendant.

The second part of the twelfth house, according to Hermes, is taken by day or night from the lord of the house of enemies to the house of enemies[1] and is projected from the ascendant. And Albumassar said that both these parts ought to be used, but if they are in opposition or the square aspect of the lords of their houses[2] or of the lord of the ascendant, the native or querent will have many enemies. However, if they are both free from their lord and from the lord of the ascendant, he will have enemies for a reason.[3] The same thing happens in revolutions because if they are evilly disposed, as had been said, men will make enemies of each other in that revolution.

The third part of the twelfth house is called the part of labor and affliction or *pars laboris et afflictionis*. It is taken by day or by night from the *pars futurorum* to the *pars fortunae* and by night the reverse [sic], and it is projected from the ascendant. Albumassar said that this part is similar to the *pars Mercurii*. If it and its lord are of good condition[4] and well disposed, it signifies that the native or querent will be fortunate in his labors and will make money from them and they will profit him. However, if it is corporally joined with the lord of the ascendant without a reception or is in opposition or square aspect with the lord, the native will labor endlessly all the days of his life and will not profit from his labors nor enjoy their goods or make money from them, nor will his success be beneficial to him.

Notes for Section 15

1. That is, it is taken from the lord of the twelfth house to the degree of the cusp of the twelfth house.
2. Bonatti is referring to signs here, not houses.
3. "he will have enemies for a reason": *non habebit inimicos de levi*.
4. "condition": *esse*.

16. A RECOUNTING OF CERTAIN PARTS ACCORDING TO ALBUMASSAR CONCERNING WHICH NO MENTION WAS MADE ABOVE; OR THE FIFTH DIFFERENTIA[1]

In this chapter mention ought to be made concerning certain other parts which have not been specifically named above, which according to Albumassar number ten. They are employed frequently in the work of the masters of this science when they desire to judge regarding any nativity, universal question,[2] or any revolution.

The first of these is called the part of the hyleg or *pars hyleg* and it is a matter which the ancient wise men of this science especially observed. They found it reliable.[3] It is taken both by day and by night if a nativity, a question, or a revolution is conjunctional from the degree of the conjunction; but if it is preventional, it is taken from the degree of the prevention[4] to the Moon, and it is projected from the ascendant.

Albumassar said that this part is directed in the same way as the hyleg is directed.[5] When its direction or profection arrives at the places of the benefics, it signifies good, but when it arrives at the malefics, it signifies evil and impediment and danger to the native or querent or to those whose revolution it is, or even if it is a universal revolution. And this is why many good astrologers are deceived, because sometimes they see that many adverse situations arise which ought not to according to the hyleg. They considered only the hyleg and did not concern themselves with the *pars hyleg*. You, however, will not neglect this but always direct the *pars hyleg* both in nativities and questions and also in revolutions, and you will not err. It has its own significations besides other things which are of great efficacy.

The second part of the fifth differentia is called the part of large bodies or *pars macrorum corporum*. It is taken by day from the *pars fortunae* to Mars and by night the reverse, and it is projected from the ascendant. Albumassar said that when this part is with the lord of the ascendant or with a planet which has any dignity in the ascendant or the Alcocoden's place, or if it is with a planet in its own dignity or in a humid sign, the native will be of large members. And he said that if it is otherwise and is with Mercury or Mars or these planets rule it, the native will be lean.

The third part of the fifth differentia is called the part of the military and of daring or *pars militiae et audaciae*. It is taken by day from Saturn to the Moon and by night in the opposite direction and is projected from the ascendant. Albumassar said that this part is similar to the *pars rationis ac profunditatis consilii* and the *pars regis et quid operis agat natus*. When it is sextile to Mars or Jupiter in signs of animals, it signifies that the native is daring and a soldier and procurator of animals and he will be a gladiator playing with spears, arms, and swords.

The fourth part of the fifth differentia is called the part of daring, strength, and dominion or *pars audaciae, fortitudinis, et dominii*. It is taken by day from the lord of the ascendant to the Moon and by night the contrary, and it is projected from the ascendant. When it is sextile to Mars or Jupiter, or in the house of the malefics, received in strong signs, it signifies that the native is spirited and strong in his body.

The fifth part of the fifth differentia is called the part of skill, talent, acuity, and discipline of all arts and of memory and the like, or *pars calliditatis, ingenii, acuitatis*, etc. It is taken by day from Mercury to the *pars futurorum* and by night in the opposite direction, and it is projected from the ascendant. The wise took this part in this way because all these things are signified by Mercury and are attributed to him, and they refer to the soul, and the *pars futurorum* signifies the quality[6] of the soul, and all these things proceed forth from the power of the soul. If it is of good condition[6] and well disposed, and it is with Mercury in a nativity or question, and Mercury is of good condition, it signifies that the native will be expert in a good skill, of sharp mind, easily taught, competent in many arts, learning all things which he desires and which he studies with less labor than others, and he will retain well what he has learned and all these things will profit him. But if they are unfortunate or evilly disposed, he will be able to learn, but the things he learns will not be useful to him; indeed he will get evil and distress because of the aforesaid. But if Mercury is joined to Mars by conjunction or aspect and if Mars has any testimony in the place where the part is, it signifies that the native or querent will be a thief and robber extremely subtle and that he will know how to open doors and to remove the bars from entrances by craft and subtlety of mind without a key. But if they, that is, Mars and Mercury, are trine or sextile with reception, he will know how to do all these things but will not do it for evil purposes.

The same thing happens in revolutions. When this part is thus disposed, as has been said, the aforesaid things happen more in that revolution than are customary at other times.

The sixth part of the fifth differentia is called the part of the investigation of a thing and whether it will be entirely perfected or destroyed or divulged or produced for effect, or *pars inquisitionis rei*. It is taken by day or night from Saturn to Mars and projected from Mercury.

This part is extracted from these three planets because the malefics have signification over destruction, and though they sometimes impede by square aspect or opposition, at other times they perfect the business, although perhaps with slowness or severity; but when the malefics impede, they destroy the business, and if they do not destroy, they delay it all the way to desperation, and because Mercury has participation in businesses therefore, they project this part from him.

If it is of good condition[6] and well disposed, free from the malefics, that is, from Mars by day and from Saturn by night, it signifies the completion of the matter. And if it is impeded by any of them as has been said, it signifies its destruction and that it will not be perfected. And if it is perfected, it will not last.

Albumassar said that this part is employed in unknown matters and in those of an unknown kind. However, if the business is known, consider whether it may be either substance or marriage or whatever other business, the matter will be helped from its own place[7] and the part will aid the significator signifying the matter.

The seventh part of the fifth differentia is called the part of necessity and delay of things or *pars necessitatis et dilationis rerum*. It is taken by day and by night, according to the Egyptians from Mars to the degree of the house of brothers [i.e., the third house] and it is projected from the ascendant. This part signifies the indolence and inertia of the native. If this part is thus impeded in a revolution, it signifies that men will be likewise in that revolution.

The eighth part of the fifth differentia, like the aforesaid part, is called the *pars necessitatis et dilationis rerum*. It is taken by day and night, according to the Persians, from the part of dilation[8] to Mercury, and it is projected from the ascendant. Albumassar said that both these parts are used. If they are of good condition and well disposed, it signifies that the native is moderately motivated for conducting his businesses. If, however, they are evilly disposed, joined with both the malefics or either of them, or if its lord [i.e., the lord of the Part] is with a malefic and especially with Saturn, or if the part and its lord is with the lord of the ascendant, it signifies that the native will be indolent and lazy and is scarcely moved to do anything and especially to those things which are necessary for him unless necessity forces him; nor will he do voluntarily any of those things which men do with hope of utility, nor will his heart suffer to let himself into any mercantile speculations or other lucrative matters for fear that he will lose as a result; nor will he believe that he is able in any way to make money, and he rarely or never believes that he is able or even knows how to make a living.

Albumassar said that if the dispositor of the malefic impedes the lord of the house of substance, the native will destroy his own substance and he will not know how, or will be condemned in it as much as is indicated by the condition[6] of the part.

The same thing happens in questions and revolutions. For if the part is as was said, men will be more indolent and timid than usual in that year.

The ninth part of the fifth differentia is called the part of retribution or *pars retributionis*. It is taken by day from Mars to the Sun and by night the reverse, and it is projected from the ascendant. If it is of good condition[6] and well disposed in an angle, especially in the first or the tenth or in the houses succedent to the angles and especially in the eleventh and fifth with the lord of the ascendant in any of their dignities, it signifies that the native will repay freely to those who do well for him or offer some suitable service to him. However, if they are of evil condition[6] in cadent houses and especially in the sixth or the twelfth and not with the lord of the ascendant nor in any of his dignities, it signifies that he will receive something for free from someone and will not repay well what was done for him. You may say the same in revolutions, if the part is so located, because men will serve in that way during that revolution. Understand the same in questions.

The tenth part of the fifth differentia is called the part of truth and good works or *pars veritatis et bonarum operationum*. It is taken by day from Mercury to Mars and by night in the opposite direction, and it is projected from the ascendant. Albumassar said that this part is similar to the *pars rationis et sensus*. If it is of good condition[6] and well disposed, fortunate and strong and in an angle, it signifies that the native or querent will be observant of truth, zealous in good works, and abhorrent of the opposites of these, and utility and profit result from his actions. However, if this part is impeded in an angle, the native will be practicing and observing the truth and good works, but evil and harm follow as a result. And if it is outside the dignities of the lord of the ascendant, he will be one who knows the truth but does not practice it. If it is so disposed in revolutions, men in that revolution will be so disposed and working likewise. Albumassar said these parts, which the ancients related and which they employed in nativities and in many places in the revolutions of years and in interrogations wherever they are necessary, have thus been made known to you. And he said, know that in many matters of the significations of the twelve houses and interrogations, and initiations [i.e., elections] and revolutions of years, there are parts concerning which we have made no mention because it is necessary that we speak of them in other books. And he said that the significations spoken of in this book are collections for the purpose of investigation because the places of the parts change their significations in good or evil according to the signs they are in and the conjunctions or aspects of the planets with them. And he said that he would relate the investigations of their significations in their places in the signs in each book as necessity required.

Notes for Section 16

1. The term *differentia* was sometimes used for a subdivision of a chapter or book. The fifth differentia mentioned here is the fifth chapter of Albumassar's *De magnis conjunctionibus annorum revolutionibus ac eorum profectionibus octo continens tractatus* (Venice, 1515). The reference to it suggests that Bonatti used a Latin translation of Albumassar's work.

2. "universal question": Albumassar's method of establishing a natal figure when the birth time is unknown.

3. Bonatti has already discussed this part in section 4.

4. Conjunctional nativities, questions, revolutions, etc., are those occurring between the time of the New and Full Moons. The degree of the conjunction (or conjunction of the luminaries) is the degree of the New Moon. Preventional nativities, etc., are those which occur after the Full Moon but before the New Moon. The degree of the prevention (or prevention of the luminaries) is the degree of the Full Moon.

5. "in the same way as the hyleg is directed": that is, by profection of degrees or by direction according to degrees of ascension (or primary directions).

6. "quality," "condition": *esse*.

7. "from its own place": that is, for substance, the second house; for marriage, the seventh house.

8. "the part of dilation": the seventh part of the fifth differentia.

17. ON THE KNOWLEDGE OF CERTAIN EXTRAORDINARY PARTS CONCERNING WHICH NO MENTION WAS MADE ABOVE

In this chapter we ought to look at certain extraordinary parts which were not mentioned in the parts of the seven planets or in the section on the parts of the twelve houses, nor in the recounting of the ten parts of the fifth differentia of Albumassar. These parts are exceptionally useful in revolutions, in determining which things one who wishes to make money is more able to profit from that year. By means of these parts you are able to judge the cheapness or mediocrity of price of whatever vegetables or of any other thing which it is usually necessary that men have for their sustenance and needs such as grain, wines, oil, etc. You will even be able to see whether there will be an abundance of these things or a shortage. Again, you will be able to know why it happens that the thing sometimes abounds and is expensive and at other times is cheap. Sometimes it does not abound and indeed there is a shortage in those things and it is cheap, and sometimes it is expensive. The aspect or corporal conjunctions of the benefics to the part or its lord, or even to the Moon, signify abundance of the thing, and so much more so if the benefic which aspects the part or its lord or the Moon is the ruler of the house in which the part falls. Shortage or want of these is signified by the aspect or corporal conjunction of the malefics to the part.

You are able to judge the cheapness of the thing by the place of the lord of the house or exaltation or of the significator in which it falls. For if it is in its house or exaltation, or is otherwise fortunate and strong, or is in an angle, and especially if it is in the tenth, it signifies the high price of that thing. However, if one is fortunate, the other unfortunate, it will change the quality[1] of that thing a little. But if the lord of exaltation is below[2] the lord of the house, the lord of the term and the lord of triplicity add or subtract something. If it is in the twelfth house in its fall or detriment or cadent from the angle,[3] and all the more certainly if it is in the twelfth or is combust, it signifies the cheapness and low price of the thing. And to the degree to which the significators are debilitated, the lower the price of the thing they signify and its worthlessness will be. If, however, they are in houses succedent to the angles, unless something impedes, the price will be neither very depressed nor much raised up. But if all the significators are fortunate and strong, the thing will be expensive and will exceed measure in price, and all the more so if they are in the tenth house as I said. But if they are unfortunate and weak and evilly disposed, they signify the extreme worthlessness of the thing and the cheapness of it. And always take care to consider the situation of each significator because each of these gives and takes away according to its condition[1]. The significators are the lord of the sign, the lord of exaltation, the lord of the term, the lord of the triplicity of the planets from which the part is extracted and the planet which is the lord of the house from which you begin to project the part. There is, however, little strength in the lord of the face, so that you need not concern yourself much about it. However, the lord of the sign in which the part falls is to be preferred above all others, and the matter ought to be judged more according to it, although the others add and take away just as was said, and the more so if it is one of the planets from which the part is extracted, because the part is greatly strengthened thereby.

Notes for Section 17

1. "quality," "condition": *esse.*
2. "below": that is, in terms of rank of dignity and the degrees of effect.

3. That would necessarily be the effect of being in the twelfth. Bonatti means by this to include *all* the cadent houses.

18. AN EXAMPLE OF THE METHOD OF EXTRACTION OF SOME PARTS

Now I shall give you an example of one of the parts for all the extraordinary parts, and I shall begin with the part of grain or *pars frumentum*. When you wish to know the state of grain in any revolution, whether it will be cheap or expensive or will have a moderate price, take the place of the Sun from the place of Mars and add to this the degrees and minutes of the sign of the ascendant and project the sum from the beginning of the sign of the ascendant,[1] giving each sign 30 equal degrees,[2] and where the number ends, there will be the part of grain. Consider, therefore, how the lord of that sign is disposed, because the better he is disposed, of so much less worth will it be and the less will it be valued. Look to the other significators which I named for you[3] and see how they are disposed. Because those which are well disposed make for increase in price and for shortage of the thing, and those which are evilly disposed make for the lowness of the price and for appropriate abundancy. And according to this you will judge regarding other things from whatever, namely according to its place and condition[4] with the aforesaid good aspects and the Moon or concerning whatever other part you wish. But if the significator of the part of grain or of any other part, namely the lord of the house[5] in which it falls, is impeded and of evil condition[4] and evilly disposed and if a benefic, fortunate and strong, and the Moon aspect the part, it signifies that the grain or whatever other thing whose part you are considering will abound and it will be cheap. If, however, a malefic aspect the part, it signifies that the grain, or whatever other thing whose part you sought, will be expensive and that there will be shortages of it. But if a benefic aspects the malefic,[6] it signifies that it will abound, but nevertheless it will still be expensive. Understand the same regarding all and each of the other parts.

On the Part of Barley or Pars Ordei
When you desire to know whether barley will be cheap or expensive in a revolution, or what its condition will be, take the place of the Moon from the place of Jupiter and add to what remains the degrees and minutes of the ascending sign and project from the ascendant, and where the number ends, there will be the part of barley from which, according to the condition[4] of the lord of that sign, you will judge by the aforesaid conditions.

On the Part of Beans or Pars Fabarum
When you desire to know whether or not beans will be cheap or expensive in the revolution you seek, take the place of Saturn from the place of Mars and add to the remainder the degree of the ascendant, giving 30 degrees to each sign

according to equal degrees, and where the number ends, there will be the part of beans. Judge then as was said regarding the others.

On the Part of Onions or Pars Ceparum

You will discover that the part of onions and the part of green peas or *pars robelliae* are the same [as the preceding part]; therefore it is not necessary for you to make another rule for these.

On the Part of Lentils or Pars Lentium

When you desire to know what the status of lentils will be, take the place of Mars from the place of Saturn and add the degree of the sign of the ascendant to the remainder, and project this from the ascendant, and where the number ends will be where the part is. Judge it as was said of the others.

On the Part of Rice or Pars Risi

You take the *pars risi* from Jupiter to Saturn and project it from the ascendant, and where the number falls, there will be the *pars risi*. Judge concerning it as was said regarding the others.

On the Part of Sesame or Pars Sisami

The *pars sisami* is taken from Saturn to Jupiter and projected from the ascendant. It is a seed very like the flaxseed, but it is white and physicians use it in certain antidotes.

On the Part of Sugar or Pars Zuchari

The *pars zuchari* is taken by subtracting the place of Mercury from the place of Venus, and what remains is added to the degrees of the ascendant and is projected from the ascendant, and where the number ends, there is the *pars zuchari*, which you will investigate as was said of the others.

On the Part of Dates or Pars Dactilorum

If you desire to know the market of dates, take the place of the Sun from the place of Venus and add the degree of the sign of the ascendant to the remainder, and project this from the ascendant. Where the number ends, there will be the part.

On the Part of Honey or Pars Mellis

If, however, you desire to know the market for honey, take the place of the Moon from the place of the Sun and add the degree of the sign of the ascendant, and project from the ascendant, and where the number ends, there will be the part.

On the Part of Wine or Pars Vini

If you want to know the market for wine, which is had from the condition[4] of the grapes, take the place of Saturn from the place of Venus and add the degree of the sign of the ascendant to the remainder, and project from the ascendant. Where the number ends will be the part which you seek. Judge it as has been said regarding the others.

On the Part of Olives or Pars Olivarum

If it is your heart's desire to know whether or not there will be an abundance of olives in the revolution which you seek and you desire to know whether olive oil will be cheap or expensive, take the place of Mercury from the place of the Moon, and to the remainder add the degree and minute of the sign of the ascendant, and project from the ascendant, giving to each sign 30 degrees according to equal degrees, and where the number ends, there will be the part.

On the Part of Nuts or Pars Nucum

When you desire to know whether or not there will be an abundance of nuts in that year or revolution, take the place of Mercury from the place of Mars and add the degree of the sign of the ascendant, and where the number ends will be the part. Judge this as was said regarding the others.

On the Part of Silk and of Other Similar Things or Pars Bambaxii et Aliorum Conjunctorum

If you desire to know the disposition of silk or its "quality"[4] and the line of lesser things lacking extremely in dryness and loving temperate humidity, such as millet, Italian millet, honeys [(?) *melica*], beans[7] and the like; although silks do not aspire to great dryness, they are nonetheless counted among these. It is taken in this way: You take the place of Mercury from the place of Venus, and to the remainder you add the degree of the sign of the ascendant so that where the number ends, there will be the part.

On the Part of Melons, Lemons, Cucumbers, and Gourds or Pars Melonum, Citrullorum, Cucumerorum, atque Curcurbitarum

In order to know whether or not there will be an abundance of melons, lemons, cucumbers, and gourds, take the place of Mercury from the place of Saturn, and to the remainder add the degree of the sign of the ascendant, and where the number ends there will be the part. Judge this as was said regarding the others.

On the Part of Hunters or Pars Venatorum

When you desire to know whether or not there may be hunting in that revolution, take the place of *caput draconis* [the dragon's head] from the place of Saturn, and to the remainder add the degree of the sign of the ascendant, and begin to project from the ascendant, and where the number ends, there the part will be. Judge it as was said regarding the others.

On the Part of Humidity and Dryness or Pars Humiditatis atque Siccitatis

For having the knowledge of the humidity or dryness of the revolution, take by day the place of the Moon from the place of Venus and by night the contrary, and to the remainder add the degree of the sign of the ascendant, and project from the ascendant, and where the number ends, there will be the part which you seek. The judgment of it is as was said regarding the others.

On the Part of Salted Things or Pars Rerum Salitarum

For knowing the market of salted things, by which you are able to know the state of them and of salt, although perhaps not exactly but still for practical purposes,[8] take the place of Mars from the place of the Moon, and add to the remainder the degree of the ascendant, and where the number ends will be the part.

On the Part of Sweet Foods or Pars Ciborum Dulcium

For knowing the market of sweet foods, take the place of the Sun from the place of Venus and to the remainder add the degree of the sign of the ascendant, and where the number ends will be the part.

On the Part of Bitter Foods or Pars Ciborum Amarorum

For knowing the condition[4] of bitter foods, take the place of Mercury from the place of Saturn, and to the remainder add the degree of the sign of the ascendant, and where the number ends will be the part.

On the Part of Pungent Foods or Pars Ciborum Acrium

For knowing the condition[4] of pungent foods, take the place of Saturn from the place of Mars, and add to the remainder the degree of the sign of the ascendant, and project this from the ascendant, and where the number ends, there will be the part.

On the Part of Sharp Foods or Pars Ciborum Acutorum

For knowing the condition[4] of sharp foods and herbs having a sharp taste, take the place of Mars from the place of Saturn, and add to the remainder the degrees of the sign of the ascendant, and project from the ascendant.

On the Part of Sweet Medicines or Pars Medicaminum Dulcium

For knowing the condition[4] of sweet purgative medicines, take the place of the Sun from the place of the Moon, and add the degree of the sign of the ascendant to the remainder, and where the number ends, there will be the part.

On the Part of Pungent Medicines or Pars Medicaminum Acrium

For knowing the condition[4] of pungent medicines, take the place of Saturn from the place of Jupiter, and add the remainder to the degree of the sign of the ascendant, and project from the ascendant, and where the number ends, there is where the part will be.

On the Part of Salty Medicines or Pars Medicaminum Salsorum

For knowing the condition[4] of salty medicines, take the place of Mars from the place of the Moon, and add to the remainder the degree of the sign of the ascendant, and project this from the ascendant, and where the number ends is where the part will be.

On the Part of the Disposition of the Year or Pars Dispositionis Anni

There is another part which is seen to comprehend all the aforesaid, and it is seen that it is a correlative with them and they with it, because it is generated from them and because they are generated from it. This part is called the part of good disposition or of the fertility of the year. It is taken from the Moon to Mercury and is projected from the ascendant, and where the number ends, there is where the part will be. Its judgment is like that of the others.

But if it happens at some time that the planet whose place you wish to extract from the place of another may be more in signs and degrees and minutes than that from which you must subtract it, add twelve signs to the lesser from which it is taken, and after this you will be able to take what you wish, and to this remainder add the degrees and minutes of the sign of the ascendant and project from the ascendant, giving to each sign 30 degrees according to equal degrees, and where the number ends, there is where the place will be. Judge as was said concerning the others.

On the Regions Where These Things Will Be

For knowing in which regions the aforesaid *accidents* will occur, consider from which part the lord of the ascendant or of the tenth or of the seventh or of the fourth may be—whether they are in the eastern part or the southern, or western or northern or in oriental signs, which are Aries and its triplicity, or southern signs, which are Taurus and its triplicity, or western which are Gemini and its triplicity, or northern signs, which are Cancer and its triplicity.

On the Time When These Things Will Be

For knowing the time in which the significations of the aforesaid parts will be and in which quarter of the year the signification will come, see the part which you want, and if it falls in the ascendant or betwen the ascendant and the fourth house cusp, its signification will occur in the first quarter of the revolution of that year or of the time in which that signification ought to occur. However, if it is in the fourth, or between the fourth and the seventh, it will occur in the second quarter. But if it is in the seventh or between the seventh and the tenth, it happens in the third quarter. But if it is in the tenth or between the tenth and the ascendant, it will happen in the last quarter of its time, and the closer it is to an angle, the sooner it happens, and the further away from an angle, the later it happens.

Notes for Section 18

1. Here again, this is really the same as projecting from the ascendant, for if the ascendant is 15 Aries and there are 35 degrees between the Sun and Mars, it is all the

same if we add 15 degrees to 35 degrees and project the sum (50 degrees) from 0 Aries, or if we simply project 35 degrees from 15 Aries. Either way we get 20 Taurus.

2. "30 equal degrees": that is, according to ecliptical longitude.
3. "which I named for you": see the end of section 17.
4. "condition," "quality": *esse*.
5. Bonatti is here referring to sign, not house.
6. "malefic": *eum* (literally "him"). Grammatically this must refer to the malefic.
7. "beans": *faseoli*.
8. "for practical purposes": *ad utilitatem*.

19. CONCERNING THE NUMBER OF SIGNIFICATORS OF EACH OF THE PARTS

Each part has at least two significators naturally,[1] although there are some of them which are sometimes content with only one, such as the part of substance or *pars substantiae* when it falls in the second house, or the part of journey or *pars itineris* when it falls in the ninth. There are some parts which have three significators, the two from which the part is extracted and one from the house in which it falls, where the latter planet is not one of the other two. There are other parts which have four significators: two from which the part is extracted, a third to which it arrives, and a fourth from which the projection is begun.

A part which is content with one significator is strengthened when its significator aspects it. But a part which has two significators is strengthened when both its significators aspect it, and they give greater hope of perfecting what the part intends; however, the lord of the house in which the part falls will be more worthy. But if the part has three significators and two aspect it but the third does not, the part will not be so strong in perfecting what it intends. But if only one of the three aspect it and the other two do not, its strength will again be less than before. But if none of them aspect it, it will be even weaker, and it will do what it intends with difficulty and harsh effort in that revolution. You may say the same if the significators are healthy according to their own condition.[2] But if they were impeded, say according to their impediment. For if they are all impeded, the signification of that part will hardly ever or never appear. And if the significators aspect the part with a favorable aspect, he will see from it the hoped-for result. If, however, they aspect the part with enmity, evil and adversity will happen to him from that cause [indicated by the part]. It is possible that none of the planets having dignity in that part aspect it and that another which naturally signifies that which the part signifies does aspect it; then from this [configuration] something will occur, although not the entire effect. For instance, if Jupiter aspects the part of substance or *pars substantiae;* for Jupiter naturally signifies substance, and if no other significators aspect it or if Venus aspects the part of marriage or *pars coniugii* and no other significators aspect it, it signifies some kind of effect of the thing. If you would have knowledge of the part of servants or handmaids or *pars servorum seu famulorum* and no significator aspected the part, but Mercury, which naturally signifies servants and handmaids, does aspect the part [some effect can be expected]. But this will be within the signification of the significator of the part, and it will be by someone who arrives on the scene unexpectedly and becomes involved in the matter on his own. And if the planet aspecting the part has any dignity in the house in which it is, this happens from that party which the querent hoped it would be, or from one of his acquaintances. However, if it is peregrine, he knows not whence it happens to him. And if the planet aspecting the part is unfortunate and not receiving the part or is impeded, there will be commotions and rumors concerning it, but nothing of what the part signifies will be perfected.

Albumassar said, after this, look to the malefic and see if it is in an angle or in a succedent house, and if it is direct, there will be destruction or impediment after [the thing] will be thought perfected. But if Saturn is that malefic, the impediment will be because of someone's old age. If Jupiter is the planet, it will be because of religious men or judges and of others entering between them. But if it is Mars, there will be some kind of contention between them because of it. If it is the Sun, it will be because of the king or wealth. But if it is Venus, it will be because of women. But if it is Mercury and he is impeded, it will be because of other businesses. And if it is the Moon, since she is the authoress of light and number, it will be because the thing may be increased. And if it is of little light, it will be because the thing is deteriorated and diminished.

Alchabitius said that the part called the part of kingdom and empire or *pars regni atque imperii,* which is used in the revolution of the year, is taken from Mars to the Moon and is projected from the ascendant of the conjunction. It signifies the change of the kingdom. Understand the same in religious sects because they are like a rule or dominion. But according to others, it is taken from the degree of the ascendant of the conjunction and is projected from the degree of the ascendant of the revolution. However, according to yet others, it is taken from the degree of the Sun to the degree of the Medium Coeli of the revolution and is projected from the degree of Jupiter, and this opinion seems more appropriate to me.

The part of the time of the rise of the kingdom or *pars temporis elevationis regni,* which signifies its duration, is taken from the hour of its rise or coronation from the Sun to the 15th degree of Leo by day and is projected from the degree of the Moon. But by night it is taken from the degree of the Moon all the way to the 10th degree of Cancer and is projected from the degree of the Sun.[3]

There is another part of the kingdom or empire which is taken by day in the hour of its rise or beginning from the Sun to Saturn and by night in the contrary, and it is projected from the ascendant of the revolution of the year in which the king or emperor is elevated or anyone else is promoted to a political office.

Alchabitius said that if Jupiter is in a common sign and the revolution is diurnal[4] and Jupiter is cadent from the angles, the *pars regni et imperii* is taken from Saturn to Jupiter and 30 degrees are added, and it is projected from the ascendant of the revolution of the year in which the king ascended. But if they oppose each other and are both cadent, then half of the degrees which are between them is taken, and this is projected from the ascendant. But if Jupiter is in Cancer and the revolution is nocturnal,[5] this part is taken from Jupiter to Saturn and is projected from the ascendant.

Alchabitius said that the first of the two parts from which the duration of the kingdom is judged, is found by observing where the profection of years comes. Begin from the conjunction of the triplicity which signifies the kingdom or religious sect, at the time of the rise of the kingdom [i.e., the king's coronation]. Of this number you give one year to every 30 degrees and one month to every 2 degrees and 30 minutes. When you know in what sign or degree this is, note this and save it for the moment because this will be the place from which you will calculate the first part, and when you desire to apply it, you will employ the ascendant of the revolution of the year in which the king, or whoever was chosen, rose. Next take the distance of the planet oriental from the Sun, from Saturn, or from Jupiter in that year[6] all the way to the degree of the equation of the part which you saved, and project this from the ascendant of the revolution. Where this comes to will be the place of the first part.

But the second part[7] is found in this way: Look from the conjunction in which the kingdom or empire arose to that sign or degree to which the profection of the years comes. Of this number, give every 30 degrees one year to the month and day in which the king arose, and this is the place of the equation of the second part. Mark this point. Next, take the distance from a planet oriental of the Sun, Saturn, and Jupiter, all the way to the place of the equation of the second part which you marked, and project this from the ascendant of the revolution,[8] and where it arrives is the place of the second part.

These are the parts which signify the duration of the king and his strength.

Notes for Section 19

1. "two significators naturally": that is, the two from which the part is extracted.
2. "if the significators are healthy according to their own condition": si fuerint significatores salvi secundum eorum salvationem.
3. I have not yet been able to figure out just how this part and those that follow actually indicate the duration of a king's rule. Nevertheless, I have included what Bonatti says on these parts for the sake of completeness and in the hope that someone else will be more fortunate than I. Such predictions were a central part of the medieval astrologer's stock in trade and would be of as much use today as they were then if we could discover the key to their employment.
4. "if...the revolution is diurnal": that is, if the Sun is above the Earth at the time of the revolution.
5. "if...the revolution is nocturnal": that is, if the Sun is below the Earth at the time of the revolution.
6. "in the year": that is, in the year of the rise of the king or sect.
7. The "second part" shows the strength of the king in a given year.
8. "revolution": that is, of each of the reign of the king or sect.

5

THE EXTRACTION OF PARTS FOR PURPOSES NOT LISTED

As there are over one hundred parts given in this work, one would hardly expect that many more could be needed. It cannot be overemphasized that the parts ought not to be resorted to until the "external aspect" of the figure has been thoroughly delineated and is understood. Yet it is conceivable that in special cases a part may be desired for which the text gives no specific instructions. Again, in horary work it may be thought worthwhile to find a part which may serve as a summation or epitome of a configuration. Such would be analogous to the midpoints used by some modern astrologers and is one of the reasons parts were used at all, as Bonatti quotes Albumassar as saying at the opening of section 1 of the translation.

The reader interested in projecting parts for purposes other than those given should study section 2 of the translation and consider carefully the following. The key to the parts is the understanding of the planets primarily (the house cusps secondarily) as causal factors or agents. These factors have certain universal significatorship by which they are said to rule this or that. For instance, the Sun rules gold, Saturn rules minerals. Thus a part of gold might be found by taking the distance from the Sun to Saturn and projecting it from the ascendant. As the Sun actually rules gold, and Saturn merely answers to the mineral aspect of gold, which gold has in common with all other minerals, I consider that these two significators cannot be said to rule the thing for which the part is sought equally, and therefore there can be no question of taking the part one way by day and another by night. The "part of gold" would be found by taking the distance from the Sun to Saturn by day *and* by night.

On the other hand, a part of coal might be plutonian as easily as it might be saturnian, and thus it would probably be best to derive the part from Saturn to Pluto by day and vice versa by night.

We ought not to be surprised or upset if one part serves many purposes. The text of the translation itself exhibits this already. It was not uncommon for this to be the case. As it did not disturb the medieval astrologer, it ought not disturb us.

Nor should we be concerned that someone else devises another way to find a part for something we have sought. Again the text already exhibits this sort of variation among the astrologers of the Persians, the Egyptians, Hermes, and others. The only real measure here is if it works. Thus if the theory is sound and repeated experience coincides, use it.

PART III

PRACTICAL ILLUSTRATIONS

6

NATAL FIGURES

We begin the practical illustrations with one of the most exotic and at the same time one of the most mundane parts that Bonatti lists. This will serve to emphasize the essentially practical nature of this astrology and show that its metaphysics are not ivory-tower speculations but rather have immediate causal importance in the seemingly disordered experiences of life. It is, in fact, one of the primary tenets behind the study of astrology that all experiences—from the most refined, spiritual, and uplifting to the most miserable, debased, and limiting—are caused by the action of "Heaven" on "Earth," the event itself arising as the third point in accordance with the metaphysical principles laid out in Chapter 2.

THE PART OF RELIGION AND THE HONESTY OF WOMEN

Our first illustrations involve the part of religion and of the honesty of the woman, or *pars religionis et honestatis mulieris* (discussed in section 10 of Bonatti's treatise). If this part is "in a fixed sign or in the aspect of any of the lords of the dignities of the sign in which it is [placed] or of any benefic, the woman will be honest and religious even if she may be longing for coitus. But if the malefics aspect it without reception and it is in a mobile sign, the woman will be excessive in her desire for coitus, giving herself to men...for a cheap price, and she will be in every way a fornicatrix." The part is found by taking the distance from the Moon to Venus, in the order of the signs, by day or night and then by projecting this from the ascendant.

I shall give four examples of this part. Since the part when in poor condition indicates sexual license and promiscuity and Bonnati's wording implies the acceptance of remuneration for the sexual act, we may therefore expect to find this part so placed in the horoscopes of prostitutes.

Figure A is the horoscope of a woman who, in addition to a more conventional line of work, engages in prostitution as a second source of income. The pertinent positions are these: Moon—16 degrees Scorpio; ascendant—16 degrees Cancer; Venus—0 degrees Scorpio. The distance between the Moon and Venus in the order of the signs is 344 degrees. This, projected from the ascendant, again in the order of the signs, brings us to 0 degrees Cancer—the sought-for part of religion and honesty of woman.

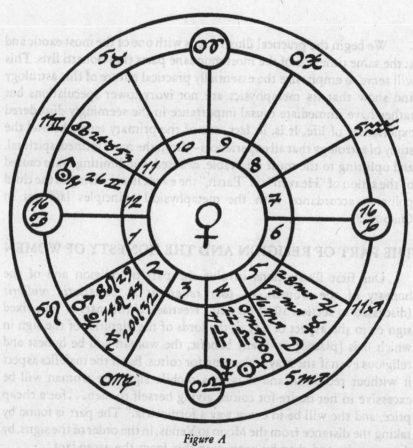

Figure A

NATAL FIGURES / 141

In practice the astrologer will be seeking information given here for the sake of illustration, namely, whether or not the woman in question is involved in illicit sexual practices. Thus it cannot be emphasized strongly enough that although the part falls in a mobile sign and is accompanied by many or all of the requirements Bonatti gives, the astrologer must never even consider concluding that the native is a prostitute unless the indications of the figure support the possibility. Even then the circumstances surrounding the case must be weighed. To show off what one knows is to serve nothing but one's own ego and in some situations can be dangerous.

Therefore the figure *must* be delineated and understood first. Let the reader, then, note (1) the water sign Cancer rising, and (2) the position of the ruler of the ascendant, the Moon, in the fifth in fall. Both the Moon and its watery sign, Cancer, are connected with generation, that is, sexual activity. The position of the Moon indicates that fifth-house activities will be the area where the native attempts to fulfill her instinctual drives. This is not particularly unusual. (3) However, the methods used in the realization of this desire, and the quality of the desire, are indicated by the relative degree of refinement or dignity of the influence. Here the Moon in fall and thus in Scorpio augurs debased activity. (4) Its dispositors, Mars and Saturn, are not in good condition in Leo and aspect the Moon adversely. Moreover, the ruler of Scorpio, Pluto, is afflicted by a terribly placed Saturn. Thus matters go from bad to worse. But still, while the native's desires are corrupt, there is no indication of prostitution, strictly speaking. This comes from (5) the fact that the rulers of the fifth house, Mars and Pluto, are both in the second. Thus the love life is connected with the native's finances. (6) The ruler of the second, the Sun, is in fall in Libra, and its dispositor, which might improve its quality if it were in good condition, is itself in detriment in Scorpio. From this we get several subconsiderations: (a) The native's self-image (Sun) is poor and particularly venal. (b) Because of its angularity and condition, it desires to improve itself, however it may. (c) Its afflictions from Neptune, Pluto, Saturn, and even the trine from Uranus do nothing to suggest that anything other than the worst methods will be used in this "improvement." Therefore, considering the Sun as the ruler of the second, we find that finances are made through illegal or venal methods.

(7) The planets Mars and Pluto dispose the Moon, indicator of the behavior used in realizing the primary drive, and thus link this too to both sex (Scorpio) and money (second house). Their poor condition reinforces the above considerations about the second house. (8) The ruler

of the fifth house (Mars) is also the ruler of the tenth (Aries). Thus the native's actions and profession are linked to the fifth and again to the second house. (9) The Moon is conjunct Mercury, god of thieves and merchants, in the fifth. (10) Mercury rules the twelfth house (secrets). Therefore, the twelfth house is linked to the fifth, indicating secret venal activity. Finally, Mercury's dispositors are Mars and Pluto in the second. Thus the secret venal activity results in profit for the native. Therefore the figure as a whole certainly does support the statement that the native engages in prostitution. With this established, it is appropriate to consider the part.

We calculated the position of the part of religion and honesty of woman as 0 degrees Cancer in this figure. This falls in the twelfth house of the figure.

The first step is to see if the conditions set forth by Bonatti are fulfilled. He states that when (1) the part is in a movable (cardinal) sign, (2) not in aspect to any of the lords of the dignities or (3) with any benefic, the woman will be "excessive in her desire for coitus, giving herself to men...for a cheap price, and she will be in every way a fornicatrix." Now, (1) Cancer *is* a movable sign. (2) The part, at 0 degrees Cancer, is not aspected by the Moon (which rules the sign), by Jupiter (which is exalted in Cancer), or by Mars or Pluto, which have honor of triplicity there. (3) Though the part can be said to be in aspect with Venus here, Venus's poor zodiacal condition by sign (i.e., detriment) and by aspect (Venus is square to Mars) and by combustion make Venus *accidentally malefic* and serves only to increase the venal character of the part. Thus, Bonatti's requirements are fulfilled.

The part in the twelfth house, indicating that the activity is secret, if further afflicted by the conjunction with the malefic Uranus, and this Uranus is the ruler of the eighth house. Therefore, the clandestine sexual activity involves other people's money (eighth house as second from the seventh—other people). As Uranus is disposed by Mercury in the fifth, the money goes to her for sexual activity. Mercury's dispositors are in the second, therefore the money increases her financial condition. The final dispositor is the Sun; therefore, as the Sun is the ruler of the second, it reaffirms the fact of the financial gain from such activities. Since it is in the fourth house, we may say that this money is used to beautify her home. Since the Sun is the significator of the ego, we may say that since her finances serve her ego or her drive for improvement, the money gained in such activities will be used for these purposes.

In this example, then, we find that there is agreement of the natal chart with the indication of the part and with the native's admitted actions (for she did in fact tell me about her avocation). This is an example of the proper use of the parts. They are valid secondary indicators of things indicated in the natal figure and may be used profitably as such, their significations being synthesized into the significations of the natal figure. Not all natal figures are so clearly defined, of course. It is in such cases that the parts may make the difference between a yes and a no on a given matter.

Figure B is the horoscope of a woman who works in bars as a prostitute. She claims as well to have several "sugar daddies."

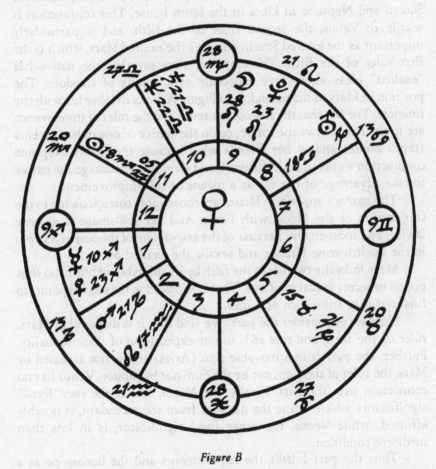

Figure B

The part of religion and honesty of woman falls at 4 degrees of Aries. The Moon is at 28 degrees Leo and Venus is at 23 degrees Sagittarius so there are 115 degrees between them in the order of the signs. Projecting 115 degrees from the ascendant brings us to 4 Aries.

Now, first we examine the natal figure. We find that Sagittarius ascends, so we know that the primary motivation is for freedom. We find that the ruler of the first is in the fifth. This is the same pattern we found in Figure A. Jupiter, the ruler of the ascendant, is peregrine in Taurus. Therefore, while things are not so corrupt as with the last case, still the quality of the motivation is not good. The mutual reception between Venus and Jupiter improves things somewhat but inextricably links the fifth house with the first, thus making the native especially venal and welding firmly in her mind the idea of fifth-house activities as a means of freedom. Moreover, Venus is harmed by the conjunction of Saturn and Neptune in Libra in the tenth house. This conjunction is sextile to Venus, the second ruler of the fifth, and is particularly important as the exalted Saturn disposes the exalted Mars, which is the first ruler of the fifth. Therefore we may say that the native has "exalted" ideas about love especially as a means of freedom. The position of Mars in the second, as in Figure A, links the love life with the finances. The fact that the ruler of the tenth and the ruler of the eleventh are in the first shows the influence on the native of one of her parents (tenth house) and of her friends who, because the Saturn-Neptune conjunction works in both the tenth and eleventh, encourage the native to take advantage of her sex as a means of self-improvement.

The native's appetites (Moon) are thoroughly corrupt owing to the conjunction of the Moon with Pluto. And her self-image is at once lawless and independent because of the association of the Sun in Scorpio in the twelfth trine Uranus and sextile the exalted Mars.

Mars links the twelfth to the fifth by its rulership of both and thus points to secret sexual relations. That it is placed in the second points to financial gain from such activities.

Now let us consider the part. We find that it is disposed by Mars, ruler of the fifth, and this adds to our expectation of illicit sexuality. Further, the part is in a movable sign (Aries) and is not aspected by Mars, the ruler of the sign, nor by the Sun, nor by Jupiter. Venus has no connection with the part. Finally, the Moon, one of the two "fixed" significators which define the distance from the ascendant, is notably afflicted, while Venus, the other fixed significator, is in less than mediocre condition.

Thus the part fulfills the requirements and the horoscope as a whole supports the native's self-declared profession of prostitution.

Figure C is the horoscope of a woman whose sexual adventures are notorious. Since I have no reports or admissions from her that she has ever taken money for the sexual act, I present the figure merely as an example of sexual promiscuity and extremism.

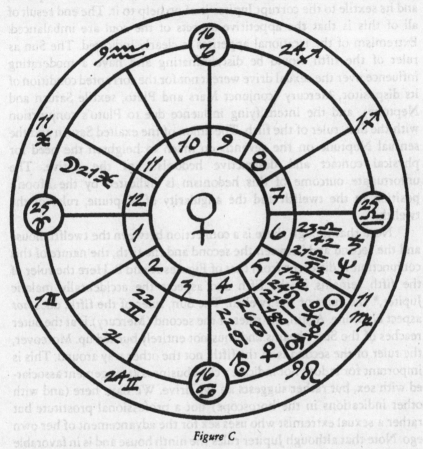

Figure C

We note immediately the same pattern seen in the last two cases: the ruler of the first in the fifth. The ascendant is Aries, so the drive is for power, freedom, and influence. The native attempts to realize this drive through the fifth house, through sexual activity. We note that the Sun is conjunct Pluto while, like Mars, Pluto rules Scorpio in the seventh house. Such an indication shows that the native has an extremely strong need to manipulate others. The conjunction's position in the fifth house, with Mercury, the ruler of Virgo, twelve signs away from the seventh sign, shows that manipulation of others through their subconscious needs leads to and is connected with sexual activity. The Moon is in Pisces in the twelfth house, square to Jupiter in detriment in the second house. Neptune is trine to Jupiter and conjunct Saturn on the seventh-house cusp in Libra. Venus, which is connected to the ascendant by a square aspect, is heavily afflicted by Uranus, Saturn, and Neptune, and its sextile to the corrupt Jupiter is of no help to it. The end result of all of this is that the appetitive aspects of the soul are imbalanced. Extremism of the irrational appetites is clearly indicated. The Sun as ruler of the fifth would be discriminating and have a moderating influence over the sexual drive were it not for the corrupted condition of its dispositor, Mercury (conjunct Mars and Pluto, sextile Saturn and Neptune), and the intensifying influence due to Pluto's conjunction with the Sun, ruler of the fifth. The union of the exalted Saturn and the sensual Neptune on the seventh do much to heighten the need for physical contact and destructive hedonism of the native. The unfortunate outcome of this hedonism is indicated by the Moon's position in the twelfth and the angularity of Neptune, ruler of the twelfth.

Note that though there is a connection between the twelfth house and the second and between the second and the fifth, the nature of this conjunction is different from that of Figures A and B. Here the ruler of the fifth remains in the fifth and aspects the accidentally malefic Jupiter,* the ruler of the twelfth. The Sun, ruler of the fifth, does *not* aspect Neptune. Again, the ruler of the second (Mercury) is at the outer reaches of the Sun's beams and thus not entirely burned up. Moreover, the ruler of the second is in the fifth, not the other way around. This is important for it does not indicate a clear business arrangement associated with sex, but rather suggests an ego drive. We have here (and with other indications in the horoscope) not a professional prostitute but rather a sexual extremist who uses sex for the advancement of her own ego. Note that although Jupiter rules the ninth house and is in favorable aspect to the ruler of the ascendant, Mars, Jupiter is in poor condition. Thus the moderating influence it might have on religious or philosophical grounds is minimized, especially since its dispositor, Mercury, is besieged by the malefics Mars and Pluto and afflicted by the sextile to Neptune and Saturn.

As the Moon is at 21 degrees of Pisces, and Venus at 26 degrees of Cancer, there are 125 degrees between them in the order of the signs. Thus the part is 125 degrees from the ascendant in the order of the signs, which brings it to 0 degrees of Virgo. This then, is the place of the part of religion and honesty of woman in this figure.

---

*By *nature* a benefic, Jupiter is "accidentally" malefic here because it is in such poor zodiacal condition.

We immediately note that Virgo is not a movable sign, and we find Venus sextile to the part. Therefore, strictly speaking, we do not have the negative indications we expect.

But do we have the positive ones? Bonatti offers positive indications which, if fulfilled, would lead us to expect that the woman is both honest and religious. They are these: (1) that the part be in a fixed sign and (2) that the part be aspected by any of the lords of the dignities of the sign it is in or (3) by any benefic.

The first of these does not apply, since Virgo is not a fixed sign. The second and the third do, as Venus is both a benefic and has honor of triplicity in Virgo. However, we cannot say that the woman is religious and honest and that she will remain so "even if she may be longing for coitus," for to do so would violate the clear indications of the natal chart to the contrary. Thus we have a situation which is instructive, for the woman in question is not a prostitute. She may exhibit extreme sexual promiscuity, and may even profit from it, but she is not in the business of selling sex. On the other hand, she is not a chaste and religious virgin. The horoscope has ruled out serious philosophic and religious pursuits. The conjunction of Mercury with Mars and Pluto and its precise sextile to Neptune rule out honesty. Therefore, to rely on the part's favorable indications of religion, honesty, and implied sexual fidelity would be fatuous. The signification of the part must be considered secondary to that of the figure. Were the other indications to the contrary lacking, the story (and the native's behavior) would be different.

If we consider the condition of the "fixed" significators, the Moon and Venus, the aspects to the part itself, and the condition of the part's dispositor, we can see how weak the case for religion and honesty is in fact.

First, neither the Moon nor Venus, the two "fixed" significators, are in good zodiacal condition (the Moon in aspect to malefic Uranus, along with Saturn and Neptune, afflicts Venus). Since these two planets are the causal factors upon which the part depends, they already by their poor condition condemn the part to a limited indication for good. Again, the part itself is besieged between Pluto and the Sun. The first of these, Pluto, is malefic by nature and unassisted by its lower octave, Mars. The second, the Sun, is accidentally malefic both by the position of Mars and Pluto in its sign, Leo, and by its conjunction to the latter and by the terrible zodiacal condition of its dispositor, Mercury (besieged by malefics Mars and Pluto, in Leo, the sign twelfth from its own). Thus, what significant benefit can the part have?

Thus we have established that Figure C represents one of the many possible intermediary degrees between the two extremes Bonatti implies in his description of the possible behavior characteristics associated with this part. Figures A and B fulfilled the lower end or extreme. We shall now look at an example of the upper end. It is a commentary on our times in this Dark Age that when the astrologer seeks an example of virtue, he must look long before he finds one. Traditional astrology in connection with the proper understanding of the teaching can provide an objective measure of where we as a race are in relation to purity, if we would accept it as such. However, today it is all but universal practice to redefine those values in our society and in our lives lest they jar us in our sleep of ignorance and cause us to see ourselves as we have become. Sodom and Gomorrah were the paradigms of Hell on Earth up to the beginning of our century. Today in our major cities they are the paradigms of sophistication. Whenever this obvious inversion of values is forced into the consciousness of the masses, the less learned respond with violence or apathy, while the learned leaders of society redefine the terms to permit the hypnotic sleep to deepen.

Figure D is an example closer to the higher of the two extremes Bonatti offers us. This woman, according to her report, has never been involved in extramarital sexual activities and is actively involved in religious and philosophical matters. The horoscope and the parts support her statements.

Looking at the figure we see, first, that the ascendant is Aquarius and that its rulers, Saturn and Uranus, are respectively in Leo on the cusp of the seventh and in Gemini on the cusp of the fifth house. With regard to Saturn, we see the extremely strong need for a partner—a drive that is part of the need for self-improvement indicated by Saturn's condition in detriment on the cusp of the seventh. This drive is terrifically intensified by the angular Pluto, with which Saturn is joined. This Pluto, while essentially malefic and threatening, is nevertheless somewhat modified by the fact that its lower octave, Mars, is in mutual reception with Jupiter, and both Jupiter and Mars are connected with Pluto: Mars by a trine and Jupiter by a square. Now, Jupiter is the ruler of the tenth, the dispositor of the entire chart, and is in the ninth house. Thus all areas of life eventually serve the higher mind. Scorpio, on the cusp of the ninth, is a water sign; thus the religio-philosophical activity involves intense devotion. Both rulers of the ninth are angular; Mars in the tenth and Pluto in the seventh. Therefore the native's religious ideals have considerable influence on her actions (tenth house) and dealings with other people (seventh house). From this angularity and from the predominance of fixed signs in the figure and the ultimate

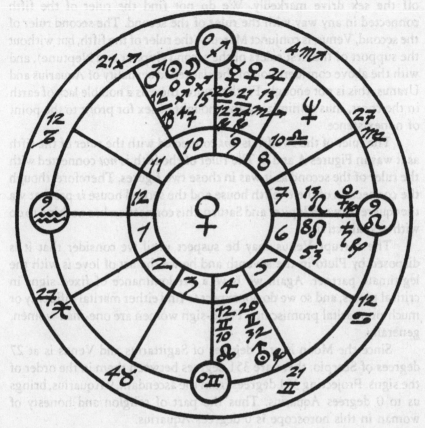

Figure D

disposition of the entire chart by Jupiter placed in the ninth, we may conclude that the native has a very firmly fixed code of behavior which is ultimately based on and serves the philosophic or religious views.

Because Jupiter and Mars are in mutual reception, Mars's disposition of Mercury is not as harmful as it might otherwise be. Moreover, Mercury's conjunction with Venus, even though accidentally malefic owing to its poor zodiacal condition, is still rather helpful. Finally, Mercury is afflicted otherwise only by the Sun, and this is not too severe an affliction since Mercury is so frequently very close to the Sun. All in all, then, there is no outstanding reason in the natal to suspect the native's honesty. On the contrary, the importance of Jupiter, here in honor of triplicity albeit afflicted by the Saturn-Pluto conjunction, augurs well for her honesty and religious sincerity.

We *do* find the ruler of the first in the fifth, but neither Aquarius nor Uranus are known for sexual activity. Quite the contrary, both cool off the sex drive markedly. We do not find the ruler of the fifth connected in any way with the ruler of the second. The second ruler of the second, Venus, is conjunct Mercury, the ruler of the fifth, but without the support of the first rulers of the second (Jupiter and Neptune), and with the above consideration of the slackened sexuality of Aquarius and Uranus, this is not enough. Furthermore, there is a notable lack of earth in the chart, thus minimizing any thought of sex for profit to the point of nonexistence.

The ruler of the twelfth is *not* connected with the ruler of the fifth as it was in Figures A and B. The ruler of the fifth is *not* connected with the ruler of the second as it was in those two figures. Therefore, though the connection of the twelfth house and the second house *is* present via the square between Jupiter and Saturn, this connection has nothing to do with sexual activity.

The corrupt Venus may be suspect until we consider that it is disposed by Pluto in the seventh and hence the act of love is with the legitimate partner. Again we have a predominance of fixed signs in critical places, and so we do not expect to find either marital infidelity or much premarital promiscuity. Fixed-sign women are one-man women, generally.

Since the Moon is at 0 degrees of Sagittarius and Venus is at 27 degrees of Scorpio, there are 351 degrees between them in the order of the signs. Projecting 351 degrees from the ascendant, 9 Aquarius, brings us to 0 degrees Aquarius. Thus the part of religion and honesty of woman in this horoscope is 0 degrees Aquarius.

This places the part in a fixed sign. Thus we have the first of Bonatti's requirements. Mercury is in aspect to 0 degrees Aquarius by a sextile, albeit a loose one. Since Mercury is in honor of triplicity in Aquarius, we have the second requirement. We might also want to accept the opposition of Saturn to the part, since Saturn is angular and the ruler of Aquarius. The third requirement is that the part be aspected by a benefic. Now, both the Sun and the Moon aspect the part exactly to a degree; of the two, the Moon is closer. Thus, even if we decide to consider that the position of Pluto and Saturn in Leo afflict the Sun sufficiently to override its disposition by Jupiter (who rules Sagittarius, in which the Sun is placed)—especially given Jupiter's position in Scorpio, Mars's and Pluto's sign—nevertheless the Moon, the woman's luminary, still fulfills the role of benefic and cuts off all other aspects by the precision of its own. No matter how we consider it, the requirements Bonatti sets are in some way fulfilled, and we are forced to conclude that the woman is virtuous, religious, and honest.

We could say further that she is dedicated to her husband, industrious, and that she serves him (note that Saturn, the ruler of her ascendant is disposed by the Sun, while Mercury, the dispositor of Uranus, is conjunct the Sun). Moreover, though the husband is indicated by the malefics in her seventh house, the ruler of the seventh aspects Saturn, the ruler of the ascendant, with a trine and therefore the marriage works.

This figure, then, clearly indicates someone much closer than the three preceding cases to the ideal which Bonatti indicates in his discussion of the part. Once more we see the signification of the parts is supported both by the other considerations of the natal figure and by the behavior of the native.

THE PART OF FORTUNE

The parts, especially those of the Sun and Moon, give a profound understanding of the inner experience of the native.

In the natal figure, the part of fortune or lunar ascendant is a shadowy point pertaining to the emotional, instinctual, or inner motivation of the individual. As such it is of as much importance for temporal considerations as for spiritual matters. Just as the ascendant of the horoscope shows the primary or outer motivation of the individual, which determines his or her outer behavior toward this or that, so the part of fortune indicates the nature of the inner world of the individual and the quality and nature of its realization. In the same way that the position and state of the ruler of the ascendant shows the area of life in which the native will attempt to realize the primary motivation as indicated by the ascendant, so the inner world's primary desire will seek realization in the house wherein its ruler is placed. The success, failure, or history associated with this inner drive will be indicated by the nature and state of the ruler of the sign in which the part of fortune falls.

Moreover, the house in which the part of fortune falls will indicate the area of life with which the native is emotionally concerned inwardly. Thus, when the part of fortune is in the first house, matters pertaining to the body take preference over the other possible significations of the part of fortune. This might mean health, or it might mean life/death concerns. I know a young lady who is a New-Moon birth in Aries. Aries rises in her natal figure. Mars, however, is in the eighth house. The fear of death is a constant concern for her.

When the part falls into the second house, then financial concerns are predominant. And so with the rest of the houses. Universally the elemental nature of the sign in which the part falls will indicate the kind of motivation; the mode (cardinal, fixed, or mutable) will indicate the kind of emotional activity, and the gender will show the activity or passivity of the drive, just as with the ascendant.

The indications of the part with respect to health arise from its function as an indicator of the health of the subtle body. The part of fortune may be considered as a reservoir which may or may not contain a vast amount of energy on which the native may draw. Again this is to be determined by the nature of the sign in which the part falls and the condition of its ruler. Heavy afflictions to either will deplete the reservoir and adversely affect the inner state, thereby weakening the health of the individual.

It is apparent from observations of transits over the part of fortune that its orb is approximately 3 degrees on either side.

It is also apparent to both reason and experience that, except in New-Moon births, the "outer" behavior and motivation indicated by the ascendant and its ruler will vary from the "inner" motivation and behavior indicated by the part of fortune and its ruler to the extent that the luminaries are distant from each other. Thus in New-Moon births we find a singularity of purpose which results from the coincidence of the part of fortune and its complement, the part of the Sun (or *pars futurorum*), with the ascendant. The direct connection of the subconscious and conscious minds in such people—resulting, as Volquine has remarked,[1] in sometimes disturbing psychic experiences, such as dizziness, strange dreams, and in extreme cases clairvoyance and clairaudience—arises from the fact that the physical body (ascendant) becomes the sole outlet for the three major levels of being. When a strong Neptune is also involved, mediumism may be expected. Whether such a state will be wholesome or not will have to be determined from the figure in question. Such individuals are quite vulnerable to disturbances of a subtle nature.

Those persons in whose natal figure the Moon is prominent will be those in whom this inner world, signified by the part of fortune and its ruler, acts most strongly.

Let us look at Figure E. This is the horoscope of an industrious, hard-working young lady. It is apparent that with Pisces rising, this native's primary motivation is for emotional security and that she attempts to realize it through hard work in her profession. She is trained as a designer but has also worked as a public relations liaison and was for a time involved in placing high school students in colleges. The conjunction of Jupiter, with the exalted Mars, second ruler of the ascendant, in the tenth house; the elevated Sun, ruler of the sixth house (employment); Jupiter's trine to the stationary Saturn in Virgo in the sixth; and the powerful Uranus square the ascendant and opposed to the tenth house cusp—all point to the extreme importance of the profession to this native.

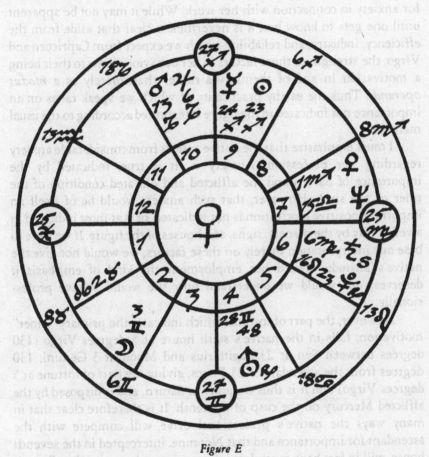

Figure E

I have known this lady for several years and have always been impressed by her industry, dedication to her work, and practicality. She frequently puts in more time on a job than anyone else to ensure its success and to make sure that all details have been taken care of.

The native is extremely high-strung. This is due to the sensitivity of her constitution (as indicated by the Piscean ascendant), the stationary Saturn trine to the ruler of the ascendant, Jupiter, and above all else to the disturbing Uranus opposed to Mercury and square to the ascendant.

Conversation with her inevitably turns to work. This is to be expected with such a horoscope, especially considering the Capricornian influence, the strength of Saturn, and the elevated Sun. However, there is always a note of anxiety in her voice whenever work is discussed, and her behavior is clearly aimed at overcoming difficulties or future causes for anxiety in connection with her work. While it may not be apparent until one gets to know her, it is nevertheless clear that aside from the efficiency, industry, and reliability which we expect from Capricorn and Virgo, the strength of these factors in her behavior points to their being a motivation in and of themselves rather than merely as a *modus operandi*. Thus the earthy practicality of which we speak takes on an importance not indicated in the figure interpreted according to the usual methods.

I must emphasize that the native suffers from considerable anxiety regarding her profession. Anxiety is, it is true, indicated by the importance of Saturn and the afflicted and elevated condition of the ruler of the sixth. However, that such anxiety would be of itself an important positive motivation is not indicated, or is at most indicated in a veiled way by the planets, signs, and houses of the figure. If we were to base our interpretation merely on these factors, we would not give the native's attitude toward her employment the kind of emphasis it deserves, nor would we understand how she would behave professionally.

However, the part of fortune, which indicates the primary "inner" motivation, falls in the native's sixth house at 5 degrees Virgo (130 degrees between Sun at 23 Sagittarius and Moon at 3 Gemini; 130 degrees from the ascendant at 25 Pisces, giving the part of fortune at 5 degrees Virgo) and it is thus conjunct to Saturn, and is disposed by the afflicted Mercury on the cusp of the tenth. It is therefore clear that in many ways the native's professional drive will compete with the ascendant for importance and that Neptune, intercepted in the seventh house, will in fact have much *less* influence over the native than Saturn, even though Saturn is cadent! This is in fact my experience. Although Neptune does affect the native's interpersonal and emotional affairs, Saturn exerts far more influence over the professional experience and even interferes with the Neptunian sensuality in the native's relations with others. Thus while the native is undoubtedly sensitive and sensual, she is not slothful or indolent at all but rather strongly motivated to work, and work hard, by her inner anxiety. To attempt to counsel her without taking this into consideration would be to miss the mark.

In a situation such as this, where the inner motivation coincides with factors in the chart determined powerfully toward particular matters, such as the profession, it is as if we are dealing with two different people: one indicated by the ascendant and one indicated by the part of fortune acting in concert with the strongly determined influence. The astrologer must be circumspect in such cases, since too much of a discrepancy between the two drives might cause problems for the native.

THE PART OF THE SUN

The complement to the part of fortune is the part of future things (*pars futurorum*) or part of the Sun. Bonatti indicates that even in his time this part received little attention. Yet he says that the ancients (by which he means primarily Albumassar) considered it second only to the part of fortune in importance. Specifically it was held to signify the soul and body (after the part of fortune), faith, prophecy, religion and culture of God, secrets, cogitations, intentions and hidden things, etc. Thus it is quite clear that this part relates to spiritual concerns even more than the part of fortune. This is undoubtedly the cause of its having been largely ignored by the medieval Western astrologer, whose trade emphasized the temporal benefits stemming from occult learning.

If the part of the Moon, or part of fortune, relates to the passive, vegetative aspect, to the subtle body, then the part of the Sun, its complement, must relate to the active powers of the soul. Thus these two parts are of primary importance in discovering the "inner" conditions of the native. The part of fortune indicates the inferior appetitive aspects of the soul, and the quality and determination of the motivations associated with these, while the part of the Sun indicates the quality and determination of the active, conscious, divine powers of the soul and their motivation and realization. Both parts will have their significations over the inner experience which may or may not bear any relation to the outer phenomena of the native's life. The outer phenomena arise from the concourse of the planets as causal factors interacting with themselves, the signs, and the ascendant. Thus the nature of the native's inner world may vary considerably from his or her outer world. Precisely what the relation between the inner and outer worlds of any figure is must be determined by how the parts, especially those of the Sun and Moon, relate to the rest of the figure by house position, disposition, and aspect.

Just as two or more houses may be connected by common rulership and by the position and aspects of the planets, so the parts may be connected in the same way, thus forming an intricate web of interrelationships of motivations on various levels.

As the part of the Sun is connected with the culture of God, faith, and religion, we may employ it to learn what ideas the native has about these things. Specifically, experience shows that the condition of the part of the Sun accurately indicates the native's concept of Divinity. Since all creatures consciously or unconsciously love some particular aspect of Existence, and by their adoration of this aspect draw closer to it and become ever more like their object of devotion, all creatures including Man may be said to be continually worshiping something as a god. The part of the Sun may be said to indicate the god the native worships. This is because the part of the Sun—that is, the part indicating the numerical relationship existing between the causal factors of the Sun (as Author of Life, Active Cause, and Source of Existence) and the Moon (as the feminine aspect of the Creator, or the Reactive Cause and Outward Manifestation of the possibilities latent in the First Cause)—represents, by its qualification according to zodiacal condition, those qualities associated with this aspect of life in the mind of the native. This numerical relationship is taken in the direction opposite to that used for discovering the part of fortune. Therefore, while the part of fortune indicates a descending of divine influence (in order of the signs), the part of the Sun indicates that to which the native aspires: his or her god. Thus, in spiritual work, purity is of great importance, for if the concept of Self [Sun] and/or of desire, or instincts [Moon] are fouled, there will be a corresponding limitation or corruption of the ideal of Divinity: the highest possible goal to which the individual can aspire.

This being the case, the reason the part of the Sun signifies secrets, cogitations, and intentions will be apparent: Since this part indicates the highest ideals of the native, and since these ideals influence the native's most secret yearnings, and since all creatures seek what they hold to be the highest Good, the part of the Sun indicates the native's plans and aspirations for these things in strict accordance to its condition, position, and disposition.

Let us look to Figure F as an example of this. The part of the Sun falls at 3 degrees of Gemini. The native is profoundly religious and at the same time philosophical. This may be seen from the fact that the ruler of the ascendant, Mercury, is in the ninth,* while the ruler of the ninth, by

*Mercury is in the eighth house. However, that it is in the ninth sign is more pertinent here since the signs indicate the soul (sky) and our subject is a specifically spiritual one.

exaltation, the Moon, is rising. Thus we have a "double determination" toward religious or philosophical matters. The Sun is in the ninth, and this adds to the native's view of herself as a religious person.

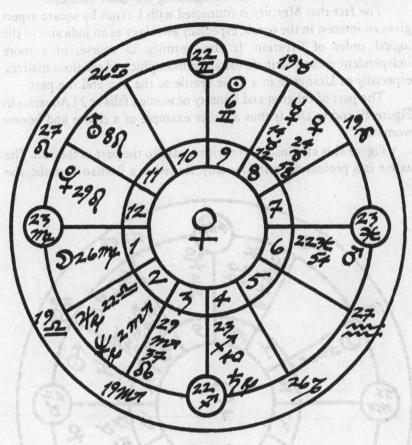

Figure F

Now, note that both the luminaries, from which the part of the Sun is taken, are in mercurial signs. Note also that the part falls in Gemini, ruled by Mercury. Thus it is clear that Mercury will have great influence over the signification of the part of the Sun. Finally, note that the part is conjunct the Sun in the ninth. Thus, the native's concept of religion and her Divinity will be essentially solar and mercurial. We may expect her to be inwardly and outwardly interested in religio-philosophical matters because both the outward indications (the planets, signs, and houses) point to such pursuits *and* the part emphasizes the same factors.

The native was raised as a Roman Catholic but has strong inclinations to philosophy, especially to the dialectical philosophy of

Plato. Her interest in religion is thus not entirely one of devotion, which would be essentially a lunar emphasis, but rather one of reason, learning, discussion, *and* devotion. Thus the primary elements are solar and mercurial—without, however, disregarding the lunar element.

The fact that Mercury is connected with Uranus by square aspect gives an interest in the occult, especially astrology as an indicator of the logical order of Creation. It also permits, of course, of a more independent mental attitude toward philosophic and religious matters, especially as Uranus is in a loose sextile to the Sun and the part.

The part of religion and honesty of woman falls at 24 Aquarius in Figure F, and so this is thus another example of a chaste and honest woman.

Figure G is also instructive with regard to the part of the Sun. The native is a profoundly religious lady. Raised as a Roman Catholic, she

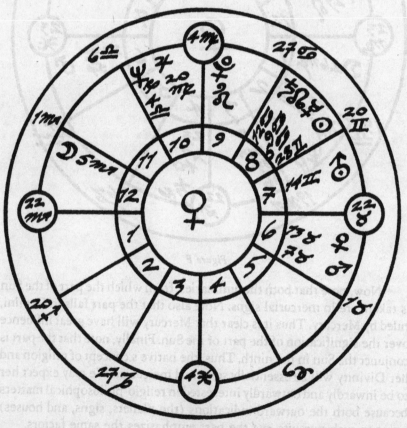

Figure G

turned in her twenties to a different approach toward religion. Note that the ruler of the ascendant, Pluto in the ninth house, is involved in a "T square" with Mars and the Moon, connecting the twelfth, sixth, and ninth houses. By rulership the first, twelfth, ninth, sixth, and fifth houses are all connected with the strain involved with the T square. The religious activities of this lady involve the transformation of the emotional ground, as is apparent from Pluto's and the Moon's involvement in the configuration. Tremendous emotional pressures are clearly indicated. Given the zodiacal condition of the planets involved, we can be sure that the process will involve a great deal of "cleaning house." Because of this and the fixity of the signs involved, we do not expect this process to be easy or pleasant.

Now, here we have an instance in which the consideration of the part of the Sun will throw light on the native's goals and concept of Divinity.

The part of the Sun falls at 15 degrees of Cancer. The part is therefore sextile to a good, albeit afflicted, Venus in the sixth house. The conjunction with the malefic Saturn is technically cut off,* but as we shall see it still has an effect. The part's dispositor is the Moon, which is also ruler of the ninth and afflicted by the T square with Pluto and Mars.

The native's concept of Divinity is by her own admission associated with fear and emotional turmoil. The fear is directly the result of the conjunction of Saturn with the part, which is greatly mitigated from what it could be by the sextile from Venus. However, that it still causes anxiety is a mark of its power and influence.

That this anxiety concerns religion is of great importance considering the other indications of religiosity and spirituality in the figure. Considering the quality of the planets involved (Moon, Saturn, Mars, and Pluto) there is no doubt some refining of being necessary. This refining process will take a considerable emotional toll on the native. The part of the Sun indicates that the native has accepted the idea that fear and misery will be involved with the process. How this all works out will be determined in the end by the context within which the activity takes place. If the spiritual teaching that she follows can provide her with the kind of uplifting reassurance necessary to help her through the difficulties which are bound to arise and she can steady her commitment to spiritual labor, then no doubt a radical transformation

---

*The sextile from Venus falls at 13 Cancer and hence technically cuts off the effects of the conjunction with Saturn. However, since Saturn is more powerful than Venus, it still causes the native some problems, although less so than it would if Venus did not cast her sextile between the part and Saturn.

can and will occur. If not, especially if the ideal of God as fear and misery cannot be dislodged, then the outcome will not be successful. Should her efforts fail and the weight of the past reassert itself, the result could be quite destructive.

We should note that the concept of religion and Divinity as fear and misery cannot be explained by consideration of any of the factors in the figure other than the part of the Sun. For we find Scorpio rising, and though both its rulers are involved with the affliction to the Moon, such an affliction, while causing intense conflict, struggle, and disturbance, will not cause fear. Fear is Saturn's production and Saturn's position in Cancer alone is not sufficient to cause the anxiety expressed by the native, although it will bring her doubts about her own inner worth.

This part may be expected to yield additional helpful information especially in figures that reveal other indications of spiritual activity. In spiritual counseling this part and several others can give invaluable assistance.

THE PART OF THE HYLEG

Bonatti mentions the *pars hyleg* in section 4 of his treatise, which deals with the parts of the first house. As with the *pars futurorum,* Bonatti's discussion indicates that the *pars hyleg* is associated with considerations that extend beyond the merely temporal. His commentary tells us that the part is the *radix vitae,* the root of the native's life, and that it is the root of the other parts. "It comprehends entirely the whole being of the native." However, because this part is "so involved with other things," the ancients did not care to make much mention of it.

Clearly, then, this part, like the *pars futurorum,* is an example of astrological doctrine associated with levels of being that pertain more to the spiritual than to the temporal. Even at the early dates at which Bonatti's sources wrote, this part, like the spiritual context it belonged to, were already falling into disuse among astrologers.

Investigation of this part in numerous natal figures supports Bonatti's statements regarding its specially esoteric nature. According to the text, if the part is well disposed, the native's "being" will be good; if poorly disposed, the contrary. By this is meant that although the true nature of all human beings is identical with the Self, whose nature is entirely Good, nevertheless individuals suffer differentiation from this essential Good by the superimposition of various qualities. These qualities can be such that they lead to the Good or away from it. The former are by definition good, the latter evil. Now, the *pars hyleg* gives an accurate synthesis, in the form of one consideration, of the quality of being of the native. But this is not all. Aside from providing such a handy index of the native's being, this part and its dispositor also indicate the purpose of the native's life—the reason for his or her incarnation! I shall illustrate this with several notable examples below. Let me first point out that in those figures where the drive of the ascendant coincides with the purpose indicated by this part and its dispositor, we find exceptional motivation in the direction indicated, such that we will have to assume its successful realization. As always, the quality—the benefic or malefic nature—of the drive depends upon the nature and state of the significators.

In Figure H we have the natal figure of a young lady who deeply and sincerely believes that she was placed upon this Earth to raise up the level of consciousness of others, to heal them through the life-giving

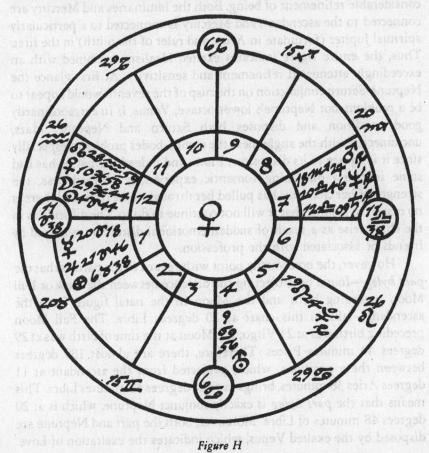

Figure H

power of Love. She feels that many people would benefit from this activity, however small her contribution might be. In her own words: "I have never really believed that I was put here for my own entertainment or amusement...I have always felt that I had something to do which involved large numbers of people."

This exalted idealism is an apt expression of the natal figure. Here we find Aries rising with the Sun, and Mercury and Jupiter actually in the sign of Aries, while the Moon, in the last few minutes of Pisces, is just about to join with the Sun. Mars, the ruler of this stellium, and dispositor of the chart (except for Neptune and Saturn), is in the seventh but works for the eighth as well because of its proximity to that house.

The quality of this figure is truly outstanding. Five planets are in some kind of honor, three of them exalted. This native is an individual of considerable refinement of being. Both the luminaries and Mercury are connected to the ascendant, and Mercury is connected to a particularly spiritual Jupiter (fortunate in Aries, and ruler of the ninth) in the first. Thus, the entire figure indicates exalted idealism combined with an exceedingly attenuated refinement and sensitivity. At first glance the Neptune-Saturn conjunction on the cusp of the seventh would appear to be a problem, but Neptune's lower octave, Venus, is in extraordinarily good condition and disposes both Saturn and Neptune. Mars, unconnected with the angles near the eighth, bodes problems, especially since it is square to its dispositor, Pluto, and indeed the native has had some intensely disturbing romantic experiences. Nevertheless, the strength of her character has pulled her through these trials and there is no reason to assume that it will not continue to do so. The difficulties in the chart arise as a result of sudden emotional disturbances caused by friends or associated with the profession.

However, the noteworthy point with regard to the parts is that the *pars hyleg*—found by projecting the distance between the New or Full Moon preceding birth and the Moon in the natal figure from the ascendant—falls in this chart at 20 degrees Libra. The Full Moon preceding birth was at 21 Virgo; the Moon at the time of birth was at 29 degrees 44 minutes Pisces. Therefore, there are almost 189 degrees between these positions, which, projected from the ascendant at 11 degrees Aries 38 minutes, brings us to 20 degrees 38 minutes Libra. This means that the *pars hyleg* is exactly conjunct Neptune, which is at 20 degrees 48 minutes of Libra. Moreover, both the part and Neptune are disposed by the exalted Venus, which indicates the exaltation of Love.

Neptune disposed in this way indicates Universal Love, and its conjunction with the *pars hyleg* in the seventh house means that the native desires to bring to others the message of the unifying power of Universal Love. Thus we can see how the statements made by the native herself arise. However, since this part indicates the task of the native's life or the cause of the incarnation, we would expect that if the native should be aware of this urge, she would in some way seek to find a way to express it perfectly, especially since the ruler of the tenth house is conjunct the part and Neptune.

This is so. Having decided upon an acting career, the native is at present arranging her economic situation to enable her to devote herself completely to acting. She has consciously decided that this is the best way she can bring her message to other people. This decision is clearly a spiritual one at the deepest of levels, as is indicated by the fact that Venus, the ruler of the *pars hyleg*, is conjunct the *pars futurorum* (which indicates the native's idea of God and of religion), which falls in the twelfth house at 16 degrees Pisces. Moveover, both Venus and the *pars futurorum* are disposed by Neptune on the *pars hyleg!* Clearly there is a link in the native's mind between God, whom she sees as Love, and her task, which she feels involves bringing this message of Love to others. Again, the part as an indicator of the level of being coincides with the level indicated by the chart as a whole and points to a heart of extraordinary purity.

Here, then, is an indication of the profound importance of these parts. Beyond any doubt they permit far deeper understanding of the inner world of the native, when they are properly understood and used, then would otherwise be possible. In Chapter 11 I shall discuss the possibilities that arise in connection with the use of these parts for spiritual counseling.

In conclusion, it must be acknowledged that there are difficulties with Figure H. The company the native keeps is a critical factor. Purity is far more easily corrupted than corruption is purified, and the native is a finely tuned instrument which requires care. Properly tuned, Apollo's lyre can charm the beasts and magically transform the heart of Man. If this native can work against habit and sleep, she can certainly overcome any obstacles to her own development and therefore accomplish the work for which she has been born.

The individual's recognition of the task she or he is to accomplish is the true moment of maturity. It seems always to involve a significant change in the course of the native's life which is sometimes associated with emotional, economic, or other disturbances. This is because such a recognition is essentially the recognition of one's own true self. While such a level of understanding still involves a limited condition of the individual soul—that is, the individual is not yet fully realized—it is nevertheless a view of the individual as related to the Whole, perceived as family, society, humanity, the cosmos, or some such entity, in light of the unconditioned Absolute Self. The effect of such a realization is to present to the individual a new view of his place in the Whole.

This recognition need not occur entirely on the conscious level. The individual need not become fully aware of all the ramifications of his new vision of himself until long after the initial steps in the new direction have been taken. Often, there is a dramatic event which moves him off in a new direction. But he need not understand that this will eventually lead him to the realization of his task. The Higher Mind apparently considers that understanding is not as critical to the lower mind as action. Therefore, while the individual must know on some level what is going on, he need not consciously have access to such knowledge. In practice this means that the astrologer may know better than the native that this or that change in the direction of one's life will bring him closer to his goal or not. Of course, the individual *may* know from birth what his life task is. In this case we are dealing with a soul of considerable development.

Usually the native becomes aware of the task sometime after he has begun to move in its direction. Therefore, the question of timing becomes important. Experience shows that the initial change toward the task occurs when the ascendant or tenth-house cusp comes to the part by profection. The conscious recognition of the new direction as the proper one may correspond with the powerful transits of major planets over the part or the point opposite to it. This may be expected especially when the transit has a disturbing effect.

Figure I is the natal figure of a man who has labored hard and long to establish a scholarly society that will encourage independent research of spiritual and philosophical matters. As we see frequently in the horoscopes of such people, the airy Libra ascends, inclining the native to intellectual pursuits, giving a drive for intellectual freedom, and bestowing the diplomacy and leadership necessary for such enterprises. Venus, the ruler of the ascendant, is in the tenth house, indicating the great drive for realization. Jupiter, the ruler of the third, having culminated at the top of the chart, is in the ninth house. Pluto's position, exactly on the cusp of the tenth, intensifies the drive to the point that

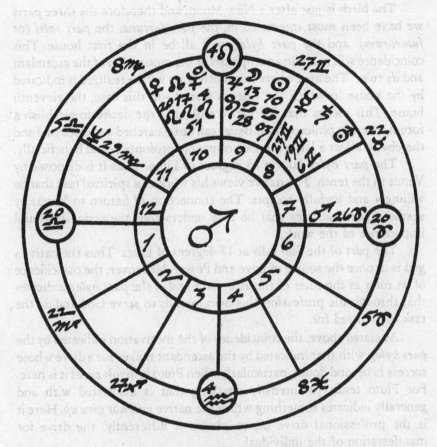

Figure I

there can be no doubt but that it shall succeed. Finally, the Sun and Moon are in the ninth in Cancer, and Mercury, the ruler of the ninth, is in Gemini on the cusp of the ninth house.

The native is deeply spiritually motivated and seeks to organize his friends and associates into a body of scholars dedicated to spiritual and philosophical research. If we consider the ninth house from the eleventh as his friends' spirituality, we find that this falls at his seventh house, wherein Mars rests in Aries. Thus his friends have a militant sense of spirituality which agrees with his own more intellectual, analytical, and philosophical inclinations, as we see from the sextile between Mars and Mercury.

Here again it is well to note the number of planets in significant degrees of dignity: six.

The birth is just after a New Moon, and therefore the three parts we have been most interested in, the *pars fortuna*, the *pars solis* (or *futurorum*), and the *pars hyleg*, will all be in the first house. This coincidence will result in an emphasis of the motivation of the ascendant and its ruler. The area where this motivation will be realized is indicated by the house in which the ruler is placed—in this case, the eleventh house. This means that the native embodies the desire to establish a forum wherein philosophical issues can be researched and discussed and thereby to affect a large number of people profoundly and beneficially.

The *pars hyleg* falls at 23 degrees of Libra. Thus it is disposed by Venus in the tenth. The native views his work as a spiritual task that he willingly and joyfully accepts. The connection of Saturn to Venus by sextile aspect indicates that he fully understands the seriousness and importance of the work.

The part of the Sun falls at 17 degrees of Libra. Thus the native's god is at once the source of Love and Power. Moreover, the coincidence of its ruler as the ruler of the ascendant and of the *pars hyleg* indicates that through his profession this man intends to serve God and do the task he is fitted for.

As stated above, the coincidence of the motivation indicated by the *pars hyleg* with that indicated by the ascendant makes for a drive whose success is beyond doubt, particularly when Pluto is involved, as it is here. For Pluto tends to intensify anything that is associated with and generally indicates something which the native *will not give up*. Here it is the professional drive or, to phrase it differently, the drive for manifestation of the individual.

The good or evil nature of the drive is indicated by the benefic or malefic nature of the planets involved. Here both Venus and Jupiter are clearly benefic. Pluto may be considered as such also, owing to the excellent zodiacal state of Mars, Pluto's "lower octave."

The being of the native, indicated by the *pars hyleg*, is Libran (i.e., Venusian), hence benefic, and so all indications point to refined spirituality, purity of motivation, and success of the enterprise. That these will still be attended by intense struggle and even danger to the native is indicated by the angular Pluto and Mars as well as the planets in the eighth house.

PARTS OF THE EIGHTH HOUSE

Figure J—that of a young lady who was raped and beaten on the sixth of December 1975 in New York City and who died on the way to

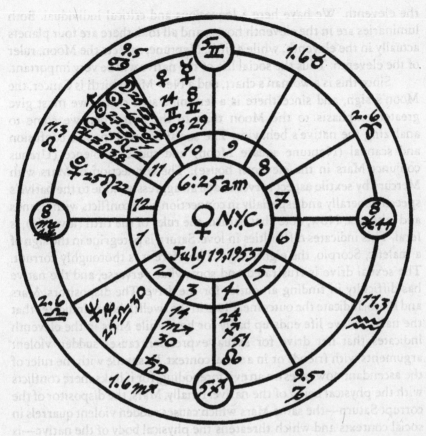

Figure J

the hospital—affords an opportunity for studying the significations of several parts of the eighth house as well as some that we have already looked at. As the parts can be applied both to revolutions and to nativities, we shall look at them both in the natal figure and in the solar return.

Figure J is the natal figure. The birth data are: female, born 6:25 A.M. EDST July 19, 1955, New York City.* We find critical Virgo ascending and its ruler, Mercury, in the tenth house sextile to Mars in

*Other pertinent facts are that the fixed star Prima Hyadum, fourth magnitude and of the nature of Saturn and Mercury, culminated at 5 Gemini 25 at the time of birth. Skat, third magnitude, of the nature of Saturn and Jupiter, was setting at that time, 8 Pisces 29. Procyon, first magnitude, of the nature of Mars and Mercury, backed up the Moon. The South Scale, third magnitude, of the nature of Jupiter and Mars, at 14 Scorpio 42, backed up the feral Saturn, which had just gone direct in the third house. Of these, Procyon is most important, being a first-magnitude star and having association with "quarrels with friends," which indeed the entire natal figure presignifies.

the eleventh. We have here a loquacious and critical individual. Both luminaries are in the eleventh house, and all told, there are four planets actually in the eleventh, while a fifth, Neptune, aspects the Moon, ruler of the eleventh. Thus the social life of the native will be very important.

Since this is a woman's chart, and a New Moon birth is Cancer, the Moon's sign, and since there is a feminine sign rising, we must give greater emphasis to the Moon than to the Sun when we come to analyzing the native's behavior. The social life will involve confusion and scandal (Neptune square Moon) and sudden violence (Uranus conjunct Mars in the eleventh house). The connection of Mars with Mercury by sextile aspect serves to add an aggressive tone to the native's speech generally and especially in connection with conflicts with friends and with sex. Now, note that Saturn, the ruler of the fifth (love life), is feral. This indicates difficulties in love. Saturn is peregrine in the sign of a malefic, Scorpio, the eighth sign. Therefore it is thoroughly corrupt. The sexual drive is frustrated and somewhat perverse, and the native has difficulty in finding an outlet for the drive. The dispositors, Mars and Pluto, indicate the outcome. Pluto in the twelfth house indicates that the native's love life ends up badly for her, while Mars in the eleventh indicates that her drive for sexual expression causes sudden violent arguments with friends or in a social context. Its sextile with the ruler of the ascendant now takes on an evil foreboding, for it links there conflicts with the physical being of the native. Finally, Mars, the dispositor of the corrupt Saturn—the same Mars which causes sudden violent quarrels in social contexts and which threatens the physical body of the native—is ruler of the house of death, the eighth house. Moreover, this Mars is disposed by the Sun, which also disposes Pluto, the other dispositor of Saturn. The Sun is also in the eleventh house. This is significant, for the Sun is also ruler of the eighth house by exaltation and partial ruler of the eleventh house. Thus the native's sexual drive and her social life are clearly linked with death.

I believe the native consulted me because she had had forebodings about her imminent death. The square between a strongly elevated Moon and Neptune and a feminine ascendant frequently gives clairvoyance, albeit uncontrolled and attended by disturbances. Unfortunately, I never got a chance to notify her of the dangerous facts in her horoscope. She died the night she gave me the birth data.

She was at least bisexual, if not exclusively homosexual, as is indicated by the prominence of the modern planets and Mercury, and by the fact that the Moon is decreasing in light and afflicted by Neptune (the planet of female homosexuality), as well as by the connection of the eighth house with the fifth through Mars in two ways: (1) Mars rules the eighth (Aries) and is exalted in the fifth (Capricorn), and (2) Mars disposes the feral Saturn. We must not ignore the conjunction of Uranus with the Sun in this regard, as it imparts an unconventionality and willful iconoclasm to the ego, encouraging the inversion of values. Note that many of the same factors which indicated violence and death in connection with the love life are also here associated with the native's homosexuality. This is of course not always the case, but here it is significant as it implies a connection of her sexual preference with the cause of her death.

Not much is known about the details of her death. One of her friends informed me of her fate and said that she had been at a party in upper Manhattan and had left after an argument. Precisely what the argument was about has never been made clear to me or to the police. She was followed after she left the party, by whom it is unclear, but apparently by someone from the party. She was raped and beaten by this person, who has never been apprehended, near a playground and managed to find her way to the house of a friend, bleeding profusely. She died on the way to the hospital.

Ptolemy and all astrologers accept that the eighth house and its ruler indicate the circumstances surrounding the native's death. Here the actual circumstances and those the astrologer would conjecture could not agree more completely. The eighth house is Aries (conflict) ruled by Mars (beatings, stabbings, loss of blood). Mars is in the eleventh house and associated with violent arguments arising in a social context, or at a party. The attack was public, as is indicated by the involvement of the Sun.

Now let us look at the testimony of the parts. The birth is a New Moon one. Therefore both the part of fortune and the part of the Sun fall at the same place, on the ascendant at 8 degrees Virgo. Mercury is therefore of considerable importance for four reasons: (1) it is ruler of the ascendant; (2) it is dispositor of the part of fortune; (3) it is dispositor of the part of the Sun; (4) it is the highest planet in the figure and the ruler of the destiny and actions of the native (tenth house).

The part of life—which as Bonatti says in his section 4 is found in diurnal charts by taking the distance from Jupiter to Saturn and projecting it from the ascendant—falls at 15 Sagittarius. This part will indicate the "longness or shortness" of life as it is well or badly disposed and aspected.

The part of death (described in Bonatti's section 11) falls in this chart at 12 degrees Pisces. It is found in diurnal or nocturnal figures by taking the distance of the Moon from the cusp of the eighth house. It tells us more about how the native will die.

The part of the killing planet (see Bonatti's section 11) also gives more details on the manner of the native's death. It is found by taking the distance from the lord of the ascendant to the Moon (by day) and projecting this distance from the ascendant. In this chart it falls at 26 Libra.

Now, Bonatti tells us that when the part of life and its dispositor are not well placed, "it signifies paucity of life and the shortness of it." Here the part falls at 15 Sagittarius, which is good enough, but its dispositor is afflicted by its conjunction with Mars and its own disposition by the Sun, and both Mars and the Sun are associated with death in this chart. Therefore we cannot expect much in the way of longevity from this part.

The part of death is at 12 Pisces. Note that it, too, is disposed by Jupiter, which is connected with the death-bringing Mars and Sun.

Saturn, ruler of the fifth house, trines the part of death, adding to our belief that the native's death is connected with a love affair.

Both Neptune, which rules Pisces, and Venus, which is exalted there, are involved with the part of the killing planet. This part falls at 26 Libra, and even though a part cannot affect a planet (for parts have a passive existence), the dispositor of Neptune will be the same as the dispositor of the part of the killing planet, namely Venus. Now, the "killing planet" here is Venus, for being the ruler of the sign in which the part falls, it becomes thus denominated, indicating that its characteristics will be involved in the native's undoing. This shows another connection between the native's death and love, as Neptune indicates "how" the native dies through its rulership of the part of death and its connection with the "killing planet," Venus. Again, Neptune is Venus's "higher octave," and whatever affects Venus, affects Neptune. Finally, "the killing planet," Venus, is ruler of the part of death by exaltation. Thus we see how the planets and parts interweave a kind of net or web of destiny indicating interconnected factors, inner and outer, which all conspire to the given end, in this case death.

Now let us look at the solar return for the fatal year, the native's twentieth (Figure K). Let it be noted that the tenth sign of the natal is rising in this figure. Thus the native's destiny is seen to unfold in this year.

The ruler of the first, Mercury, is in the second sign from the ascendant, and close enough to the cusp of the house to be considered in the second house. The second house, as the house opposite the eighth, is associated with death. Moreover, Mercury applies to the sextile of Mars, a repeat of the dangerous sextile in the natal figure. Mars is ruler (by exaltation) of the eighth house, death, and is placed in Taurus, the sign opposite the eighth sign, Scorpio. Mars's position in the eleventh and its association with the eighth is another repeat of the natal configuration.

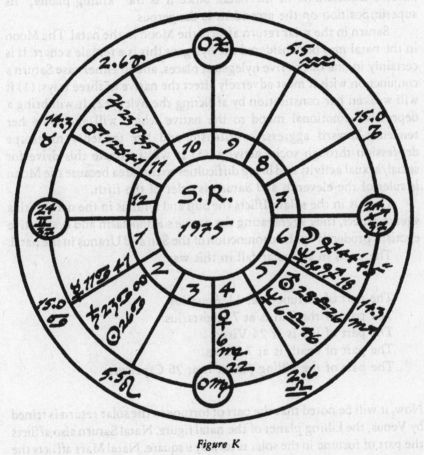

Figure K

The ruler of the tenth house, Jupiter, is connected with the ruler of the eighth house, Mars. This is yet another fatal repeat of the natal. Venus, angular in both figures, is connected to Mercury in both figures, by conjunction in the natal and by sextile in the solar return. Neptune is again connected with the Moon, this time in the unfortunate sixth house. This connection only serves to intensify the native's licentiousness and to cloud her judgment in regard to related matters.

Comparing the natal and the solar return, we find that Venus in the solar is conjunct the natal ascendant. Since Venus rules the fifth house in the solar and is angular, we can be sure that the native's sex drive will be strong in her twentieth year. The fact that this angular Venus conjoins the natal ascendant considerably amplifies the drive. Moreover, this drive cannot have a beneficial effect on the native because of Venus's adverse associations in the natal. Since it is the "killing planet," its superimposition on the ascendant is dangerous.

Saturn in the solar return afflicts the Moon in the natal. The Moon in the natal may be considered the hyleg, as this is a female's chart. It is certainly in one of the five hylegeical places, and in either case Saturn's conjunction with it must adversely affect the native in three ways: (1) It will weaken her constitution by afflicting the hyleg. (2) It will bring a depressive emotional mood to the native which will aggravate her tendency toward aggressive criticism and her tendency to escape depression through social activity. (3) It will frustrate this drive for social/sexual activity and bring difficulties to this area because the Moon is ruler of the eleventh and Saturn is ruler of the fifth.

Uranus in the solar afflicts the Sun and Uranus in the natal with a square aspect, thus aggravating the native's iconoclasm and destructive egotism produced by the conjunction of the Sun and Uranus in the natal.

The parts in the solar fall in this way:

The part of fortune is at 11 Aquarius.
The part of the Sun is at 7 Sagittarius.
The part of life is at 24 Virgo.
The part of death is at 7 Pisces.
The part of the killing planet is at 26 Capricorn.

Now, it will be noted that the part of fortune in the solar return is trined by Venus, the killing planet of the natal figure. Natal Saturn also afflicts the part of fortune in the solar return by a square. Natal Mars afflicts the part of the Sun in the solar return by a trine. It might be argued that the trine from the natal Jupiter is closer, but I have already pointed out that natal Jupiter's conjunction with Mars and its disposition by the Sun (ruler of the eighth) limits its beneficial contribution. I now point out that Jupiter is the ruler of the natal fourth house (the end of life). Therefore it is questionable how much help this Jupiter can be. I add that the dispositor of the part of the Sun in the solar return is Jupiter, which is placed in Aries in the solar return, and is thus ruled by Mars, which has honor in the eighth houses of both figures and falls in the natal eighth by its position in Aries. Moreover, the solar-return Jupiter rules the tenth house (destiny and actions) and is square to the solar-return Saturn, ruler of the house of death.

The part of death at 7 Pisces in the solar return is opposed to Venus in the solar return, and Venus, be it noted, is in the fourth house (end of life). Solar-return Jupiter, the dispositor of the part, is square to the solar-return Saturn, ruler of the eighth house of the solar return.

The same considerations apply where we note that the part of the "killing planet" in the solar return falls in Capricorn, thus making solar-return Saturn especially malicious. Thus both the benefics, Jupiter and Venus, are clearly associated with death in the solar return, a fact that precludes any mitigation of the evil signified by the malefics Mars and Saturn.

Finally, we see that at the time of death the native was undergoing a primary direction of Mercury, ruler of the natal first and tenth, to the Sun, ruler of the natal eighth, by exaltation. Thus the evidence overwhelmingly indicates the native's death. We see, too, that a death associated with a quarrel arising in a social setting and in some way connected with the native's sexual preference is clearly indicated, as is the manner of death—attack in a public place and a violent death from loss of blood due to a stabbing or beating.

The timing of the native's death is always a tricky business and is best passed over here. My primary purpose is (1) to demonstrate that the parts supply accurate support of those things indicated in the natal and solar return figures; (2) to show that the parts may be used in both natal and revolutional figures and to show how their testimonies ought to be interwoven with those of the natal and solar-return figures;* (3) to emphasize that in judgment of the parts, whether of natal or revolutional figures, it is necessary to remember that the parts are *affected by* the planets of both figures and *do not affect the planets*.

In closing this discussion, let us notice the transits on the sixth of December 1975† (see next page).

Especially worthy of note here are the transits of the planets associated with death in the natal, solar return, and primary direction—that is,

*An analogous procedure can be adopted in lunar returns.

†In the following list, N = natal, and SR = solar return.

☉ 13 ♐ 44' 22" (opposed N ♀ ; ♂ N part of life; 1° past □ N part of death)

☽ 3 ♒ (earlier in the day it had transited the opposition to N ☽ , ☉, ☋ opposed N ♂ and ♃ .)

☿ 17 ♐ (conjunct N part of life)

♀ 0 ♏ (□ N ♂)

♂ Re 26 ♊ (⚹ N ♀ ; 2° past △ N part of killing planet, 2° before ⚷ SR part of killing planet, 1° past △ N ♆)

♃ Re 14 ♉ 47 (⚹ N ♀)

♄ Re 2 ♌ (☌ N ♂)

☋ 5 ♏ (□ N ♂)

♅ 11 ♐ (☍ N ♀)

♇ 11 ♎ (△ N ☿ ; ♀ ; ⚹ N ♂ ; ☌ SR part of fortune)

Mars, Sun, Mercury, and Saturn. Note that three of the four planets mentioned make significant transits both to one or the other of the planets named *and* to various of the parts in either the natal or solar return, or both.

Note

1. Alexandre Volquine, *Lunar Astrology*, trans. John Broglio (New York: ASI Publishers, 1972).

7

COMPARING NATAL FIGURES

The use of the significations of the parts in comparing natal figures highlights the "inner" nature of the parts and their essentially passive nature. In such comparisons it quickly becomes apparent that the significations of the parts belong to the native's inner world and that unless there has been sufficient spiritual development on the native's part, he will himself objectively doubt the reality of these subjective opinions, moods, and experiences. We are here in the realm of mind, a realm that almost every individual mistakenly believes to be his own separate experience totally divorced from "reality," which he equates with the physical/economic outer world.

Hence in those cases where the part of fortune differs significantly elementally and otherwise from the ascendant and its ruler, the Sun and the Moon, it is quite possible for the native to become conditioned through family, education, and peer pressure to deny his inner motivation (indicated by the part of fortune) in favor of one of the outer factors mentioned (Sun, Moon, ascendant), believing that only those factors associated with "outer" sensible things are real, while the "inner" motivation is unreal. This is in fact the ordinary condition among the majority of us. It inevitably leads to trouble, for the inner tends to express itself somehow, and where it cannot do so constructively, it does so destructively.

On the other hand, when we compare two charts, we usually find that at least one planet of one chart falls on or aspects some part in the other chart. In such cases—and it is most apparent where such coincidences involve the part of fortune—it is clear that the person whose part is contacted (let's call him X) is affected by the person (Y) whose planet contacts the part rather than vice versa. Moreover, the affect of such contact is in conformity with the nature, state, and local determination of the planet in Y's chart.

Such an interaction between two people is experienced as deeper and more subtle than an interaction between two planets in their figures, or Y's planets on one of X's house cusps (e.g., ascendant or Medium Coeli). The affected party, X, will feel as though he has been deeply affected or "touched," although he may or may not immediately exhibit anything to indicate that this is so. That X has in fact been influenced will eventually come out in discussions in which he will frequently make remarks about Y's character and/or her reaction to him which will not be explainable by reference to the comparison of the "outer" side of their natal charts.

Subjectively, of course, the individual so influenced will recognize the reality of such an interaction, but objectively he may not, depending, as I said above, on how much reality he will ascribe to such experiences. Such behavior is frequently seen in natives with Gemini, Aquarius, or Aries rising, where other factors in the figures accentuate the desire to rely only on objective perception and logic in problem solving and human interactions.

All this will become clear in the examples that follow.

Since the parts represent secondary "inner" characterisitics arising from the interaction of causal factors (the planets) in the irrational sphere (the zodiac), the delineation of the significations of the parts in a single figure must be postponed until after the judgment of the significations of the "outer" aspect of the chart (the determinations of the planets, houses, and aspects) has been made. Thus, in the comparison of natal horoscopes, the delineation of the "outer" aspects of each chart singly and then together must precede the delineation of the interraction of the planets of one chart on the parts of the other. The parts, it must be remembered, have no more active causality than the Moon's nodes or the house cusps, and so we cannot think of the part of fortune, for instance, in chart Y affecting, say, Venus in chart X. But we may consider that Venus in chart X affects the part of fortune or any other part which it conjoins or aspects in chart Y.

For the sake of clarity and ease of reference, the procedure for comparing two natal figures may be summarized as follows.

1. Interpret each natal figure individually without reference to the other, from its outer aspect first.

2. Interpret each natal figure individually without reference to the other figure with regard to the combined "inner" and "outer" testimony (i.e., the signification of the parts of that figure in the context of the determinations of the planets, house aspects, etc.).

3. Consider how the outer aspect of one chart affects the outer of the other and vice versa.

4. Consider how the inner aspect of one chart is affected by the outer aspect of the other chart and vice versa.

Thus the consideration of the signification of the parts in comparisons must be the last consideration. This is because the outer side of the chart sets the context here, while the inner shows how the inner person meets the outward circumstances of life.

In this way the parts—especially the part of fortune, the part of the Sun, and the part of the hyleg—can explain a great deal of the "why"of human interactions, while the outer aspects of the chart—especially the Sun, Moon, ascendant, and ruler of the ascendant—indicate the "what" of the interraction.

By the "what" of the interaction is meant the objective observation of what actually occurs. By the "why" of the interraction is meant the "inner" motivation, opinions, etc., which need not be identical to the nature of the outer behavior. The following example will make this clear.

Figures L and M are the natal figures of lovers. Figure L is the female partner, Figure M the male. (Figure L may look familiar; we looked at it before as Figure E.) This couple came to me several years ago. At that time they were living together and, although they did not say so, were considering marriage. Since they asked no specific questions, the consultation consisted mainly of personality analyses of their charts and a general discussion of their professional prospects. The comparison of their charts I kept basically to myself, since it was evident from both figures that no long-lasting partnership between them was possible.

Both partners admit to having difficulty with the idea of a lifelong commitment. Note in Figure M: Aquarius rising; the angular Uranus, one ruler of the ascendant; and the other ruler, Saturn, in Cancer in the fifth house. Note also the square between the ruler of the fifth, the

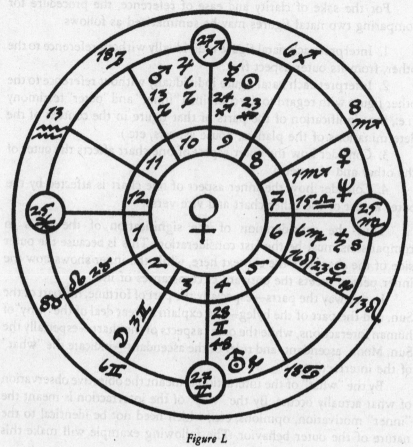

Figure L

exalted Moon, and the Sun-Pluto conjunction in Leo. Finally, note the three planets in the seventh house. All these things point to two factors in M's personality: a reluctance to form any limiting commitment, and a deep need for female companionship and love.

In Figure L we see Pisces rising with one ruler, Neptune, in Libra in the seventh, and the other, Jupiter, in Capricorn in the tenth. Here is the basic conflict in this native, one commonly met with in the modern woman: a dual need for a professional life and for a partner. This theme is repeated by the square between L's Moon in Gemini and the stationary Saturn in the sixth house. Here the Moon is the ruler of the fifth (love life), and Saturn is determined by its position in the sixth and rulership of the tenth toward the profession. Thus there is a conflict between love life and work.

We discussed the importance of the profession to L (as Figure E) in Chapter 5 (see page 153), so we need not review it here. However, with

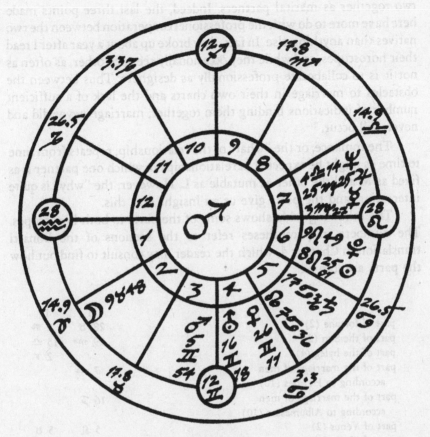

Figure M

regard to the breakup of any partnership in which L feels trapped, note the angular opposition between Uranus on the cusp of the fourth and the combust Mercury, ruler of the seventh (partnerships). The Sun is also involved in this opposition, and its position in Sagittarius reduces the likelihood of a successful marriage all the more. Finally, the Moon's position in Gemini gives an aversion to any deep emotional bond.

Now, comparing the figure outwardly—in accordance with the rules laid out by Ptolemy[1] and Morin,[2] we find that there is no connection between the ascendants of the two figures. However, the ruler of M's ascendant, Saturn, is square to L's ruler, Neptune, while M's other ruler, Uranus, is trine to L's Neptune. L's other ruler, Jupiter, is trine to M's Moon in Taurus. L's Moon is sextile M's Sun, while M's Mars is conjunct L's Moon. L's Saturn trines M's Moon, which falls precisely on L's second-house cusp. There are several other concurrences between the figures, but the more we look, the less we see to bind the two together as marital partners. Indeed, the last three points made here have more to do with the professional cooperation between the two natives than anything else. In fact, they broke up about a year after I read their horoscopes, and while they occasionally see each other, as often as not it is to collaborate professionally as designers. Thus between the obstacles to marriage in their own charts and the lack of a sufficient number of indications binding them together, marriage never did and never will occur.

The romance, or the "what" of the relationship, repeats from time to time as might be expected in relationships in which one partner is as fixed as M and the other as mutable as L. However, the "why" is quite interesting, and the parts give us an insight into this.

The following table shows some of the parts in both horoscopes. The numbers in parentheses refer to the sections of the Bonatti translation in Chapter 4, which the reader may consult to find out how the parts are located.

	M	L
part of fortune (2)	28 ♉	5 ♍
part of the Sun (2)	29 ♍	15 ♎
part of the hyleg (4)		2 ♉
part of the marriage of men according to Hermes (10)	7 ♒	
part of the marriage of men according to Albumassar (10)	16 ♑	
part of Venus (2)	5 ♌	5 ♉
part of Mars (2)	6 ♓	3 ♐
part of luxury and fornication of men (10)	19 ♓	
part of Pleasures and amusements (10)	0 ♉	16 ♒
part of the marriage of women (10)		29 ♑

The table illustrates the use of the parts in comparing horoscopes on the basis of my knowledge of the nature of the relationship between L and M.* This is stated because the reader may well wonder why these particular parts were chosen when, as Chapter 4 shows, there are one hundred from which to choose. Suffice it to say that if we were delineating two such charts "cold"—that is, for the first time, with no knowledge of the relationship—we would either project *all* the parts,

*Note that in some cases a part is listed here for one partner and not for the other. This is because occasionally one part seemed pertinent for one partner and not for the other.

which is tedious, or decide which parts we would look at on the basis of which area of life or "house" we were interested in.

Now, M has had a very central role in influencing L's professional career, in changing the direction in which her life was going, and she has admitted that he exerts a deep influence over her in those respects despite the history of their relationship and their breakup. Reference to the outer aspects of these charts cannot sufficiently explain this admission. L is clearly a sensitive, changeable person; M is the stronger partner, and that he would have an effect on L's work is to some degree indicated by the conjunction of his Mercury with L's Saturn and by the fact that two of M's planets fall in L's sixth house, that M's Jupiter aspects L's tenth house cusp by a square aspect, and that L's horoscope indicates that her friends influence her professional life. This is shown in L's chart by the fact that Saturn, in her sixth house, is the ruler of her eleventh (friends) and disposes Jupiter, the ruler of the first and tenth. However, M is not her friend (eleventh house) but her lover (fifth house), and L's admission was not of an outward fact so much as of an inner experience. L's inner life is of great importance to her, as indicated by the Piscean ascendant and the strong Saturn and Neptune. Therefore, when we consider that the ruler of M's ascendant, Uranus, is conjunct L's part of the Sun (which indicates the highest success she dreams of attaining, her "secrets and cogitations," as Bonatti puts it), we begin to see that M is exerting an influence on L at a very deep level indeed. Since we determine what the influence is by considering the nature, state, and determination of the influencing planet in M's figure, we first note that Uranus is in Gemini in his fourth and is feral; then we conclude that M influenced L by encouraging independence (feral Uranus) from her family (fourth house) and freedom to detemine the course of her life (Uranus in Gemini opposed to tenth house— profession). That he suggested a professional partnership with him which would be very successful is surmised from the fact that Uranus is disposed by an exalted Mercury in his seventh house in Virgo. As it occurs, this Mercury to which I refer, in M's chart, falls closely (2 degrees) on L's part of fortune. This is quite significant, for as the part of fortune is the "lunar" ascendant and indicates the native's inner motivation, M's placing his Mercury (intelligence) on L's inner ascendant has three effects:

1. It means that L will consider M very clever, especially in business matters.

2. It encourages L to develop the professional part of her life,

which we have already seen she wanted to do as a means of achieving independence (note Uranus in her figure and its aspects).

3. It corresponds with a desire L has for forming partnerships which benefit her professionally. This is indicated by the combust Mercury, ruler to the sixth and seventh on cusp of the tenth. That these partnerships are doomed to the same fate as the marriage is indicated by the angular Uranus in her chart.

From these connections, M is seen to ring bells deep within L. His success must have been as inexplicable to him as it was inescapably logical to L.

Now let us consider L's part of the hyleg. It was said earlier that this part indicates the task that the native has to accomplish in this life, that is, the reason for the incarnation. In L's chart, the part falls at 4 degrees Aries, which is in her first house, and the ruler, Mars, is exalted in the tenth house and conjunct the ruler of the ascendant, Jupiter. I take this last fact to be an indication that the native knows what she must do in this life and has from birth had at least some fairly clear precognitions or ideas that she would have to develop an aggressive, industrious, goal-oriented behavior to overcome her otherwise destructive, lethargic Neptunian sensuality. We have seen that she has made efforts and progress in this direction. Now we find that M's Neptune opposes L's *pars hyleg,* while his Mars aspects it by sextile. From this we conclude that he stimulated her artistic abilities and encouraged in her a more aggressive attitude in her artistic endeavors. In fact, there was a period in their relationship when M labored considerably with L to get her to take her artwork to galleries and art directors and encouraged her to be more confident of her abilities and energetic in getting them accepted for sale and use.

It could be remarked that the connection of M's Mars and Neptune with L's *pars hyleg* is not entirely beneficial, since the Mars-Neptune influence is especially seductive and as such aggravates L's hedonism. It is worth noting that L's Moon, the ruler of her fifth house, is the planet in her chart which most closely aspects her *pars hyleg* and that her Mars is square her Neptune, thus indicating that her partner and other people (seventh house) interfere with her professional drive by stimulating her sensuality. Such is in fact the case: M and L's relationship has been a full one, but that it is so just goes to show the depth of insight which the parts offer us into the inner world of the native, and the necessity for proceeding in a methodical way.

More could be said on the theme of sensuality with regard to the parts and their role in the comparison of these two figures, but it would be tedious. Enough has been said to illustrate how the parts may be used and to permit the reader to discover their significations for himself.

In concluding this chapter, I should like to mention that three parts above all others ought to be considered in any work with the parts: the part of the Sun *(pars futurorum)*, the part of the hyleg *(pars hyleg)*, and the part of fortune *(pars fortunae)*. Of these three, the part of fortune is the most apparently influential. In comparisons of natal figures, the conjunctions and aspects of the planets of one chart with these three parts should be carefully noted, as the native's behavior will certainly be affected thereby. The connection of Jupiter with the part of fortune will engender trust in the native whose part of fortune is so touched. Mars will cause the native to feel the other's aggressiveness. Venus will bring pleasure and sexual attraction. Mercury will bring intelligence; Saturn, fear or restraint depending on Saturn's condition; Neptune, sensuality —and sometimes, when connected also with Mars, hypnotism. Uranus can bring a sense of the other's eccentricity, a homosexual attraction, or a magical influence. Pluto brings surrender of the native's will to the other or a radical transformation and refinement of the native's being, depending upon the state and determination of Pluto and Mars in the other's figure.

The effects of the planets on the part of the Sun are similar, although the native will probably not notice them so soon as their effect on the part of fortune. Their effects on the *pars hyleg* might go entirely unnoticed by the native until he realizes the fact that his life has been in fact redirected. An instance of this is the example of L affected by M.

The other parts certainly respond to planetary influences from another chart in a way entirely analogous to that outlined above. Their significations, however, are more limited in scope than the three mentioned and as such need not be specifically dealt with here.

Notes

1. Ptolemy, *Tetrabiblos,* book 4, chap. 5.
2. Jean Morin, *Astrologia gallica,* book 21, chap. 13.

8

HORARY FIGURES

The following is an example of the use of the parts by a medieval astrologer in a medical horary figure:[1]

> In the year of our Lord Jesus 1431 and on the seventh day of the month of August, which was the day of Mars, with seven hours completed from the middle of the night, in the hour of the sun, a certain master in arts and doctor in medicine named Henry Amici, a native of Brussels in the Brabant, asked on behalf of the Lord Dean at Vienne, who was ill, whether he would survive or not. It happened that the figure of the heaven above Vienne at that hour was as shown. [See figure.]

> I looked at this figure or question and I gave the ascendant and Moon to the ill Dean and saw that the Moon was applying to the conjunction of the Sun and was already under the Sun's rays. This was one testimony of death. I considered that the part of the killing planet in the 14th degree of Leo between the Moon and the Sun and within the rays of the Sun at the beginning of the twelfth house to be a sign of the evil tormenting the patient. I considered in the third place that the part of death in the 26th degree of Virgo in the ascendant, the house of life, was an evil testimony. Fourthly, I considered the part of life of the present figure in the 26th degree of Aries, in the house of death; so that there was a certain evil combination, i.e., life or the part of life in the house of death, and the part of death in the house of life; both in the same number of degrees in each sign, which degrees are the terms of the malefics. Furthermore, the part of fortune was in the 7th degree of Virgo in

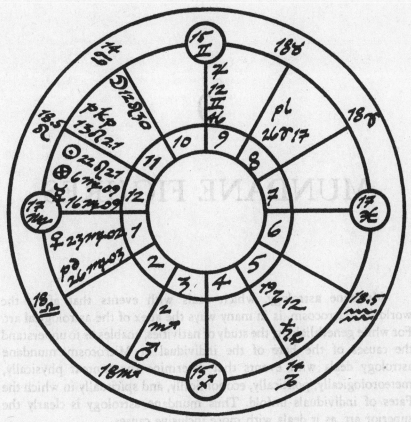

Figure 24

Figure of the question put to Jean Ganivet regarding the Dean of Vienne showing the use of the parts in such cases. As there are no standard symbols for the parts, those used by Ganivet are abbreviated and shown on the figure. Pkp stands for "part of the killing planet." Pd stands for "part of death." Pl stands for "part of life."

the twelfth house, with Mercury at the end of its direct motion coming to the beginning of its retrogradation and corrupting the ascendant. From this I judged that the patient would come to delirium within one natural day at the latest no matter how prudent he was, and so it happened that he became delirious before one natural day and died before two.

9

MUNDANE FIGURES

Mundane astrology, which deals with events that affect the world or Macrocosm, is in many ways the apex of the astrological art. For while genethlialogy, the study of nativities, enables us to understand the causes of the Fate of the individual or Microcosm, mundane astrology deals with events that determine the context physically, meteorologically, politically, economically, and spiritually in which the Fates of individuals unfold. Thus mundane astrology is clearly the superior art, as it deals with more inclusive causes.

Traditional astrological practice bases its inquiry into the condition of the Macrocosm on three primary pillars: First, the ingress of the Sun into the cardinal signs each year; of these the most important is the vernal ingress or the figure erected for the time of the entrance of the Sun into Aries at the vernal equinox. Second, the eclipses of the luminaries; the most important here are total eclipses of the Sun, although the eclipses of the Moon are also considered important, as are partial eclipses of both luminaries. Third, the conjunctions of the major planets; of these the most important are those which involve a changing of triplicity—that is, when the conjunction of two or more major planets occurs in a sign of a different triplicity from that of the sign in which the preceding conjunction of the same planets took place. These conjunctions traditionally are held to signify great changes in the world's affairs, specifically in politics and religion.

Supplementary to these three pillars are the study of the figure of the New Moon of the year or that of the New Moon preceding the Sun's ingress into the cardinal signs, and the consideration of comets, meteors, and the transits of planets and fixed stars over the angles of the place in question. However, as the parts are traditionally employed more in the ingresses and eclipses, I shall omit the consideration of all else in this work.[1]

The parts' use in mundane astrology can be simply and easily demonstrated now that we have seen their use in natal figures, provided that the reader remembers that the signification of the parts in a mundane figure must be considered in terms of the mundane context. This will be easier initially with some of the parts than with others because the comments in Bonatti's text are aimed more toward natal astrology. Some clearly deal with matters relating to mundane astrology, such as the parts of the tenth house which describe the king. These parts are easily employed in revolutions of the world (ingresses). Others, such as the parts of the twelfth and second houses, may be adapted for use where the part allows interpretation on a national level. For instance, the part of secret enemies, the second part of the twelfth house, may relate as easily to the secret enemies of a nation, in conformity with the twelfth house's meaning in a mundane figure, as to the native's secret enemies in a natal figure. The trick is to apply the parts according to the dictum "As above, so below." Some of the parts will not easily permit of this, however, and the astrologer will have to be judicious in applying the parts to the mundane figure. The business will become safer when the part is understood as an arithmetical symbol arising from the interaction of the "fixed significators" as causal factors. At this point the text will no longer be needed and the parts that cause problems can be easily applied to any figure.

THE WATERGATE SCANDAL

Let us look at the figure of the vernal ingress for 1972 (Figure N) and the figure of the solar eclipse of July 10, 1972 (Figure O). These two figures foreshadowed the Watergate scandal.

The public still remembers sufficient of the details of the sorry affair even now, so a detailed account of it is unnecessary. It should suffice to say that shortly after two A.M. June 17, 1972, five men carrying cameras, electronic bugging devices, burglary tools, and walkie-talkies were caught red-handed by the Metropolitan Police in the act of bugging and burglarizing the offices of the Democratic National Committee at the Watergate Hotel in Washington, D.C. It soon became apparent that members of the Committee to Re-elect the President (CRP) were also involved in what bit by bit was discovered to be a broad pattern of illegal covert activities for purposes of political espionage, and this ultimately led to the conviction and imprisonment of a large part of the president's cabinet, the principals of the CRP, even to the resignation on August 9, 1974, of President Richard Nixon in the face of certain impeachment and possible criminal charges. The trial of the original seven Watergate defendants (the five apprehended at the break-in and two members of the CRP) began on January 8, 1973. On March 23, Judge John Sirica, who presided at the trial of the defendants, disclosed that James McCord, one of the convicted defendants, had exposed in a letter to him the involvement of "higher-ups" in the original break-in and thus uncovered a far-reaching plot, the investigation of which ultimately led to consideration of the possible involvement of the president himself. The entire scandal lasted until July of 1975 with the conviction of former Attorney General John N. Mitchell for perjury and obstruction of justice in connection with the scandal and his disbarment from practicing law in New York State.

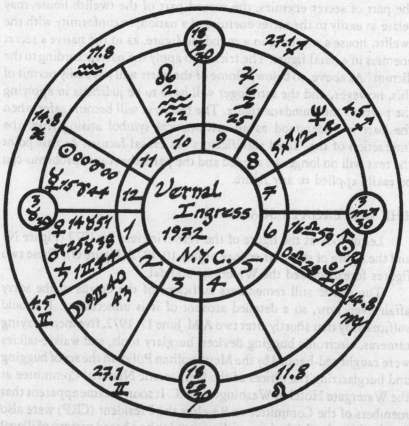

Figure N

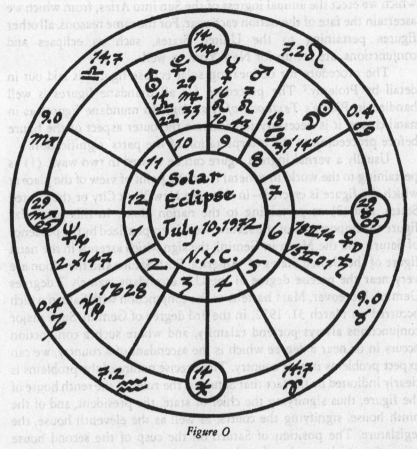

Figure O

As the vernal ingress precedes the eclipse figure, we shall begin with Figure N and then show how the two figures are related and what role the parts might have played in the delineation of them. Notice that both figures are erected for New York City rather than Philadelphia or Washington, D.C. This is because New York City has always been, and remains today, the economic capital of the United States. Calvin Coolidge bluntly stated the truth when he said, "The business of America is business." While this fact does not endear the United States to many people, it is important for us as astrologers to recognize it, for it means that mundane figures erected for anywhere else cannot reflect the heart of the nation as precisely as those erected for New York City. Washington, D.C., may be the nation's brain center and Chicago its breadbasket, but New York remains its heart, and as was stated in Chapter 2, the heart is the locus of the "stars" whose movements give rise to the fate of the entity. Thus New York City must be the place for which we erect the annual ingress of the Sun into Aries, from which we ascertain the fate of the nation each year. For the same reasons, all other figures pertaining to the United States, such as eclipses and conjunctions, are set up for New York as well.

The procedure for delineating solar eclipse figures is laid out in detail by Ptolemy.[2] The procedure for all mundane figures is well handled in Pierce's *Textbook of Astrology*. In mundane figures as in natal charts, it is necessary to delineate the outer aspect of the figure before proceeding to the interpretation of the parts' signification.

Usually a vernal ingress figure can be viewed in two ways: (1) as pertaining to the world in general from the point of view of the place at which the figure is erected—in this case New York City or the United States, and (2) as pertaining to the nation alone. In this particular figure the importance of the second view is emphasized by the presence of Saturn and the Moon in Gemini, the sign which ascends in the natal figure of the United States of America. Both Saturn and the Moon are very near the precise degree of the U.S. ascendant, namely 7 degrees Gemini. Moreover, Mars hastens to the conjunction with Saturn which occurred on March 31, 1972, in the 3rd degree of Gemini. Such major conjunctions always portend calamity, and where such a conjunction occurs in or near a degree which is the ascendant of a country, we can expect problems in that country. The precise nature of the problems is clearly indicated by the fact that Saturn is the ruler of the tenth house of the figure, thus signifying the chief of state, the president, and of the ninth house, signifying the courts, as well as the eleventh house, the legislature. The position of Saturn on the cusp of the second house brings financial considerations into the matter, and the position of the Moon, ruler of the fourth (public buildings, and especially hotels), in the second house with Saturn shows where the action takes place. Thus when Mars, the ruler of the twelfth house (clandestine activity), reaches Saturn, it presignifies that a conflict would break out involving the United States presidency and the courts and legislature as a result of a clandestine action in a public building or hotel. Considering the opposition of Neptune to the Moon, we can add the word "scandal" to our description of the event and note that its position in the eighth house connects the cabinet in some way with the problem.

Regarding the quality of advice the president would get from the cabinet, we note the ruler of the eighth,* Jupiter, in detriment in

---

*The eighth house signifies the cabinet. It can be viewed as eleven houses from the tenth, hence as "the friends of the president."

Capricorn, a postion notable for indicating a lack of discrimination as it is traditionally a sign of the abuse of power. Jupiter also rules the twelfth house, as does Neptune, thus connecting the cabinet with the "clandestine action." The outcome can be seen from the condition of the sign and its ruler ten signs away from the sign (Gemini) in which this all occurred, namely, Pisces. Jupiter, the ruler of Pisces, is in detriment in the ninth house, thus pointing to a grim judicial situation. Ten signs from the sign on the cusp of the tenth house brings us to Libra. Here we find Pluto afflicting the Sun (universal significator of the chief of state) by opposition, and Uranus afflicting Mercury, the ruler of the sign in which the conjunction took place. Both these last two configurations portend a radical change in the presidency, and indeed President Nixon was forced to step down or face certain impeachment—a process which involves the legislature and would likely have involved the courts as well. The latter were certainly involved with regard to the members of the cabinet, many of whom received jail terms and fines for their part in the scandal.

It was stated above that the conjunction of the malefics Mars and Saturn in a degree near the ascendant of the United States occurred on March 31, 1972. This was only one day after the fateful meeting of March 30, 1972, at Key Biscayne, Florida, at which G. Gordon Liddy, financial counsel to the CRP, presented his intelligence plan to the CRP campaign director and former attorney general, John Mitchell. Gordon G. Strachan, staff assistant to H. R. Haldeman, assistant to the president and White House chief of staff, later testified at the Senate Watergate Hearings that Jeb Stuart Magruder, then deputy campaign director of the CRP and deputy director of White House Communications, told him that, at this meeting, "a sophisticated political intelligence gathering system had been approved with a budget of $300,000."

This "plan," which was later to be exposed and the employment of which was to cause so much disturbance for the next several years, occurred one day before the malefic conjunction and after the ingress of the Sun into Aries, the figure of which accurately presignifies the coming crisis. The fact that the meeting referred to took place one day before the conjunction should not disturb us, for Mars frequently brings things to a head about one day or so before its conjunction. Moreover, the context for the event already existed in the ingress figure (Figure N).

Now, what is the testimony of the parts in Figure N? Specifically, how do we find the tenth house, the house of the chief of state, disposed in this matter? First, let us take the third part of the tenth house, called the part of kingship, kings, and dispositors. Section 13 of the translation tells us that it is found by day by taking the distance from Mercury to Mars and projecting it from the ascendant. As Mercury is at 15 Aries and Mars at 25 Taurus, the distance between them is 40 degrees, which added to the ascendant brings us to 13 Gemini (only 6 degrees from the ascendant of the United States). Bonatti tells us that the part is taken in this way because the signification of "prohibiting a matter from reaching the consulate" has been given to Mercury and "fear and terror" to Mars. Nefarious activity is thus associated with the significations of the part. When the part and its lord are well disposed and in good condition, the native (in this case the chief of state) will achieve high status, and "the affairs of men will be according to his hand." The part falls in the second house; it is sextile its ruler, Mercury, which is in the twelfth house, and afflicted by the double approaching opposition from Uranus in the sixth. Thus the part connects the chief of state with covert (twelfth house) operations and opposes him (through the ruler Mercury) to the legislature (eleventh house) through its ruler, Uranus in the sixth.

Let us look at the sixth part of the tenth house, the part of nobles and those who are known among men. This part is taken by day and night from Mercury to the Sun and projected from the ascendant. When it and its lord are in good condition and well disposed, the native will be noble and honored among kings and the wealthy and powerful. We find that the part falls at 18 Aries. This is again in the twelfth house, while the part's ruler, Mars, is in detriment in Taurus in the first house, applying to the fateful conjunction with Saturn, ruler of the tenth house (chief of state). The Sun, ruler of the part by exaltation, also falls in the the twelfth and is opposed by the covert and highly destructive and manipulative Pluto. Moreover, the 18th degree of Aries, the part itself, is exactly square to the place of the July 10, 1972, eclipse. It is also conjunct Mercury and opposed to Uranus. Hence it is connected in every possible way with the coming scandal.

Since we have such an emphasis on the twelfth house, let us look there and see what twelfth-house parts are involved. First is the first part of the twelfth house, the part of enemies. It is found by day and night by taking the distance from Saturn to Mars and projecting this from the ascendant. That distance is 6 degrees, so the part falls at 27 Aries. Again the part falls in the twelfth house and its ruler, Mars, threatens the presidency. The next part, the part of enemies according to Hermes, is found by taking the distance from the lord of the twelfth to the cusp of the twelfth and projecting this from the ascendant. Let us use Jupiter (already afflicted by its zodiacal position) as the ruler of the twelfth. It is approximately 68 degrees from the twelfth house cusp and thus the part falls at 11 Cancer. This is conjunct the coming eclipse and square to Uranus. Albumassar states that if these two parts of enemies are opposed as they are here, at least by sign,* "men will make enemies of each other in that revolution." Given the Plutonian caste of the conflict, we have probably not heard the entire end of the matter even now.

However, though the parts indicate that there are numerous connections between the chief of state and the covert activities to the twelfth house, the astrologer must be wary of concluding from the testimony of the parts that the president had any active role at this stage of the scandal in directing such activities. The parts indicate the "inner" experience of a figure, not the outer or behavioral side of it. Thus the most that can be affirmed is that attitudes were such that there was a community of spirit concerning these matters. In this general atmosphere, behavior arose which was in keeping with the spiritual tone (such as it was). Those who committed the acts did so, of course, of their own volition, but with the inner assumption that they would be supported because this was what was desired "all the way to the top." When will men recognize that superiors rule inferiors and thus the "tone" set at the top sets the context for the organization as a whole and determines more subtly and effectively the actions of the individual members of the organization than all the policy statements and direct orders that may be made?

I must admit that the preceding delineation is the product of hindsight. In 1972, I was only beginning to experiment with mundane figures. It did not occur to me at the time to look at ingresses. The figure we have just looked at was not erected until rather recently when I was studying the mundane applications of the doctrine of the parts. It occurred to me to compare the eclipse figure of July 10, 1972, which I had erected in the first part of 1972, with the ingress for that year. We shall see below the results of the comparison. However, first we should look at the figure of the solar eclipse for July 10, 1972, erected for New York City (Figure O), which as I have said I erected early in 1972 and discussed with several of my friends. At the time I was somewhat baffled at the dramatically dangerous indications I found and, being new at this art, I was very keen not to overreact or jump to any hasty conclusions. I proceeded carefully in delineating the figure, step by step according to

*We assume that any discordant aspect would have similar results such as the square which we have here by sign.

the rules laid out in *Tetrabiblos*.[2] Indeed, I came exceedingly close to forecasting precisely what was to occur, but, not having confidence in my judgment at that time, I did not publish the results; instead I anxiously waited for them to play themselves out. It was the awesome and eerie experience of watching the predicted events unfold on radio and television and in the newspapers during the expected time periods and frequently to the day that convinced me that the destinies of nations, indeed of mankind, were predictable by means of mundane astrology.

Let us now turn to the figure of the solar eclipse of July 10, 1972 (Figure O). We first delineate the figure according to the rules given by Ptolemy. As the eclipse was not seen as total in the United States, its effects would not have been total either. The eclipse occurred at 18 Cancer, exactly on the cusp of the fourth house in the vernal ingress figure (Figure N)—the fourth representing public buildings and also the party out of power at the time (that is, the Democratic party). This is also exactly square to the sixth part of the tenth house (the part of nobles and those who are known among men) in the ingress figure. Thus the relevance of both figures to each other is clear.

The ingress sets the stage on which the eclipse acts. The eclipse lasted two and a half hours and so, according to Ptolemy's rules, its effects were to last two and a half years. Since it occurred about halfway between the western horizon and the zenith, the events forecast by the eclipse were thus to begin around the tenth of January 1973.[3] The "major intensifications" of the events, as Ptolemy puts it, would occur in May 1973. As the very last degree of Scorpio ascends in the figure and such degrees are ineffectual because of a lack of polarity, being merely the end of a sign, we may consider Sagittarius to ascend. This necessarily places Gemini on the western horizon. Gemini is thus the "angle which precedes the eclipse," and from it, as Ptolemy states, we determine that the class to be affected by the eclipse is the human kingdom, Gemini being an air sign. Since the eclipse takes place in the sign of the summer solstice, Cancer, the changes indicated by the eclipse (all eclipses indicate some kind of change) would affect political customs.[2] This was certainly the effect of the Watergate scandal, which prompted a widespread effort to take power away from the presidency and to distribute it to the legislative branch in particular. It also effected change in the laws regarding fund raising for political campaigns. A great many people were to be affected by the change, as is indicated by the oriental position of seven planets, Uranus, Neptune, Pluto, Jupiter, Mercury, Venus, and Saturn.[5]

At the time I drew up Figure O, I noted that Pluto ruled the eclipse,[6] while Neptune in the first house indicated the condition of the people. We were in those days at the height of a liberal era. Neptune, associated with extreme left-wing politics, accurately indicated the influences guiding the American people in those days, while Pluto up to now associated with far-right politics,* holding the tenth house (presidency), indicated that covert conflict was going on between two powerful political forces. I use the term "covert" since both Neptune and Pluto have this characteristic and since Pluto originates in the twelfth house of this figure (Pluto rules the twelfth). As Pluto always polarizes whatever it effects, I wrote, in 1972, "Government split into two factions resulting from secretive manipulation of people. People duped and confused as fanatics attempt to usurp power. Legislative and court battle over cabinet appointee or in some way connected with cabinet, possibly resulting in change in Constitution."

The elements of the coming scandal were present in more abundance than I could then synthesize with precision. Yet even the rough approximation given above was shockingly close to the mark.

All solar eclipse figures have *some* reference to the chief of state because of the Sun's universal significatorship with the king or head of state. Thus the position of Pluto in the tenth house of such a figure clearly points to three things: (1) radical change in government, especially in the presidency, (2) factions in government and (3) the idea of manipulation connected with the presidency. The third point is seen in the case in two ways: (a) The presidency is manipulated by twelfth-house elements—possibly secret societies and certainly de facto clandestine and covert political groups and (b) the executive branch itself is manipulative because of Pluto's position in the tenth. In this latter case, note that Mercury, ruler of the tenth, is sextile to Saturn, ruler of the second house (nation's finances), while Pluto in the tenth is in double-forming square to Jupiter, in the second. Thus the tenth house (executive branch) is connected in two ways to the second (nation's finances). Note now that the nation's finances are ruled by the executive branch, for Saturn, ruler of the second, is disposed by Mercury (Saturn is in Gemini, ruled by Mercury), or the executive branch. Again, Pluto, characterizing the executive branch, is elevated over Jupiter in the second and connected to it by malefic aspect. These factors clearly

*As time passes, political nomenclature changes. Pluto, being a pressure cooker, will soon bring about a new kind of politics, for which no present term suffices. I have coined a term to describe this kind of political activity, which will be felt more after Pluto's entrance into Scorpio: "the politics of transformation."

indicate the manipulation of the wealth of the nation by the executive branch. One of the facts that came out during the Senate Watergate investigations was the "attempt" to politicize the Internal Revenue Service as a means of harassing people on the "enemies list"—a decidedly Plutonian object kept by the White House (executive branch).

We could go on and on with the delineation of this figure, but to do so would take up undue space. Those interested should study these figures closely, for much is to be learned, especially when one compares the universal significatorships with the house positions and house rulers. Our interest is primarily with the parts and so, having first delineated the figure, we shall now pass to consideration of the same parts we looked at in the ingress figure (Figure N).

Let us begin with the third part of the tenth house, the part of kingship, kings, and dispositors. In the eclipse figure (Figure O) it falls at about 20 degrees Scorpio, in the twelfth house again. The closest aspects to the part are the opposition from Venus and the trine from the eclipse. Of the two, the eclipse aspect is stronger.

Thus we find the part indicating by its signification the government, in aspect to the eclipse, clearly showing that the change in government affects the executive branch (tenth house) and again connects the tenth house with the twelfth. Moreover, the rulers of the part, Pluto and Mars, are in the tenth and ninth houses, signifying aggressive manipulation of government and courts (ninth house). The presence of Mars in the ninth also signifies the association of religious figures in the scandal. It will be remembered that three of the president's strongest supporters were the evangelist Billy Graham; a Jesuit priest, Dr. John McLaughlin, special assistant to the president; and Rabbi Baruch Korff, who headed an anti-impeachment campaign.

The sixth part of the tenth house, the part of nobles and those who are known among men, falls at one degree of Scorpio. This again puts the part on the cusp of the twelfth house. Its dispositors will obviously be the same as before. We should note that this part is sextile to Pluto and to Jupiter, which is in fall and thus thoroughly corrupt.

The first part of the twelfth house, the part of enemies, falls at 22 degrees of Capricorn in Figure O. This is in the second house, roughly opposed to the eclipse and also loosely trine to Pluto. Saturn, its dispositor, is sextile to and disposed by the ruler of the tenth house. This is a significant difference from the previous indications, for now we find an aspect of unity, the sextile, connecting the presidency (ruler of the tenth house) with the covert agents (twelfth house). Previously the connections were such that they could be interpreted as mere association

MUNDANE FIGURES / 197

of or interference by the twelfth house in the affairs of the tenth. Now we see unity, agreement, cooperation. We have passed from the March 31, 1972, meeting at Key Biscayne, past the break-in, to the cover-up.

The second part of the twelfth house falls at one degree of Pisces (using Mars as the ruler of the twelfth house). One dispositor of the part, Jupiter, falls on the cusp of the second house and is squared by Pluto, as we have seen, from the tenth house. Jupiter's position in Capricorn is (as I pointed out in dealing with the ingress figure) renowned for its association with the "abuse of power," here characterizing the activity of the covert group. The other dispositor of the part, Neptune, is rising, on the first-house cusp. This shows that the twelfth-house faction desires to mislead people. This is apparent from the fact that the part is a twelfth-house part by nature, and that its ruler, Neptune, acts according to its nature, which is to mislead, confuse, and lull to sleep in the area of life associated with the house in which it is placed, that is, the first house or the population of the nation. The retrograde condition of both Neptune and Jupiter shows the frustration of this desire to mislead and confuse.

The thrust of all this is to firmly associate the tenth house (presidency) with the twelfth (covert operations). The actual resignation of the president in the face of inevitable impeachment is of course part of the "outer" aspect of the figure, specifically the Pluto-Jupiter square and the eclipse itself in concert with the vernal ingress and conjunction of March 31, 1972. The role of the parts here must be secondary, as in natal astrology, and thus we have subordinated their judgment to that of the figure itself as is fitting. However, there can be no doubt that, in hindsight, their application to such mundane figures does much to develop patterns, flesh out the interpretation, and even expose elements not initially apparent. What is particularly noteworthy in the delineation of the parts in these two figures is how strongly and consistently they point to a connection between the tenth and twelfth houses. The challenge to the astrologer in such cases is to have the faith in his art to judge what is indicated rather than to "figure it out" or limit his interpretation to what makes sense at the time. Such an approach must fall short of the truth, since it is the product of the limited mind. An unlimited Mind has disposed the heavens, and the astrologer must have the faith and courage necessary to simply say what is there.

Notes

1. Those who are interested in these other matters should see Ptolemy, *Tetrabiblos*, book 2, chaps. 10 and 11; and Alfred John Pearce, *Textbook of*

Astrology (Washington, D.C.: American Federation of Astrologers, 1970), where conjunctions are dealt with as well. There is considerable material on conjunctions, comets, and so on, in Latin, Hebrew, Arabic, and Sanskrit, and the translation of it would be a great aid to astrologers who know only English.

2. Ptolemy, *Tetrabiblos,* book 2, chaps. 5-10.

3. See Ptolemy's timing sequence given in *Tetrabiblos,* book 2, chap. 7.

4. See Ptolemy, *Tetrabiblos,* book 2, chap. 8.

5. Ibid.

6. Ibid.

10

COMMODITIES VARIATION

In section 17 of the translation, Bonatti offers some "extraordinary parts" which deal with the annual variation exhibited in agricultural productivity and in the variation of prices paid for these commodities. I was more than a little surprised to find what amounts to an astrological guide to commodities speculation in a thirteenth-century astrological manual. And I was thunderstruck to find that the method seemed reliable, at least with regard to the prediction of patterns of variation in the annual production of specific commodities. On reflection, however, it seemed plausible, considering that the nature of the growing cycle and the nature of speculation have not altered since the thirteenth century. Furthermore, both vegetable growth and the instinctual urges (intuition, hunches) upon which this entire activity of gambling rests are eminently connected with the realm of astrological causality, for while the speculator undoubtedly feels as though he approaches the business with the most up-to-date information and with proven methods, still in gambling of all sorts the final decision rests as often as not upon hunches, feelings, and intuition, all of which are irrational. The best brokers undoubtedly warn their clients that commodities specula-tion is "fast moving," sometimes "unpredictable," and even "danger-ous." This unpredictability is due to the fact that the commodities speculator is required to base his judgment on past performance of a specific commodity and upon sundry empirical data which may or may not bear on the issue. Thus the entire business *is* difficult to predict. However, I believe that the causal factors which have been outlined in this book act on the "lunar" aspect of nature, which by definition controls both growth and the "irrational," intuitive aspect of the mind, as opposed to strict logic; and since the action of these casual factors on this "lunar" aspect of nature is essentially mathematically precise, though usually hidden, and since there is but one Mind in which the mutations brought about by these factors on this "lunar" subject, therefore the variations of commodities *are* predictable via the astrological doctrine of parts, as Bonatti suggests.

As illustration of this, I offer Figures Q-W, the figures of the solar ingress at the vernal equinox for the years 1968-1974. All figures are erected for New York City. We shall look at the variation in the production of barley in the United States during these years.

In section 18 of the translation, Bonatti tells us that the part of barley is found by taking the place of the Moon from the place of Jupiter and adding the difference (expressed as degrees of longitude) to the ascendant. The place "where the number ends" is the part of barley. The part of barley for the years 1968 to 1974 are as follows:

1968	4 Capricorn	1971	20 Scorpio
1969	14 Capricorn	1972	0 Sagittarius
1970	20 Sagittarius	1973	17 Sagittarius
		1974	19 Libra

Figure P

Bonatti tells us in section 17 that "the aspect or corporal conjunction of the benefics to the part or its lord, or even to the Moon, signify abundance of the thing, and so much more if the benefic which aspects the part or its lord or the Moon is the ruler of the house in which the part falls." The same associations with the malefics cause shortages. To these considerations I would add that when the part or its lord is angular, it promises more yield than otherwise, and when it is cadent, it is in a sensitive condition because the aspects of the malefics may well be from angular or succedent planets, which would then be more powerful than the part and capable of severely impeding its work, and causing shortages. Moreover, applying aspects are far more important than separating ones.

It is well also to remark here that the parts do not give us absolute

measures but relative. That is, the parts may indicate an increase or a
decrease in the production of a given commodity over the previous
year's production, but to know what the measure of such an increase is,
we must know what the production was the previous year. This
information is published annually by the U.S. Department of
Agriculture and by various commmodities investment services.

After figures Q-W, on page 208, the reader will find a table taken
from the 1975 *Commodity Year Book.** The second column on the left
gives the U.S. production of barley for the years 1962-1975. Here we see
the variation in the production of barley between 1968 and 1974, shown
by the quantity of barley reported produced in thousands of metric tons
in those years.

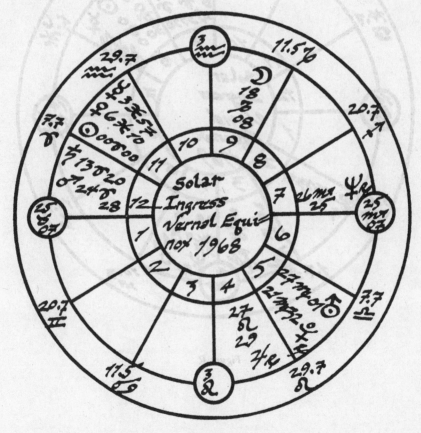

Figure Q

Commodity Year Book, an annual publication of the Commodity Research Bureau, Inc., 1 Liberty Plaza,
New York, N.Y. 10006.

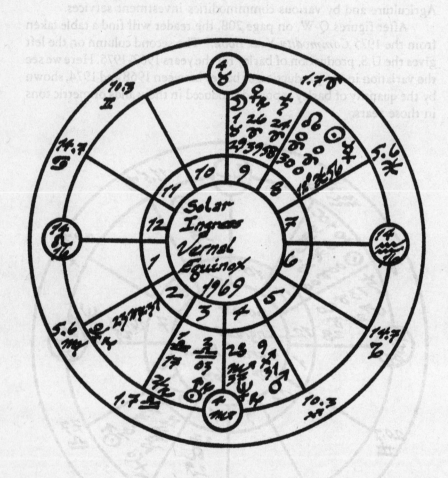

Figure R

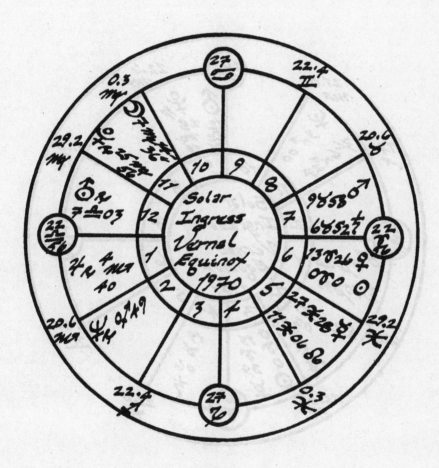

Figure S

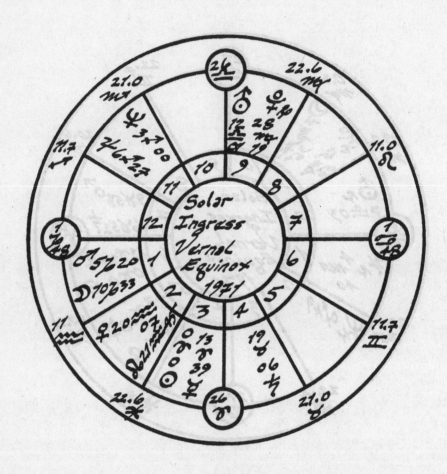

Figure T

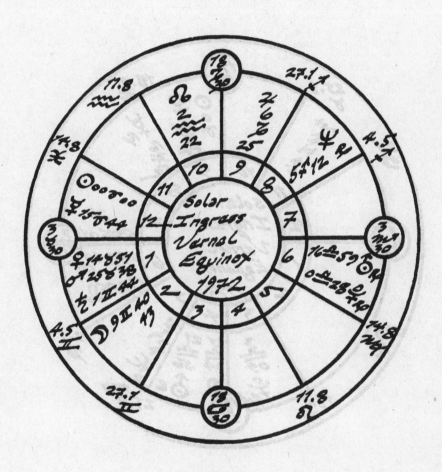

Figure U

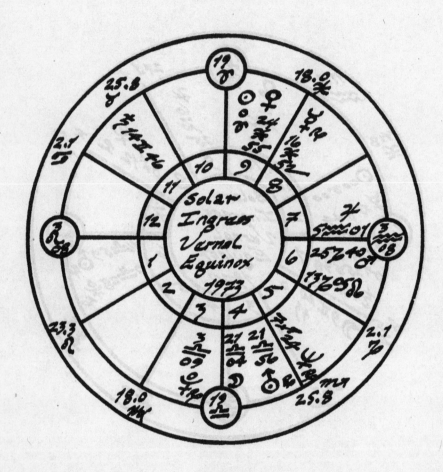

Figure V

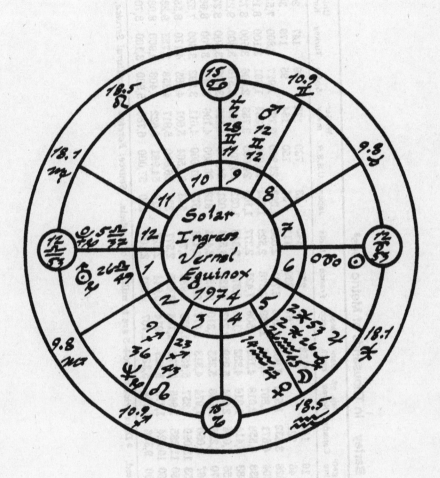

Figure W

World Production of Barley   In Thousands of Metric Tons[3]

Crop Years	United States	Argentine	Canada	Rep. of Korea	Denmark	Morocco	France	India	Japan	U.S.S.R.	W. Germany	Spain	Turkey	United King.	World Total
1962	428	16	166		152	55	271	145	73	720	172	99	147	269	3,910
1963	393	46	221		156	67	339	111	34	750	164	95	179	308	4,060
1964–5[3]	8,405	826	3,632	1,515	3,900	1,168	6,791	2,038	1,203	23,800	3,798	1,927	2,800	7,523	94,497
1965–6	8,558	404	4,671	1,807	4,125	1,189	7,378	2,523	1,234	19,000	3,264	1,891	3,100	8,191	93,779
1966–7	8,537	438	6,558	2,018	4,159	506	7,421	2,377	1,105	24,000	3,753	2,006	3,500	8,724	101,219
1967–8	8,137	588	5,414	1,916	4,382	1,100	9,874	2,348	1,032	20,700	4,592	2,576	3,800	9,215	103,566
1968–9	9,278	556	7,084	2,084	5,059	2,223	9,139	3,504	1,021	24,600	4,825	3,708	3,500	8,271	114,388
1969–0	9,298	570	8,238	2,066	5,255	1,310	9,452	2,424	812	26,800	4,796	3,969	3,700	8,663	117,354
1970–1	9,060	367	9,050	1,974	4,813	1,477	8,126	2,716	573	31,600	4,611	3,092	3,300	7,529	119,579
1971–2	10,094	553	13,099	1,857	5,458	1,675	8,930	2,784	503	34,564	5,601	4,783	4,170	8,558	136,475
1972–3	9,220	880	11,285	1,965	5,572	1,744	10,425	2,577	325	36,800	5,817	4,358	3,725	9,238	138,500
1973–4[1]	9,242	660	10,224	1,778	5,425	914	10,844	2,327	216	54,981	6,622	4,408	2,900	8,988	155,586
1974–5[2]	7,085	630	9,386	1,794	5,325	1,707	9,931	2,100	210	57,000	6,780	5,500	3,100	8,700	157,251

[1] Preliminary.   [2] Estimated.   [3] Data prior to 1964–5 are in millions of bushels.   Source: *Foreign Agricultural Service, U.S.D.A.*

Thus in Figure Q for 1968, we find the part of barley at 4 Capricorn. The part is favorably aspected by Venus and Mercury. Its dispositor, Saturn, is in detriment but cadent, and the square between the Moon and Saturn is a separating aspect already 5 degrees past and cadent as well. Hence it is not powerful enough to impede the signification of the part which, being succcedent, is stronger. We must therefore conclude that there would be significant increase in U.S. production of barley in that year over the previous year. Reference to the table shows that 8,137 metric tons of barley were produced in 1967 and that in 1968, the year in question, 9,278 metric tons were produced, a rise of 1,141 metric tons. Such a rise is truly significant and is to be found whenever a benefic, in exalted condition and at least as strong by house position as the part, favorably aspects the part as Venus in Pisces does here.

However, contrary indications will point to marked declines in productivity. Witness the table for reported production of barley; 9,242 metric tons in 1973, and 7,085 metric tons in 1974, a drop of 2,157 metric tons. In Figure W for 1974, the part falls at 19 Libra. The dispositor of the part is Venus, on the cusp of the fifth house and thus very nearly succedent, in honor of triplicity, and trine to the part. In fact, there is a grand trine between Mars, Venus, and the part, which is rising. From all this we would expect a large increase in barley production in 1974. However, we cannot overlook the double-applying conjunction of the highly malefic Uranus (note that Mercury, Uranus's lower octave, is in fall and cadent, leading us to expect the worst from Uranus), which is angular whereas the other planets mentioned are cadent *and* whose aspect applies while their aspects are separating. Therefore the negative testimony of the malefic Uranus outweighs those of the benefics and we must judge a dramatic decline in productivity rather than an increase. Such was the case, as the table shows.

We must be circumspect, for sometimes the strength of the ruler of the part, combined with other factors, will offset what would otherwise be indicated by the condition of the part itself. Thus in 1973 the part was at 17 Sagittarius. On Figure V this falls 3 degrees or less from the opposition to Saturn. It is one degree from the square to Mercury. Yet production of barley in 1973 was not greatly different from that in 1972: In 1972 reported production was 9,220 metric tons, and in 1973, 9,242, a slight increase of 22 metric tons. Now, it is important to note that the part is in Sagittarius, the sign of a benefic, and that Jupiter, the ruler of the part, is angular and aspected favorably by the Sun and Neptune. Neptune may here be considered a benefic because its lower octave,

Venus, is exalted. Moreover, the aspects of Saturn and Mercury are separating, while Jupiter's aspect to Neptune is forming. Thus while the adverse effect of Saturn was felt, the strength of the ruler was sufficient even to cause a slight increase in production.

These indications should be sufficient to show how the parts are useful in predicting the annual pattern of commodities production. Interested readers may study the other parts given here against the production reported in the table. I have shown how the parts' testimony ought to be interpreted. Bonatti explains how the annual variations of prices are to be accounted for from the same ingress figures (which he calls revolutions). I shall pass over this aspect of the business since we are here concerned with the astrological doctrine of the parts and not with commodities speculation, which is only dealt with here because Bonatti happened to include something on it in his treatise.

11

SPIRITUAL COUNSELING

The aim of spiritual counseling is the discovery of the Self. The Self, the underlying, unchanging reality of every being, is the birthright of all mankind, yet it is all but unknown to the majority of us. The function of the spiritual counselor is to lead those who seek the Self to uncover it.

This Self is at the heart of all existence and has been likened to the Sun. Indeed, it is the First Principle of our art, the *sine qua non* of the human experience. However the realization of its eternal, immanent, and immutable presence is frustrated by a kind of cloud. This cloud effectively screens our ordinary condition from the light of the Self and thereby permits the false view we have of both ourselves and the world to continue. In this ordinary condition Man labors under delusion after delusion and, cut off from his true nature, becomes the plaything of all manner of influences—all incomplete, all unfulfilling. Because he is divorced from Self, he does not know who or what he is, and thus, feeling a lack, and desiring an identity, he mistakenly adopts points of view, talents, opinions, and experiences, hoping that each will in some way fulfill his longing. In this way over a period of time a kind of conglomeration of experiences, opinions, and even physical character- istics are built up which all together constitute his picture of himself. However, being merely a picture, a "graven image" and not really the Self (as the individual himself knows deep down) the image is never perfect and requires continuous attention as it is always in need of a facelift. Moreover, as time goes on, changes are wrought uncontrollably and seemingly unavoidably by forces he cannot understand. This causes the individual great disturbance, perhaps even anguish, for by now he has become thoroughly enamored of his "god" and totally believes that he *is* the graven image and that any modification thereof involves a modification of himself. Nevertheless, try as he might, his outer experience brings change after unavoidable change, so that his original desire, to know himself, to hold fast to the unchangeable, is continuously frustrated. And all this because of the cloud which is ignorance.

The human personality is a mask. It is an ephemeral, continuously changing, and imperfect representation of Man himself. It arises mechanically via the law of cause and effect operating in accordance with the Quaternary, as the following diagram shows.

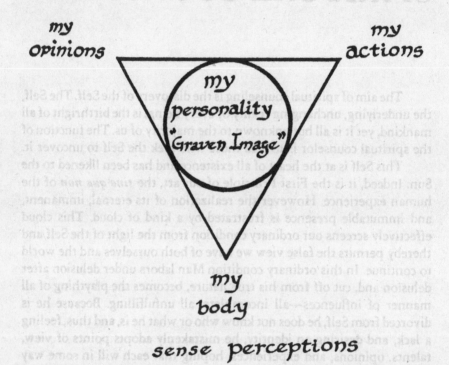

Here we have three factors—"my opinions," "my actions," and "my body"—interacting with each other, each as causes, the effect being the rise of "my personality."

Thus my opinions cause me to act in a given way. Again, my body has an effect upon both my actions and my opinions, for as I am healthy or ill, so my actions vary. But my opinions vary as well, both my opinions of myself (graven image) and my opinions about the world—as anyone may observe by getting me out of bed too early or asking me about my opinions when I am hungry, ill or in a hurry. Yet my actions may also affect both my body and my opinions, for should I go jogging in the morning—an activity quite uncharacteristic of me—I would undoubtedly feel exhausted after very little effort and would think myself an inferior and weak creature (although I would never let on so). However, were my opinions about jogging such that I was strongly motivated to jog and kept it up long enough, the exercise would have the effect of toning up my muscles and strengthening my wind, and very soon, feeling healthier and stronger than ever, I would think myself the very embodiment of manhood and not bother at all to hide the opinion.

If I learn a classical language so that I may have access to sources at present denied me, I may become a better astrologer. Thus my actions (learning the language) would affect my opinions (of my knowledge of the art) and my body (for my tongue would flap with unheard-of doctrines), and this would all dramatically change my self-image. Any number of examples can be given to make the point from any of the angles of the diagram. But these few should serve. Some reflection may be necessary to come to the realization that this diagram does in fact represent things as they are. Readers are asked to apply it with ruthlessly objective observation to themselves and others and to see for themselves what value it has. Eventually one comes to accept the premise that what we call our personality is the end result of the other three factors, and since none of these three factors are constant, personality *must* be a continuously changing facade.

This being the case, then, we must show the relation of the diagram both to the Self, which is the aim of spiritual counseling, and the art of astrology—specifically the parts.

I have stated that none of the three factors whose interaction gives rise to the graven image are constant. Clearly our body is in a constant state of change. Cells are replaced, food passes in and out, as does breath. Our body is a transformer, continuously changing matter from one state to another as food changes into flesh and bone. Indeed the body is like a stationary wave whose form appears constant yet whose substance is continuously being renewed and altered.

Our opinions also are changing. The ideas I had about things as a child no longer seem relevant. When in college, I viewed the world dramatically differently than I do now. Who is there who has not noticed the changes in his or her own opinions and those of friends in the last five years? Opinions may not change as quickly as some of the cells of our body, yet change they do.

Our actions, being related to the other two causes, opinions and body, also change. For one thing, the age of the body brings about changes in the actions as new ideas cause different behavior. But there are other factors as well which influence action. Certainly we observe that much of our behavior originates from we know not where. Habit accounts for much of it, but so do changes in the external environment. Thus up to now we have viewed the diagram incompletely, for no man exists entirely cut off from his environment, and changes in the latter necessarily effect changes in the former. Thus an economic change, such as a depression, will have dramatic effects on the man's actions, opinions, body, and self-image. Now, seasonal changes are certainly changes of the exterior environment, and these have no other causes than astronomical movement. Slowly, inexorably, it is becoming accepted that economic variations are also cyclic and associated as intimately with planetary motion as are the biological and the physiological cycles of bodies human and animal. If we permit objective study of this diagram to go on long enough, we shall realize that to the degree we are able to expand the view from that of "my opinions," "my actions," "my body," and "my personality" to the opinions, actions, body, and "personality" of the world, to that degree we can see that the entire diagram, and every aspect of the world (except for One) participates in cyclicity. That is, as "my body" has biological and physiological cycles, so too does the body of world—that is, the Earth, our Mother, and the sky, our Father. For undeniably these are cycles of fertility and growth, cycles of famine and disease.

Then, too, "my actions" belie a cycle, at least that of waking and sleeping, but also those of sex, of eating, of work and leisure; even my "occasional" visits to relatives and friends will be seen to be cyclic—but then so are war and peace in the world, the Earth's rotation on its axis, its revolution about the Sun, its wobbling poles.

Finally, just as my opinions are cyclical, so are the world's. Though men make the opinions other men hold, yet the length of a man's life is measured and once the exponents of a philosophy are dead, the world is a field in which new seeds are sown. A new crop is reaped in season. Thus the world at any one time has an identity which varies and is as ephemeral as my own.

Yet it was said that to the degree that we expand our observation away from ourselves and out toward the manifested Creation, to that degree we may see that every aspect of the world *except for One* participates in cyclic mutation. What is this One thing which is immutable, the same, always present? What indeed, other than the Self, the observer of the change, whose uncovering is the aim of spiritual counseling. This alone is the thread which strings together the pearls of experience. This is the fountain, the spring from which the Light flows into this world, enlivening the drama.

This, then, is what must be uncovered by the spiritual counselor, first in himself, then in others. This is what is covered by the "cloud of unknowing," the pale of ignorance which may only be dispelled by the very Light it veils. Here is where astrologers may be of great assistance. Who better than they can convincingly show that all the myriad experiences, events, and accidents of this life are cyclical in nature, arise by law with mathematical precision, and are of their very nature finite, ephemeral, and above all else observed by the unchanging Self?

That which the many take for the self is not the Self but only a graven image, an automaton, thoroughly and boringly predictable, a red herring to distract our attention from the Source of our Being.

The human personality is like a cloudy day. One looks up but cannot see the Sun for the clouds. Yet if during the night, the clouds should blow away, one may look up and see the constellations, the planets, and the Moon and know the season and the causes of actions and events here below. Yet, though this knowledge is useful, it is infinitely inferior to the knowledge of the Day, for which the knowledge of night is but a prelude, and which vanishes—as do the stars and darkness at the rising of the Sun. And yet until the Sun has risen and set repeatedly and one has frequently watched the orderly movement of the stars and planets in the night sky and witnessed the concomitant mutations among men, he will not recognize the order of the world and the One Source from which it all flows. Having recognized the order, he draws nearer the Source until at last the Sun rises and does not set.

This is the aim. The Dawn of the Light of the Sun, of the Self, which may be uncovered through the repeated observation of cyclic phenomena for the purpose of differentiating Same and Other. All other efforts are vain until this occurs. All talk of escaping various aspects of one's Fate are ignorant. All attempts to manipulate Destiny according to our whims are madness.

Now, all that has been said regarding this matter up to now may be employed in turning the view away from the purely physical and the unsatisfactory "graven image" and toward the Self. Indeed, whatever will achieve the aim may be used, provided always the welfare of the individual is considered.

It must also be regarded as a cardinal rule that one does not impose his views on others. No one who does not specifically ask for guidance can be led. It is fruitless to attempt to guide those who do not wish it. Worse, it is dangerous, for in forcing the sleeper to awake, one encourages a violent reaction against Truth which is likely to seriously scar a person who might otherwise have awakened in his own time. Thus afflicted, he becomes a destroyer of Truth rather than a cultivator of it. Assuming, then, that spiritual counseling is truly wanted, the process may begin.

For this process, observation must be developed. Observation is impossible without attention. Attention does not occur until the mind is stilled. Thus the astrologer who would be a spiritual counselor must, first, get the native to still his mind. Second, he must direct the native's attention to the causes that give rise to phenomena. (As discussed in Chapter 2, these causes are principally the Ternary Law operating in an observed field—that is, the activity of numbers 1, 2, and 3, with 4 seen as the embodiment of the action.) Third, he must permit observation to occur.

The first item is the toughest. If it is achieved, the rest may follow. There can be three obstacles to a still mind: (1) physiological defect, (2) hyperactivity, and (3) wrong opinion. The first is a medical problem due to nervous disorder, improper hormonal secretions, or some other imbalance. The astrologer can only refer the individual to a physician. Hyperactivity may be a physical or a psychological problem, or it may be merely habit. If it is habit, it may be handled, but great care should be taken not to encroach upon the territory of the medical profession. The only way to handle such cases is to engender a calming atmosphere and practice repeated exercises to still the body, such as meditation and relaxation. If there is no response to this, there may be a psychological disturbance and the person should be referred to appropriate professional services. Spiritual work cannot be beneficial to anyone who is not stable and in control of himself. We are dealing here not with healing but with counseling, and unless the individual is whole, he should not commence such work.

Wrong opinion, however, is another matter. An individual's opinions generally reflect his character, which is to say that we gravitate toward opinions that justify our emotional structure. Since the natal figure is a diagram of this emotional structure, just what the individual's opinions are likely to be is fairly easily known by comparing his natal figure (the solar returns, primary directions, and transits) with the opinions of the day. The third point will be the native's ideas of things. Armed with this knowledge, we may have an idea of what to expect. However, it is rarely advisable to attack these ideas head on, for in so doing we invariably attack the self-image in such a way that excessive and unnecessary resistance to anything we may say is built up. The goal here is a stilled mind. If the body can be brought to stillness, so can the mind. Knowledge of the natal figure and the native's opinions thus becomes a way of establishing prestige, and this is ultimately what encourages agreement and relaxation.

The parts come in when one understands that one reaches peace through doing what one is qualified for, not by struggling against Fate. Not until the individual has found or made his or her niche in the Whole can the mind find peace. Thus the astrologer must know the outer side of the natal figure, for this will surely give the talents and motivations of the native. But he must know also how these outer drives relate to the inner longings of the native. The inner continually attempts to become outer, and surely life is hell when one must do what is contrary to one's desires. Fate *sometimes* imposes this, but not always, and to assume that one draws nearer to God to the degree that he experiences misery is masochism, not piety. Study particularly closely the ascendant, the Sun, and the Moon. As the Sun is the heart, so its condition shows the condition of the native's heart and thus his spiritual work. The ascendant shows how he must relate to the world given his heart's desire, and the Moon shows what he has become through his past lives. It indicates the general quality of his being and particularly as regards his instinctual drives, sex and appetites. Next note the relation of the part of fortune to the figure as a whole. See what characteristics are linked to the part of fortune by aspect, conjunction, or common rulership, for these the native surely has an inner longing to express. See if there are any obstacles to the manifestation of these drives. For instance, what relation, if any, do these drives have to the primary motivation as indicated by the ascendant, Sun, and Moon?

Then consider the part of the Sun. What god does the native worship? Is the nature of his highest hopes in keeping with the drive of the ascendant, the Sun, the Moon, and part of fortune? Finally, consider the *pars hyleg* and especially the profections to it and its ruler, for when the ascendant comes to the *pars hyleg* or its ruler by profection, the native may be expected to come to an understanding of what he must do in this incarnation, especially if there is any association in the natal figure between the *pars hyleg* or its ruler and the Sun.

From these considerations it should be possible to aid the native to find that place in the world which he himself seeks. From the other parts, a pretty clear picture of how all this is likely to end up is possible. (The means for delineating them has been given in the examples.) This done, the native may be encouraged to develop sufficient facility at what he does that his mind is not disturbed by the routine. Then he may observe more and more precisely his relation to his surroundings and to penetrate inwardly into the nature of his own "graven image" and its relation to the three causes which give rise to it. Ultimately he may see that part of him observes all he does and all that goes on around him without ever becoming involved in the activity.

To this observer we must all repair and become grounded therein. Should we get this far, we will find that our diagram will have been redrawn thus:

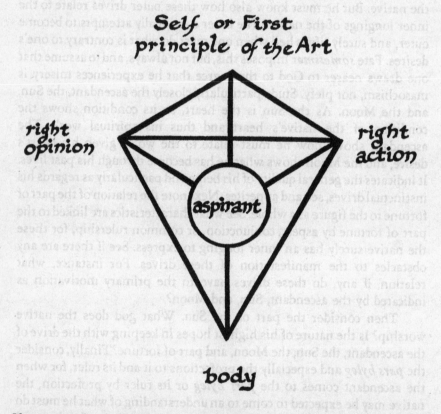

If we succeed in achieving this, another may come who may guide us yet further; for it is said that when the student is ready, the teacher appears.

EPILOGUE

Much of what has been included in this work is unusual in an astrological work for two reasons. First it transcends the merely astrological and finds the roots of the astrological tree in metaphysics and philosophy, and makes no attempt to offer a physical explanation for astrological influence. This must be the case. Astrology as a predictive art is but the exoteric astrology. Its rationale is not to be found in the physical world, even though many astrologers of this century sincerely believe so. They labor under a misconception impressed on them by an education which serves a materialism alien to the principles on which the art rests. Ultimately this will change as men learn to reconcile science and religion. In the meantime, much valuable material stands to be lost because of ignorance of the languages in which the really important astrological texts are written. Astrologers as well as others have come to this present state of ignorance of the classical languages because our Western educational system has excised from its curriculum all subjects not directly geared to the advancement of atheistic technological materialism. Although American education is most seriously deficient in this respect, the trend in the West as a whole has only been a little slower than in the communist countries. The pattern in education is the same whether the politics are capitalist or communist. The astrologer has become the victim of the industrial revolution.

Astrologers must awaken to this pattern and to the fact that it threatens the art as much as it destroys all other forms of scholarship, for it limits astrological research to the realm of empiricism. There are indeed few who can see beyond the physical to the realms wherein astrological causes operate. Thus limited, astrology has withered. A wealth of astrological material was written by men who were part of traditions which handed down better than ours the fruit of men of vision. But it is rotting in the libraries of the world. Those who wrote it guided nations and maintained a link between Heaven and Earth. Our inability to tap this reservoir condemns us to the pulp "astrology" of the newspapers (and now the telephone), which, as we all know, is useless superstition.

If we are ever to raise up the level of the art to its former prestigious position, astrologers will have to have access to material written for that art. This, then, is the second reason that this book contains much material that is not usually met with in modern works on astrology. I have drawn on Latin sources as well as English and English translations of Hebrew and Sanskrit. It is to be hoped that others seriously interested in refining the present condition of the art will avail themselves of the knowledge of languages so that that which was contributed by our ancestors will not be entirely lost.

Finally, the astrologer cannot afford to lose sight of the First Principle of the art, namely the One. Astrology is essentially a sacred art. The astrologer is essentially a priest, a mage. His duty to the client is not merely to predict events but to continually point up toward Heaven and thereby to remind man of his Divine origin.

APPENDIXES

A

ON THE LOTS OF MANILIUS

The twelve lots of the twelve signs referred to by Manilius in chapters 2-4 of book 3 of his *Astronomicon* are merely a twelvefold determination of the ecliptic based upon the part of fortune as the starting point. On first observation I thought them to be "lunar" ascendant. They are not. Rather they indicate twelve sensitive points on the ecliptic—much like the parts. Their influence is limited primarily to the degree in which they fall, and they seem to be totally passive. In this passivity they again show a resemblance to the parts. All twelve lots fall in the same degree of their respective signs as the part of fortune holds in its; there is one lot per sign. This means, of course, that if the part of fortune is at 5 degrees of Taurus, the second lot will be at 5 Gemini, the third at 5 Cancer, the fourth at 5 Leo, and so on. The twelfth will be at 5 Aries. Thus the "lots" of Manilius are purely numerological entities, being the determination of degrees on the circle of the ecliptic toward specific meanings through the office of the Duodenary, using the part of fortune as the One from which the twelvefold determination begins. The use of the Duodenary as a primary division of the circle has obvious precedents in the twelve signs and twelve houses. Modern astrologers, having forgotten the true nature of numbers and the nonphysical nature of astrological causality, are not used to thinking of numbers such as the Duodecad as causal agents in themselves. Normally, we use numbers merely to count or identify. However, as asserted in Chapter 2, number is ultimately the differentiating cause of all things. Here again we see the Duodecad acting so as to detemine these points on the circle toward specific natures.

The specific natures given to the different parts arise solely from the nature of the numbers underlying the particular lot. Thus, the lot of "fortune" is the first. It is the "field" or place, the "given" from which the native must work. It is thus naturally One. The second lot, "warfare," receives its signification from the antipathy embodied in the Dyad. Civil employment, the third, is so designated from the mutable reconciliation and activity inherent in both the Ternary and in commerce. Manilius tells us that this lot "shows what rewards our services may gain, and how too often we may court in vain," by the relation of the planets to this point. The fourth lot is called "pleading" and is associated with "fortunes of the bar." The number 4, like the Octad, was called Justice by the ancients and thus the concept of weighing, which is the activity of discrimination and so associated with the court, arises from the Quaternary. The fifth lot is associated with "marriage" because it is the marriage of the first even number, 2, and the first odd, 3. The sixth lot is called "plenty" and comes from the "procreation" or abundant fertility of 2 and 3. Six is of course the number of Creation. The seventh opposes the first and is thus "danger," for the Dyad underlies it. The eighth is "nobility, fame, honor," etc., because being the Octad, it is the just reflection of Man's desires, as explained in Chapter 2. The ninth is "children" because there are nine stages to manifestation. The tenth is called "Man" and "act of life" because of the nature of the Decad in association with manifestation. The eleventh lot is called "health." This is a euphemism. The eleventh stage, following manifestation, is dissolution. It is represented by two Unities—a clear absurdity—and thus should be called "disease." The nature of the native's illnesses would be known from it. Manilius indicates that it is useful for timing the administration of drugs. The last lot, "wishes," is a sum total of those that went before, just as Pisces is the "dust bin of the zodiac" or the repository of good fortune.

These lots are to be judged as all parts are, namely from the favorable or unfavorable aspects of the planets to them. As Manilius makes no mention of their rulers or house position, they may be ignored. Their use thus becomes quite restricted and ancillary, as is fitting.

B

ON FIRMICUS' DUODECATEMORIA

In Professor Bram's translation of J. Firmicus Maternus' *Mathesis**
is found Firmicus' exposition of an ancillary system of delineation much
like the parts in that it, like Manilius' "lots," relies upon a numerical
extrapolation employing the Duodenary. In this system a planet's
duodecatemorion is found by 12, and the number thus produced is
projected from the beginning of the sign in which the planet is placed.

Firmicus himself gives an example of the discovery of the
duodecatemorion of the Sun when posited at 5 degrees Aries 5 minutes.
Since $5° \times 12 = 60°$ and $5' \times 12 = 60$ or $1°$, therefore the product is 61.
Sixty-one degrees from 0 Aries brings us to 1 degree Gemini, which is
the Sun's duodecatemorion.

These duodecatemoria seem to be treated as aspects of a sort, for
Firmicus seems to imply that when the duodecatemorion of a benefic is
afflicted, so is the benefic, according to the nature and state of the
malefic.

Whatever the rationale for these duodecatemoria was in practice
(for I know of no one who uses them now), their theoretical existence is
essentially numerical. Thus if the duodecatemoria were believed to
exert or indicate any influence at all, it was only by virtue of the active
nature of number. In this case, as with Manilius' lots, with the predictive

*In *Ancient Astrology: Theory and Practice* (Park Ridge, N.J.: Noyes Press, 1975).

technique of profection, with the division of the ecliptic into twelve signs and the house system employed by Western astrologers, the active number is the Duodenary. It is number, considered as causative of differentiation, as the principle of measure operating in the Circle of the Other of Plato's *Timaeus*.

C

ON PROFECTION

Profection is a useful predictive method by itself or in conjunction with the parts. The following translation from Bonatti's *Liber astronomiae* deals with the method in detail.

ON THE PROFECTION OF YEARS OF THE WORLD AND OF NATIVITIES

Mention having been made above concerning the number of years which are attributed to any native, it seems convenient to me and right to speak after this on the profection of years of the native. Profection is the signification of what results from the nature of the sign which immediately follows the sign on the ascendant of the nativity or its ruler, good or evil or the mean between these as we said in previous places.[1] It is called indeed profection because it advances[2] by exchanging itself one sign for every year according to the continuing succession of the signs, the rulers of which stand for significators of the revolutions of the [corresponding] years ruling the administration of both good and evil, sometimes increasing one or diminishing it. The interpretation of this is the Alcocoden[3] which is the participator of the accidents that will come to the native in the year of any revolution, the knowledge of the discovery of which is of this sort. Consider the year, day, month, and hour of anyone's nativity and see how many solar years the native has already completed, and take one sign from the ascendant of the nativity [in the order of the signs] for each year. Begin from the hour of birth of that native according to the succession of the signs, giving one sign to each year, and where that number ends, the sign which immediately succeeds is the sign of the profection from the ascendant of the nativity. It will be the ascendant of the profection of the year which then follows, and the profection of this year will be in such a degree of a sign as was the degree of the ascendant at the time of birth. Understand likewise regarding every profection because it will always be (for every year) in the same degree of the sign as it was in the sign which preceded it in the year which had just passed. The planet which is lord of the sign is called the Alcocoden, which is the adjutor[4] of the planet which is the ruler of the ascendant of the revolution of the year which you are seeking. By such a planet the disposition of the status of the native in that year is shown to you even if it should occur that many revolutions will be made in this nativity.[5] But for the honors and dignities that will accrue to the native in each year, you look at the sign of profection from the Sun, namely to each solar year one whole sign, so that you may see his profection. But for the condition of the body or the soul of the native, you look to the sign of profection from the Moon. But for his profession and his duties you are able to look to the Medium Coeli. For knowing his wealth and prosperity, however, you are able to look to the sign of profection from the part of fortune and from the sign of the house of substance [the second house]. The profection of brothers you take from the sign of profection from the house of brothers [the fourth house]. For the profection of fathers, you look to the sign of profection from the house of fathers [the third house]. The profection of offspring you see from the profection of the sign of offspring [the fifth house]. The profection of servants and maids you take from the profection of the sign of the house of servants [the sixth house]. For the profection of the wife and for the allies and enemies, you will take from the sign of the profection from the house of the wife [the seventh house]. The profection of the substance of those you will take from the profection of the sign of the house of the substance of the wife [the eighth house]. The profection of religious things you take from the profection of the sign from the house of religious things [the ninth house]. The profection of kings you take from the profection of the house of kings [the tenth house]. The profection of friends you take from the profection of the sign of the house of friends [the eleventh house]. The profection of the hidden enemies you take from the house of secret enemies [the twelfth house]. And know that the profection will be so to speak the matter changing the revolution, which happens individually according to the succession of the signs; whatever the ascendant is, profection does not occur unless from one sign to the sign which follows it immediately, which does not happen in a revolution. And profection changes the revolution in this way, that if good is signified in that year by the revolution and good is signified by the profection, it increases the good signified by the revolution. However, if the contrary is signified by it, it diminishes the good signified by the revolution. If, indeed, evil is signified by the revolution and by the profection, the evil signified by the revolution is increased. But if evil is signified by the revolution and good by the profection, the evil signified by the revolution is diminished and so according to this profection is another revolution.

ON THE ORDER OF THE PROFECTION

The order of the profection is of this sort. We posit that someone is born with the ascendant at 10 degrees of Aries. In the following year it will be in the sign Taurus at 10 degrees. However, this will not be the ascendant of the revolution, it will be assisting it.[6] In the third year Gemini will be the sign of profection (in the tenth degree of the sign), but it will not be the ascendant of the following revolution, and so through the order all the way to the end of the signs. But after the completion of the twelve signs, the profection reverts to the first sign, and so you will dispose [the profections] all the way to the end of the life of the native. And from this I shall give you a certain true example. The native was my nephew (era of the Arabs 665, 3 months, 9 days, and era of Christ 1267, sixth day from the entrance into January). The ascendant of his nativity was 13 degrees Capricorn and Mars in it [Capricorn] at 6 degrees and 5 minutes, and the Sun in it [Capricorn] at 12 degrees and 10 minutes. The second house was 20 degrees Aquarius; the third house 2 degrees Aries. The fourth house 12

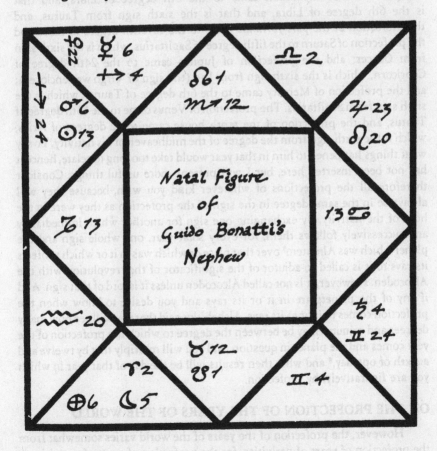

Natal Figure of Guido Bonatti's Nephew

degrees Taurus, Luna in it [i.e., in Taurus] at 5 degrees, 5 minutes; the *pars fortunae,* 6 degrees 5 minutes; the fifth house, 4 degrees Gemini. Cauda draconis [dragon's tail] in it, 1 degree Gemini, 31 minutes. The sixth house, 24 degrees Gemini, 15 minutes. The seventh house, 13 degrees Cancer. Saturn in it [in Cancer], 4 degrees, 15 minutes. The eighth house, 20 degrees Leo. Jupiter in it [in Leo], 23 degrees, 20 minutes. The ninth house, 2 degrees Libra; Scorpio, the tenth house, 12 degrees. Sagittarius, the eleventh house, 4 degrees. Caput draconis in it [in Scorpio], 1 degree, 31 minutes. Mercury in it [Scorpio] 6 degrees, 55 minutes. Venus, 22 degrees, 16 minutes. Likewise, Sagittarius, the twelfth house, 23 degrees. Whence when he had passed five solar years, I once looked at his revolution, and the fifth year from the ascendant of his nativity came to Gemini, which is the sixth sign from Capricorn, and to the 13th degree of it, and the profection of the Sun came to the 13th degree of it [Gemini] likewise; and Mercury was the Alcocoden or lord of that year or revolution, and the profection of Mars to the seventh degree of Gemini and the profection of the Moon came to the 6th degree of Libra, and that is the 6th degree of Libra, and that is the sixth sign from Taurus, and the profection of the *pars fortunae* came to the seventh degree of Libra and the profection of Saturn to the fifth degree of Sagittarius, which is the sixth sign from Cancer; and the profection of Jupiter came to the 24th degree of Capricorn, which is the sixth sign from Leo (the sign of Virgo was enclosed); and the profection of Mercury came to the 6th degree of Taurus, which is the sixth sign from Sagittarius. The profection of Venus came to the 13th degree of Taurus, and the profection of the tenth house came to 12 degrees of Aries, which is the sixth sign from the degree of the midheaven of his nativity. To say what things happened to him in that year would take too long to relate, hence it has not been inserted here, but I will present more useful things. Consider therefore all the profections of whatever kind you wish, because they will always be in the same degree in the sign of the profection as they were in the hour of the nativity. By exchanging one sign for another which immediately and successively follows them, for every solar year, one whole sign and the planet which was Almutem[7] over that place or which was in it or which profects its rays to it is called co-adjutor of the significator of that revolution with the Alcocoden. However, it is not called Alcocoden unless it is lord of that sign. And if any of the planets are in it or its rays and you desire to know when the profection comes to it or to its rays, Alchabitius said that you will see how many degrees and minutes may be between the degree to which the profection of the year comes and the planet in question, and you will multiply that by twelve and a sixth of one day,[8] and what then results will be the day of that year in which you are figuratively, by profection.

ON THE PROFECTION OF THE YEARS OF THE WORLD

However, the profection of the years of the world varies somewhat from the profection of years of nativities, for the profection of years of nativities is taken from the ascendant of any nativity, and then every solar year is exchanged for one whole sign just as has been said. However, the profection of years of the world is taken from the first minute of Aries or indeed of any inception of another great matter such as some kingdom or empire, or some sect, or some religion, as when the kingdom of Nebuchadnezzar began or the kingdom of Ptolemy and the kingdom of Phillip, Alexander, of King Yesdargit began, and the kingdom of the Romans, and so it was when the sect or religion of Augustine began and when the sect of Benedict, and the sect of the Brothers of Minors, which began in the 609th year of the era of the Arabs and the month of the lord Raba, in the era of Christ 1211 years, at the beginning of which was such an ascendant that this sect will subdue all the other sects and the other orders living under the Roman church, but I dare not speak of its end for fear that I might incite a rumor among the vulgar. It will be extremely public when it comes and there will be an immense rumor concerning it. And similar things, the beginnings of which are had, their accidents are universally known in perpetuum, and by their annual revolutions, the yearly things are known by their beginning having been considered,[9] and the profection interposes parts according to their nature[10] sometimes by adding, sometimes by subtracting or taking away from the revolution. By considering that [the profection] from sign to sign successively (as I said), you will be able to know the accidents of the matter whose revolution you are considering.[11]

Nor, moreover, is this profection of this kind of beginnings simply such as is the profection of the years of the world, but it is assimilated to it, as it were, on account of its long durability. However, concerning profection from the ascendant of profection [sic], and concerning the significator which is in any of the angles or in any of the other places besides the angles, and concerning a significator of the right circle,[12] and concerning the significator of the oblique circle, and concerning certain others which are in the fourth differentia of the *Introductionium* of Alchabitius on the judgments of this art I do not speak at all since he has dealt sufficiently with all these in that work with a long dissertation, so that it is not fitting that I sweat over them now, and indeed because that work, although it may be useful and profound in knowledge, renders it with greater labor than of manifest utility. Moreover, those things which were apparently more useful, I explained to you. The direction according to the rulers of the terms has been discussed above in the second part in the chapter on the knowledge of the life of the native and his condition.[13] Therefore we shall discuss further concerning directing significators and what kind and in what way we ought to direct them.

This method of profection is highly advantageous; has the benefit of "traveling light" since time-space conversion tables, ephemerides, and tables of houses are not needed; and illustrates extraordinarily well the causal nature of number, in this case the Duodenary. Therefore, it corroborates what was stated in Chapter 2, namely that number, measure, proportion are the ultimate cause of all manifestation.

These methods are the ones upon which most traditional astrological prediction was based. They are all essentially numerical or symbolical and require less from the astrologer than primary directions. I have seen a Hindu astrologer making use of profection in 1976 in New York City, which shows that the traditional methods are still in use in India at any rate.

Notes

1. I have translated rather loosely here to keep the meaning of the text: Profectio autem est significatum quod resultat ex his quae accidunt ex signo quod immediate succedit signo quod fuit ascendens nativitatis ac eius dominus, bonum sive malum, aut mediate, prout in superioribus dictur.

2. The play on words in the Latin, which cannot be duplicated in English, is based on the words *profectio* and *proficit*, translated above as "it advances." Bonatti is implying an etymology of *profectio* from *proficio*. The latter also means "to profit."

3. Here Bonatti is copying an Arabic term and not using it definitively. He explains in what follows what he means by the term.

4. "adjutor": or helper.

5. The sense is this: first, that the ruler of the sign found by profection, called here Alcocoden, is co-ruler of the year along with the ruler of the ascendant of the revolution of the year; second, that the planet will always be useful in profections of this sort no matter how many circuits of the circle you have to make. Thus a planet ruling the fourth house will accurately describe the affairs of the fourth, sixteenth, twenty-eighth, and fortieth years.

6. "it will be assisting it": that is, in the manner explained in the preceding section, "On the Profection of Years of the World and of Nativities."

7. Here the term "Almutem," like "Alcocoden," is used relatively to differentiate a strong co-influencing planet from the ruler of the sign of the profection, or Alcocoden.

8. "and you will multiply that by twelve and a sixth of one day": *et multiplicabis illud in 12 et sextam unius die.*

9. Bonatti speaks periphrastically of the nativity of the organization or its *principium* ("beginning").

10. "nature": *esse.*

11. Literally: *cuius revolutionem volueris in revolutione illa.*

12. "concerning a significator of the right circle": *de significatore circli directi*—i.e., of right ascension.

13. "condition": *esse.*

D

ON BONATTI'S USE OF THE PART OF THE FATHER

Bonatti gives us an indirect method of determining the approximate length of the native's life by first determining the length of the father's life. The method, which appears to work reasonably well with the horoscopes of first-born males only, seems similar to a folk method my mother mentioned to me. According to this method, one may estimate the length of one's own life by adding the number of years of life of one's parents and dividing by two. No allowance is made in this method for siblings who will live to varying ages, and to determine the length of one's parents' lives while they remain living it is necessary to go to *their* parents or even great-grandparents if the grandparents are still alive. This method is obviously only a gross approximation, but I have been assured that it works out "pretty close."

Bonatti's method is "pretty close," too. He quotes "Aomar" as saying, "You ought to look at the sign which is fourth from the ascendant and its ruler; from the part of the fathers, and from the Sun in diurnal figures and Saturn in nocturnal. Look to the *pars patrum* or part of the father and to the sign of the fourth house both in diurnal and nocturnal figures. Look at these positions and find the Almutem [that planet which rules all or most of them] and whatever planets seem to fit the bill, you take the strongest of these [i.e., strongest both ways: (1) by rulership or dignity; (2) by house position—angular, cadent, or succedent]." Bonatti gives an order of procedure: first, the lord of the fourth, then the part of the father and its lord, then the Sun and Saturn, and finally the planet in the fourth.

The stronger of those planets in the nativity will be the one which is in an angle, not further from the cusp of the angle than 3 degrees before and 5 after, or which is in succedent houses similarly or any of the rulers of the other four dignities in which the planet is. This planet will give you the quality or condition of the father's life.

Next choose a hyleg for the father from between the *pars patris*, the degree of the fourth-house cusp, and the degrees of the Sun and Saturn. Direct that planet or place by profection to the benefics and malefics, and according to this you will see the quantity of the years of the native's father. His condition in a given year will vary in accordance with the condition of this significator.

Highly suspect years, in which his life is in danger, are those in which the said significator reaches angular malefics or their harmful aspect.

Thus two significators are found, an Almutem and a hyleg. The Almutem seems to play the role of "ruler of the chart," and when it is ill affected, the native's father "has a bad year." When it is well affected, everything is fine. The hyleg, on the other hand, determines the length of life in this method as in nativities, for severe enough afflictions to it can terminate the lifespan. The length of life is then the number of degrees of ecliptical longitude which lie between the "hyleg" and the killing point. This point can be a corporal conjunction or an aspect.

E

PARTS USED BY AL-BIRUNI IN HORARY QUESTIONS

In his *Book of Instruction in the Elements of the Art of Astrology* (London, 1934; trans. R. Ramsey Wright), al-Biruni lists a number of parts used specifically in horary questions. Since the work is out of print and difficult to find, I offer here a table of parts given in it. These parts are not mentioned by Bonatti.

Part	From	To	Project From	Diurnal or Nocturnal
1. Secrets	lord of ascendant	cusp of 10th	ascendant	same
2. Urgent wish	lord of hour	lord of ascendant	ascendant	change*
3. Time of attainment	lord of hour	lord of 10th	ascendant	change
4. Information, whether true or false	☿	☽	ascendant	change
5. Injury to business	lord of ascendant	⊕	ascendant	same
6. Freedmen and servants	♃	♄	☿	same
7. Lords and masters	♃	♄	☽	same
8. Marriage	♀	cusp of 7th	ascendant	same
9. Time for action	☉	♃	ascendant	same

10. Time occupied therein	☉	♄	ascendant	same
11. Dismissal or resignation	☉	♃	♄	same
12. Time thereof	lord of affair	⊕	cusp of 10th	same
13. Life or death of an absent person	☽	♂	ascendant	same
14. Lost animal	☉	♂	ascendant	same
15. Lawsuit	♂	☿	ascendant	same
16. Successful issue	☉	♃	ascendant	same
17. Decapitation	☽	♂	cusp of 8th	same
18. Torture	☽	♄	cusp of 9th	same

*Reverse the order of fixed significators when table says "change" in right-hand column.

The following parts are associated with the years, the four quarters, and the conjunction and opposition of the Moon.

Part	From	To	Project From	Diurnal or Nocturnal
1. Earth	♄	♃	ascendant	same
2. Water	☽	♀	ascendant	same
3. Air and water	☿	lord of his house	ascendant	same
4. Fire	☉	♂	ascendant	same
5. Clouds	♂	♄	ascendant	change
6. Rains	☽	♀	ascendant	change
7. Cold	♃	♄	ascendant	change
8. Floods	☉	♄	☽	at moonrise

Part	From	To	Project From	Diurnal or Nocturnal
1. Sultan's lot	M.C., ☉	M.C. of solar revolution	♃	same
2. Again by another method	degree ascendant conjunction	degree conjunction	ascendant	same
3. Victory	☉	lord of 7th (Degree of descendant)	ascendant	same
4. Battle	♂	☊	degree of lot of victory	same
5. Second way according to Umar (b.)	♂	☊	ascendant	same
6. Third way according to al-Furkham	♄	☿	ascendant	same
7. Truce between armies	☊	☿	ascendant	same
8. Conquest	☉	♂	ascendant	same
9. Triumph	⊕	♃	ascendant	change
10. Of first conjunction	ascendant of year of conjunction	degree of conjunction	ascendant	same
11. Of second conjunction	ascendant conjunction	degree of conjunction	ascendant	same

These parts are cast at revolution of the year and at conjunctions.

METAPHYSICAL BIBLIOGRAPHY

ENGLISH

Boehme, Jacob. *Signature of All Things*. London: James Clark and Co., 1969.

———————————. *Mysterium Magnum*. London: Watkins, 1965.

———————————. *Aurora*. London: Watkins, 1960.

———————————. *The Three Principles of the Divine Essence*. Chicago: Yogi Publication Society, 1909.

Burkhardt, Titus. *Mystical Astrology of Ibn Arabi*, trans. Bulent Rauf. Aldsworth, Gloucestershire, England: Beshara Publications, 1977.

Cassirer, Ernst, et al. *Renaissance Philosophy of Man*. Chicago, 1948; 12th ed., 1971.

Dee, John. *The Mathematicall Praeface* (1570). New York: Academic Publications, 1975.

———————————. *John Dee on Astronomy: The Propaedeumata Aphoristica*, trans. Shumaker and Heilbron. University of California Press, 1978.

———————————. *The Hieroglyphic Monad*. New York: Samuel Weiser, 1975.

Euclid. *Euclid's Elements*, trans. T. Heath. 3 vols. New York: Dover Publications, 1956.

Myer, Isaac. *Qabbalah*. New York: Samuel Weiser, 1972.

Nasr, Seyyed Hossein. *An Introduction to Islamic Cosmological Doctrine*. Boulder, Colo.: Shambala, 1978.

Plato. *The Works of Plato*, trans. Benjamin Jowett. New York: Random House, 1937.

———————————. *Epinomis*. trans. with introduction and notes by J. Harward. Oxford, England: Clarendon Press, 1928.

Plotinus. *The Enneads*, trans. Stephan MacKenna. London: Faber and Faber, 1969.

Proclus. *A Commentary on the First Book of Euclid's Elements*, trans. Glenn Morrow. Princeton, N.J.: Princeton University Press, 1970.

Scholem, Gershom. *Kabbalah*. New York: Quadrangle Books, 1974.

Schopenhauer, Arthur. *The World As Will and Representation*, trans. E.F.J. Payne. New York: Dover Publications, 1969.

Scott, W. *Hermetica*. London: Dawsons, 1968.

Shankara. *Pancikaranam*. Calcutta: Advaita Ashrama, 1972.

Taylor, Thomas. *The Theoretic Arithmetic of the Pythagoreans*. New York: Samuel Weiser, 1972.

Sepher Yezirah, trans. Isidor Kalisch. New York: L.H. Frank and Co., 1877.

Zohar, trans. H. Sperling and M. Simon. New York: Rebecca Bennet Publications, n.d.

Latin

Agrippa, H. Cornelius. *De occulta philosophia*, in *Opera omnia*. Lyon, 1600.

Ficino, Marsilio. *Opera omnia*. Basel, 1576.

Fludd, Robert. *Utriusque cosmi majoris scilicet et minoris metaphysica, physica atque technica historia*. Oppenheim, 1618.

INDEX OF PARTS

GENERAL INDEX

Abbasid caliphs, 8
Agrippa, Henry Cornelius, 17
Al-Biruni, 9
Albumassar, 7, 8, 9, 81, 82, 83, 84, 85, 89, 92,
  93, 95, 97, 98, 99, 100, 101, 103, 104, 105,
  106, 107, 108, 110, 112, 113, 117, 118, 120,
  121, 123, 124, 132, 155
Alchabitius, 81, 99, 102, 132, 133
Alcocden, 121, 225, 228
Al-Kindi, 8, 9, 13
Almutem, 82, 110, 231
Angelic World: first *he* of Tetragrammaton,
  34
Arabs, 8
Archetype, 25, 41
Astrology, 1, 2, 8, 9, 11, 13, 17, 23, 65, 139, 214
Astrotheology, 12
Azemena, 108, 109

Bacon, Roger, 12, 13
Boehme, Jacob, 15, 17, 33, 41
Bonatti, Guido, 9, 10, 81
Bruno, Giordano, 18, 20

Causal World, 60; first *he* of Tetragrammaton,
  41
Celestial Equator: produced by Quinary, 57
Classical languages, 13, 14, 220
Commodities, 199-200
Conjunction of Mars and Saturn near ascen-
  dant of United States' Figure, 190, 191
Conjunctional Figure, 99
Corruption, 87

Death, 90, 107-109
Dee, John, 10, 13
De magnis conjunctionibus (On the Great
  Conjunctions), 9
Divine Virgin, 43
Duality: See *Dyad*.
Dyad, 23, 24, 29, 30, 37, 38, 41, 45, 69, 70

Eclipse (solar) of July 10, 1972, 187, 195-197
Ecliptic: 59, 71
Egyptians and Babylonians, 7, 83
Eight, 50-51, 60
Ennead, 35, 51-52, 53, 59
Ether, 27
Exaltations of planets: numerical basis for, 62-
  69

Fall of Man, 61
Fate, 29
Ficino, Marsilio, 12
Firmicus Maternus, Julius, 7
First Principle, 15, 16, 19, 21
Five, 35-38, 39, 41, 43
Fludd, Robert 13, 27, 36

Ganivet, Jean, 80, 184-185
Generation, 87
God, 18; native's concept of, 157-160
Gods, 22
Guellius, 89
Guna, 24

Heart, 18, 19 20, 21, 22
Hermes Trismegistus, 19, 20, 89, 102, 103, 104, 105, 120
Homosexuality, 168-169
Humanist tradition, 8
Hylegeical places, 7

Incarnation, 21
Ingress: Vernal *1968*, 201; *1969*, 202; *1970*, 203; *1971*, 204; *1972*, 205; *1973*, 206; *1974*, 207
Inheritances, 98

Karma, 21
Kepler, Johann, 12, 70, 71

Law of Three, 48
Liber astronomiae, 9, 10
Lots, 1, 221-222
Lull Ramón, 12
Luminaries: transcendental power in, 71

Maia, 32
Malefic and benefic: importance of terms, 78
Man, 2, 17, 20, 25, 212
Manilius, Marcus, 7
Masha'allah, 7
Microcosm, 16, 20, 21, 24, 39
Mirandola, Pico della, 10, 20
Monad, 15, 16, 20, 22, 24, 25, 28, 30, 33, 44, 47; binds together the Hexad, 45; circle is embodiment of, 57; defined, 15; importance of maintaining contact with in practice, 53; the inward spirit or first mother, 41; numerical causes are expressions of, 54-55; Sun embodies, 66
Morin, Jean Baptiste, 13, 71-73

New York City: heart of U.S. 189-190
Nine: See *Ennead*.
Number: in the Archetype, 29-69; basis of astrology, 22; source of First Principle, 23; treble state, 23; means of differentiation of Light of Consciousness, 23; measures all things, 22

Octad: See *Eight*.
OM, 24

Part: of father, 85, 97, 231-232; of fortune, 7, 85, 86, 87, 88, 89, 92, 102, 114, 116, 117, 118, 120, 121, 151-155, 175, 176; in comparisons of natal figures, 180, 183; of things to come (*pars futurorum, pars solis*), 87, 88, 89, 92, 114, 116, 117, 118, 120, 121, 155-160; in comparisons of natal figures, 180, 183; of death, 169-170, 172; *pars hyleg*, 160-166; in comparisons of natal figures, 180, 182, 183; of the killing planet, 170, 172, 174; of life, 169-170, 172-174; of luxury and fornication of men, 180; of the marriage of men according to Albumassar, 180; of the marriages of men according to Hermes, 180; of the marriage of women, 180; of Mars, 180; of Moon, see *part of fortune;* of Pleasures and Amusements, 180; of religion and of the honesty of the woman, 139-151; of Sun, see *part of daemon;* of Venus, 180

Parts: and commodities variation, 199-210; methods of projecting according to Bonatti, 83-84; and numerical relationships, 69-73; origin uncertain, 8; proliferation of, 9; reasons for extracting according to Albumassar, 82; in solar and lunar revolutions, 79; ways of extracting according to Albumassar, 82, 84
Planets: as causal factors, 59-62
Polarization: See *Dyad*.
Preventional Figure, 99
Prime mover: first *he* in Tetragrammaton, 58
Primitive qualities: generation of, 37; and planets, 47
Proclus, 51
Plato, 33, 34, 56
Profection, 225-230
Prostitution, 139, 140, 141, 144
Ptolemy, Claudius, 7
Purpose of present incarnation, 161-166
Pythagoras, 33

Quaternary: fountain of natural effects, 44
Quinary: See *Five*.

BOOKS OF RELATED INTEREST

Aspects in Astrology
A Guide to Understanding
Planetary Relationships in the Horoscope
by Sue Tompkins

Astrology and the Rising of Kundalini
The Transformative Power of Saturn, Chiron, and Uranus
by Barbara Hand Clow

Moon Phase Astrology
The Lunar Key to Your Destiny
by Raven Kaldera

Taoist Astrology
A Handbook of the Authentic Chinese Tradition
by Susan Levitt with Jean Tang

How to Practice Vedic Astrology
A Beginner's Guide to Casting
Your Horoscope and Predicting Your Future
by Andrew Bloomfield

Cherokee Astrology
Animal Medicine in the Stars
by Raven Hail

Shamanic Egyptian Astrology
Your Planetary Relationship to the Gods
by Linda Star Wolf and Ruby Falconer

Cosmic Astrology
An East-West Guide to Your Internal Energy Persona
by Mantak Chia and William U. Wei

Inner Traditions • Bear & Company
P.O. Box 388
Rochester, VT 05767
1-800-246-8648
www.InnerTraditions.com

Or contact your local bookseller